The Stewart/Colbert Effect

The Stewart/Colbert Effect

Essays on the Real Impacts of Fake News

Edited by
AMARNATH AMARASINGAM

Foreword by ROBERT W. MCCHESNEY

McFarland & Company, Inc., Publishers
Jefferson, North Carolina, and London

LIBRARY OF CONGRESS CATALOGUING-IN-PUBLICATION DATA

The Stewart/Colbert effect : essays on the real impacts of
  fake news / edited by Amarnath Amarasingam ;
  foreword by Robert W. McChesney.
      p.   cm.
  Includes bibliographical references and index.

  ISBN 978-0-7864-5886-8
  softcover : 50# alkaline paper ∞

  1. Daily show (Television program)   2. Colbert report
(Television program)   3. Television comedies — United States —
History and criticism.   4. Television comedies — United
States — Influence.   5. Television and politics — United States.
6. Television news programs — Parodies, imitations, etc.
7. Political satire, American — History and criticism.
I. Amarasingam, Amarnath.
PN1992.77.D28S74   2011
791.45'617 — dc22   2011012956

BRITISH LIBRARY CATALOGUING DATA ARE AVAILABLE

On the cover: Poster art for the Rally to Restore Sanity and/or Fear
on October 30, 2010, at the National Mall in Washington, D.C.

Manufactured in the United States of America

McFarland & Company, Inc., Publishers
  Box 611, Jefferson, North Carolina 28640
    www.mcfarlandpub.com

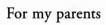
For my parents

Table of Contents

PART II. THEORETICAL CONSIDERATIONS

Foreword by
Robert W. McChesney

In the fall of 2000 Ralph Nader's presidential campaign as the Green Party candidate was in full swing. In September he came to Madison, Wisconsin, where I was living at the time, to make a speech before a packed hour of some 2,000 people. Before the speech, he held a fundraising event for his strongest supporters across the street from the theater. Traveling with Nader and giving warm-up talks at the fundraiser were Phil Donahue, the TV talk show host, and Michael Moore, the film maker. Moore was the lead-in to Nader and his talk brought down the house was his trademark wit and humor. When Nader grabbed the microphone from Moore, the audience was already giddy, hooting and hollering, and ready for more.

"I love great political humor as much as anyone," Nader began, "and there is little doubt that we live in times when there is tremendous political humor." Nader then proceeded to describe a long trip he had taken to the Soviet Union in the early 1960s so he could see firsthand what life was like under communism. "There was the best underground political humor and satire I have ever seen. It was so striking and so well received because the official journalism was so atrocious and discredited."

I have long thought Nader's assessment can be applied to understanding and situating the "fake news" phenomenon of Jon Stewart and Stephen Colbert. It is brilliant humor, to be sure, but it is based to a certain extent on how atrocious the official journalism of our times has become. Stewart and Colbert do not need to adopt the asinine professional practices of mainstream journalism, especially the requirement to regurgitate with a straight face whatever people in power say, and only allow credible dissidence when it comes from other people in power. If pro-corporate right-wing hacks like Glenn Beck or Sean Hannity can get people to talk about something preposterous, it becomes a legitimate news story, empirical evidence be damned. Stewart

1

and Colbert actually demonstrate the idiotic, bogus and propagandistic nature of what people in power and "newsmakers" say, in a manner that would be considered "ideological" and "unprofessional" were it to come from a mainstream newsroom. By avoiding the absurd professional practices, they can get us much closer to the truth. Fake news becomes real journalism.

Nader's comments were also meant as a reminder we would do well to heed: although the old Soviet Union had wonderful political satire, it was an undesirable place to live otherwise. The official culture was one of propaganda and lies, freedom as we know it was non-existent, and the quality of life was poor. Although we enjoy precious freedoms in the United States, our economy and political system are awash in plutocracy, corruption, mindless commercialism and stagnation that are ultimately incompatible with a humane, self-governing and sustainable society and the rule of law. Our future looks dark, and the woeful state of what remains of the U.S. mainstream "free press" holds no small portion of the responsibility.

Every weeknight Jon Stewart and Stephen Colbert demonstrate that corruption and idiocy with comic genius. But, as Nader reminded his audience, being able to crack jokes is great, but it can also be a sign a weakness.

We need also to bear in mind that Stewart and Colbert *are* comedians, not journalists. Their shtick depends on playing off of what appears in the mainstream news. They are not breaking stories with packs of investigative reporters. As our mainstream journalism shrivels, as newsrooms downsize and close up shop, what Stewart and Colbert have to work with may improve as low-hanging fruit susceptible to satire, but the range of issues shrinks. And the ability of thoughtful Americans to turn to these programs as some sort of corrective to and substitute for mainstream news diminishes.

These are my opinions, of course, and not necessarily those of the contributors to this superb volume. What the authors herein demonstrate is not only the significance of "fake news," but also its importance for media scholarship. The striking emergence of Stewart and Colbert has long since exceeded "flash in the pan" status, and is a long-term generational phenomenon. How fake news is evolving, how audiences respond, how it effects the political system and journalism, are all real questions that need to be studied and researched. This important volume assembled and edited by Amarnath Amarasingam contributes much to this ongoing conversation.

Robert W. McChesney is a professor of communication a the University of Illinois at Urbana-Champaign, and has written extensively about politics and the media. He is cofounder of the media reform organization Free Press, and hosts a weekly show, Media Matters, *on WILL-AM radio (from his website).*

Preface

> *"The media is supposed to be the teacher. If they're also in the back of the room throwing spit-balls, what hope do we have of educating the public?"*
> Bill Maher, *Real Time with Bill Maher*, September 11, 2009
>
> *"A comedian's attacking me! Wow! He runs a variety show!"*
> Jim Cramer, *Today's Show*, March 10, 2009

It is customary for researchers to introduce their current project by arguing that their topic of study has not received the attention it duly deserves. It would be disingenuous to argue the same for *The Daily Show* (TDS) and *The Colbert Report* (TCR). Scholarly commentary and research into the effects of political comedy is vast and growing (see, for example, Baym 2009; Gray, Jones, and Thompson 2009; Jackson 2009; Jones 2010). This book, rather than breaking new ground, seeks to cultivate the already rich landscape even further by contributing new research and providing new theoretical perspectives. It is also one of the only books dedicated solely to studying the overall social significance of Jon Stewart and Stephen Colbert. TDS and TCR have gained a reputation for hard-hitting satire and looking at current events with a dedication to fairness. As comedian Dennis Miller remarked to Bill O'Reilly after the famous exchange between MSNBC's Jim Cramer and Jon Stewart, "Jon is a mensch, and Jon doesn't like disengenous people. And I knew he was going to get eviscerated, as he should ... Cramer hates the idea that somebody as quintessentially cool as Jon Stewart thinks he's a putz. So he's willing to go on and have himself crucified." For a purveyor of fake news, Stewart has become one of the most trusted newsmen in the country. According to a 2007 Pew Research Center survey, Stewart landed in fourth place, tied with Brian Williams, Tom Brokaw, Dan Rather, and Anderson Cooper, as the journalist that Americans most admired (Kakutani 2008).

This book attempts to go beyond the current debates surrounding political comedy, a debate that often gets stalemated in a discussion about whether it is breeding cynicism and hurting political discourse or whether it is a powerful force holding politicians and media outlets accountable. It is difficult to deny that watching even a single episode of TDS leaves the viewer feeling that politicians do not care about their constituency, and that media discourse has become little more than partisan bickering. The larger question, however, is whether TDS and TCR contribute to this decline or help remedy it. Do they transcend the partisanship that is characteristic of current political discourse, or are they simply another voice on the Left? Additionally, does watching these two comedy programs increase viewer knowledge of politics, or is a fairly sophisticated knowledge of political discourse necessary for fully understanding them? There has been much research attempting to answer these questions and others. The present volume hopes to further contribute to the conversation.

In the introduction to the book, Josh Compton provides an overview of effects research on *The Daily Show* and *The Colbert Report*, exploring impacts on political perceptions, engagement, and trust. He shows that in the 1990s and early 2000s, much of the late night television political humor research focused on effects on viewers' attitudes toward candidates and impacts on viewers' voting intentions. More recent research, however, has approached late night political comedy from a wider perspective, exploring impacts of political humor on viewers' cynicism, civic participation, and perceived efficacy. Compton illustrates how scholars have also moved from treating late night television humor as a genre and, instead, have teased out unique influences of specific programs, and how TDS and TCR have been common candidates for this type of focused scholarship. He concludes with suggestions for future scholarship, including suggested theoretical launching points, effects of candidate appearances, reactions to failed humor, and implications of word-of-mouth communication of political humor.

Part I of the book contains five essays detailing the results from new research experiments done on the social significance of TDS and TCR. First, Lauren Feldman, Anthony Leiserowitz, and Edward Maibach test prior research on the political effects of late-night comedy programs which have demonstrated that by piggy-backing political content on entertainment fare, such programs provide a "gateway" to increased audience attention to news and public affairs, particularly among less politically engaged audiences. Given the heightened coverage of science and environmental topics on TDS and TCR, their essay considers whether a similar process could be at work relative to public attention to science and the environment. They use nationally representative survey data to evaluate the relationship between watching TDS and TCR and attentiveness to science and environmental issues, specifically global warming. Results indicate that audience exposure to these programs goes hand-in-hand with attention paid to science and the environment. Their essay also argues that the relationship between satirical news use and attentiveness is most pronounced among those with the least amount of formal education, who might otherwise lack the resources and motivation to pay attention to scientific and environmental issues. In this way, they argue, satirical news is an attention equalizer, reducing traditional gaps in attentiveness between those with low and high levels of education.

Michael A. Xenos, Patricia Moy, and Amy B. Becker further the scholarship on the impact of political comedy which suggests that such programming can have significant effects on viewers' attitudes and opinions. In their essay, they explore such effects through the lens of partisan heuristics or information shortcuts enabled by the association of particular comedy sources with certain perspectives on American politics. Specifically, they test hypotheses concerning whether viewers' partisan identification moderates message-consistent persuasive effects from exposure to a political comedy stimulus taken from TDS. Analyses of their data ($N=323$) provide results consistent with the notion that in cognitive terms, comedians such as Jon Stewart can provide source cues similar to those associated with more traditional political figures and pundits. In other words, comedy programs like TDS can help viewers form opinions consistent with their partisan predispositions and thus make sense of the political world.

Jody C. Baumgartner and Jonathan S. Morris argue that much of the recent focus on TDS has been as the result of its seeming potential to engage chronically disinterested young people in the political process. They suggest that TDS is far less politically relevant in this respect than most observers believe. Drawing from survey data collected during the 2008 presidential campaign, Baumgartner and Morris demonstrate that reliance on TDS does not correlate with increased political knowledge or activity among young adults. While it is true, they argue, that many TDS viewers are more knowledgeable and engaged than non-viewers, these individuals rely on other sources of news as well. Moreover, they suggest that heavy viewing may lead to greater levels of political cynicism.

Mark K. McBeth and Randy S. Clemons explore the impact of fake news on discourse, politics, and public policy. Using the 2008 United States Presidential campaign as a case study, they present an analysis of mainstream and fake news coverage of such issues as Joe the Plumber, William Ayers, ACORN, and Jeremiah Wright. They subsequently provide an extended discussion of Wright and a survey experiment that evaluates media coverage of the event from ABC News, TDS, and TCR. While their survey participants felt that they received more information about the Wright controversy from ABC

News, they believed that TDS best dealt with the complexity of racial relations and that both TDS and TCR were more neutral in their coverage. McBeth and Clemons conclude with an analysis of the impact of fake news coverage on public policy formation and the potential positive role that it plays. The results suggest that the fake news of Jon Stewart and Stephen Colbert may be more real than today's real news programs.

Dannagal Goldthwaite Young and Sarah E. Esralew examine the relationship between late-night comedy viewing and normatively positive political behaviors including political discussion and participation. Their essay (using 2004 National Annenberg Election Survey data) suggests that late-night comedy viewers, particularly of TDS, are more likely to engage in these behaviors than non-viewers. Instead of arguing about the normative implications of political cynicism or a lack of trust in government, they look directly at political behaviors that are indicative of a healthy and active democracy: participation in the campaign and discussing politics with various cohorts. They also explore the role of political knowledge as a moderator of these effects processes.

Part II of the book, consisting of five essays, provides theoretical explorations into the social significance of TDS and TCR. Richard Van Heertum argues that TDS and TCR speak the lingua franca of youth today, inflected by a strong predilection toward irony. He first deconstructs what he calls the "culture of the cool" in popular culture today, and then explores the place of political cynicism in contemporary American politics. From here, Heertum explains where these shows fit within the political landscape. He concludes by arguing that they provide a valuable resource critiquing politics and the media and helping youth navigate the formation and solidification of their political identities.

Julia R. Fox argues that Stewart's and Colbert's positions within the political system are not new, but in fact go back hundreds, even thousands, of years to those of court jesters in European and Asian monarchies. Like court jesters, Fox argues, Stewart and Colbert use humor to skewer the ruling administration. And, just as court jesters had no official social standing within those monarchies, and thus no status to risk in criticizing their rulers, Stewart and Colbert have no official status to risk within the established news media and thus are not bound to adhere to the traditional news media's norms and conventions. In her essay, Fox traces the roles and history of court jesters and argues that Stewart and Colbert function in much the same way today that court jesters in European and Asian monarchies once did.

Robert T. Tally, Jr., argues that TDS and TCR are apt examples of Umberto Eco and Jean Baudrillard's notion of hyperreality. He notes that while satire in the form of news is not new, Stewart and Colbert have become a much more socially significant force, not just poking fun at figures *in* the news, but launching a full-scale attack on the media and the messages simultaneously. Tally argues that the hyperreality of these fake news shows does not lie in the vaunted, or maligned, fact that some people get their news from Stewart or Colbert, but that these shows dramatically enact the underlying critique of the media, by showing that the mainstream news is altogether artificial, constructed according to formulae and processes easily decoded by comedy writers and attentive viewers. As such, he points out, TDS and TCR shape the social field even as they lampoon it.

Kevin A. Wisniewski examines the formats and rhetoric of TDS and TCR, with a particular focus on the segments of interviews. Deconstructing the actors of the interviews — specifically the guest, Stewart and Colbert, the studio audience, and the audience at home — Wisniewski attempts to reveal how mechanisms of imitation and contagion provide an explanation of how both a sense of self and national character and culture develop. As a comedian, he argues, Stewart's agenda is much more direct and obvious to his viewers; he often fulfills his role as dissenter, objector, and has become a sort of watchdog of American politics. Meanwhile, Colbert, a self-proclaimed actor, is much more difficult to read: masking agendas, performing characters, harshly criticizing one aspect of American politics one moment only to rally the audience into a "U-S-A" chant the next. Building on discourses of public culture and social theories around "the meme," Wisniewski examines how these contagious characters work within both systems of politics and comedy and, in doing so, have a power to unmake holistic metaphors; what is instead suggested is a power — or weakness — of these metaphors, of communicability.

In the final essay, Bruce A. Williams and Michael X. Delli Carpini explore the role of the TDS in the new media environment. They start with an example of the unsurprising, but rarely discussed reality that like any attempt to address issues of the day, the show makes mistakes. Additionally, like any other show, decisions are made about what issues to cover, what issues to ignore and what perspective to take. Williams and Carpini use this example as a departure point for discussing the criteria most appropriate for evaluating and holding accountable satirical shows, and other non-traditional sources of political information. In concluding sections they tentatively propose and apply a set of values appropriate for understanding the responsibility of those public figures — the professional journalists of CNN and the writers of TDS, but also bloggers and citizens themselves—upon which the public now depends for reliable political information

Introduction

Surveying Scholarship on
The Daily Show *and* The Colbert Report

JOSH COMPTON

From conventional late-night comedy talk shows to cable television news satire, editorial cartoons to viral online video clips; from books to bumper stickers, candidates' jokes to jokes about candidates, political humor is widespread in modern political campaigns (see Baumgartner and Morris 2008a and Compton 2008). Political humor may be at unmatched levels (Baumgartner and Morris 2008b, 622), and as this essay reveals, scholarship on political humor is at an unprecedented level as well. No outlet for political humor has received more attention in recent years than late-night television comedy, and no programs have received more attention than Comedy Central's *The Daily Show* (1996–) and *The Colbert Report* (2005–).

Some of the earliest explorations of political late-night television comedy fall under the rubric of *new media* (Davis and Owen 1998), *soft news* (Baum 2002), or *non-traditional media* (Moy, Pfau, and Kahlor 1999). In this type of research, late-night comedy is one example, joining other forms of entertainment television such as the daytime talk show. Analyses reveal that such television programs influence viewers' evaluations of political candidates (Pfau, Cho, and Chong 2001; Pfau and Eveland 1996), viewers' perceptions of certain institutions (Moy, Pfau, and Kahlor 1999), their interest in campaigns (McLeod et al. 1996), and their support for specific policies (Baum 2002, 2004). Some scholars find that people learn about politics from soft news (Baum 2003; Brewer and Cao 2006; Chaffee, Zhao, and Leshner 1994), while others conclude that learning effects, if any, are limited (Prior 2003; Hollander 2005). Research in soft news and new media offered some of the first inklings that late-night political humor mattered.

9

More recently, scholars have studied late-night television comedy in particular under the rubric of *soft news* or *new media* studies. Much of that work focuses on individual level voter variables. While most research has not revealed direct links between watching late-night comedy television and political knowledge (Brewer and Cao 2008; Cao 2008), we do find evidence that some viewers are learning during specific campaigns (Cao 2008). Other evidence suggests viewers of late-night comedy television may be *recognizing* political information (Hollander 2005), or that late-night comedy increases knowledge only of "widely known, thus relatively easy, political facts and issue" (Baek and Wojcieszak 2009, 797). When it comes to influencing candidate evaluations, viewers with lower political knowledge are more likely to be affected (Young 2004b), and late-night comedy makes negative characteristics of candidates more salient (Young 2006).

Scholars have also explored relationships between late-night television viewing and other dimensions, such as political participation and attitudes toward politics. Viewers of *The Tonight Show* and *Late Show* are more likely to be politically involved (Cao and Brewer 2008; Hoffman and Thomson 2009; Moy, Xenos, and Hess 2005) and participate in political discussions (Moy, Xenos, and Hess 2005); additionally, they are more politically knowledgeable and have more positive attitudes toward the political process (Pfau, Houston, and Semmler 2005). Viewers of late-night comedy are also more likely to be interested in traditional forms of news (Feldman and Young 2008), and viewers of certain late-night talk shows are less cynical about news media, while certain other shows seem to foster cynicism (Morris and Baumgartner 2008). Late-night comedy appears to have positive effects on viewers' perceived political efficacy (Hoffman and Thomson 2009).

In other research, the focus is even more specific — not just from *soft news* to late-night comedy, but also from late-night comedy to particular comedy television programs. "Political humor — even late-night televised political humor — is not monolithic" (Baumgartner and Morris 2008b, 624), and neither is its audience (Young and Tisinger 2006). *The Daily Show* and *The Colbert Report* are, for example, two shows that fit "the fake news subgenre" of political satire (Holbert 2005, 441). Jon Stewart (the host of *The Daily Show* since 1999) and Stephen Colbert (the host of *The Colbert Report* since its inception) are *"rhetorical critics ...* who creatively guide audiences toward democratic possibilities" (Waisenan 2009, 120, emphasis in original). Another scholar concluded: "The informed satire of Jon Stewart and Stephen Colbert can, arguably, be considered some of the most bracing and engaging commentary on the television landscape" (Colletta 2009, 872). Of the late-night comedy programs, none have received more specific attention from scholars than *The Daily Show* and *The Colbert Report*.

Although viewers do not tune in to *The Daily Show* to get political news for the same reasons they tune in to national news (Holbert, Lambde, Dudo, and Carlton 2007), evidence suggests that *The Daily Show* is, in many respects, like national news. For example, *The Daily Show* offers as much substantive coverage of political events, like presidential debates and conventions, as network news coverage (Fox, Koloen, and Sahin 2007). Additionally, *The Daily Show* spends a great deal of its time covering politics, world affairs, and news media, including focusing its attention on policy issues (Brewer and Marquardt 2007, 264). Baym (2005) contends that *The Daily Show* should be considered *alternative journalism* rather than *fake news*. Journalists often praise *The Daily Show*, even though it derives much of its humor by mocking journalists (Feldman 2007).

Scholars differentiate *The Daily Show* and *The Colbert Report* from other types of late-night political humor, such as *The Tonight Show with Jay Leno* or *Late Show with David Letterman*. "Jon Stewart's approach differs significantly from that of David Letterman and Jay Leno — and Colbert differs from all three of them" (Baumgartner and Morris 2008b, 624). When comparing *The Daily Show* and *The Colbert Report* to other late-night political comedy shows, scholars point to differences in impact, humor, and hosts. *The Daily Show* is more influential than other forms of political comedy (Baumgartner and Morris 2008b, 623), the show is more political than other late-night television programs (Young 2004a), and its host, Jon Stewart, is more vocal with his political ideology (Jones 2005; Morris 2009). Young and Tisinger noted:

> While Leno and Letterman may be predominantly entertainment programs that include political elements, *The Daily Show* should be considered — in the spirit of Monty Python — something completely different: a program designed to entertain but that functions predominantly as a political program. (Young and Tisinger 2006, 129)

The humor of *The Daily Show* is more dependent on irony, parody, and satire than the simpler jokes of late-night talk show hosts, like Leno and Letterman (Young and Tisinger 2006, 118), and viewers are more cognitively engaged (Xenos and Becker 2009, 331); yet, the complexity of its humor is achieved during a shorter time frame: a thirty-minute program versus the hour-and-a-half format of most late-night talk shows (Jones 2005). On *The Colbert Report*, host Stephen Colbert relies on deadpan satire (LaMarre, Landreville, and Beam 2009), and his approach is "a fundamentally different type of humor" (Baumgartner and Morris 2008b, 625) when compared to other late-night programs.

Viewers of *The Daily Show* and *The Colbert Report* differ from viewers of other news media. As examples, *The Daily Show* viewers are more likely to be younger (Coe et al. 2008; Morris 2009; Young 2004a), male (Coe et al.

2008; Young and Tisinger 2006), have more education (Morris 2009), and be more liberal (Coe et al. 2008; Young 2004a). They are also more likely to be interested in political news (Feldman and Young 2008; Young 2004a; Young and Tisinger 2006) and to be more politically knowledgeable (Young 2004a; Young and Tisinger 2006). One study found that viewers who are higher sensation seekers and higher in verbal aggression are more likely to watch political satire shows, such as *The Daily Show* (Banerjee, Greene, Krcmar, and Bagdasarov 2009).

But before we lump Stewart and Colbert together as an alternative conceptualization of late-night television political humor, we should recognize the differences between the two comedic hosts. Colbert hosts his program in character, relying on "deadpan satire" (LaMarre, Landreville, and Beam 2009, 216). Baumgartner and Morris distinguish the two hosts in this way: "Unlike Stewart, who plays the role of a common-sense observer who humorously points out the absurd in politics, Colbert parodies the new breed of self-indulgent, conservative news personalities" (Baumgartner and Morris 2008b, 623). Additionally, "Stewart delivers his jokes in his own left-leaning, astounded-but-amused persona, whereas Colbert's character and show are formal, stylistic appropriations of generally right-wing news reporting" (Waisenan 2009, 125). *The Colbert Report* has been characterized as "an even more extreme parody than *The Daily Show*, as Colbert more fully inhabits his persona" (Druick 2009, 304). While the hosts share similarities and stand in contrast to other types of late-night television personas, they host decisively different programs.

But more importantly for this essay, the effects of these shows are also different. Effects of watching *The Daily Show* are more pronounced and consistent when compared with watching *The Tonight Show*, *Late Night*, or *Late Show* (Morris 2009). In recognizing that *The Daily Show* and *The Colbert Report* are unique when compared to other late-night comedy programs (and even when compared to each other), this essay turns to a survey of scholarship exploring unique effects of these two programs. A review of what we know from empirical effects research on these two programs helps us to see similarities and differences between the two programs, and also helps us to move forward with future investigations of this unique type of political humor.

Learning and Information Processing

As with research into the genre of soft news (Baum 2003; Brewer and Cao 2006; Chaffee, Zhao, and Leshner 1994), scholars have looked for learning effects with *The Daily Show* and *The Colbert Report*. In their study, "Just Laugh!" (2008) Young Mie Kim and John Vishak compare effects of watching entertainment coverage of the U.S. Supreme Court Justice and Chief Justice nominations in 2005. Participants watched a clip from *The Daily Show*, news from NBC and CNN, or, in the control condition, a science documentary. Viewers of evening news segments recalled more factual statements (and more accurate information in terms of issues and procedures) than viewers of *The Daily Show*. Kim and Vishak also found that viewers in both conditions learned more information than the control group. But perhaps their most compelling finding was that viewers of late-night comedy are more likely to engage in online-based political information processing, whereas viewers of conventional news are more likely to engage in memory-based political information processing. That is, "entertainment media appeared to be used for an affective integrator (i.e., online tally), the basis for individual's political judgments" (Kim and Vishak 2008, 353). Kim and Vishak's findings add a layer of nuance to the question of whether viewers learn from late-night comedy television. Their research reveals that besides learning some factual information, viewers may be processing political information differently.

Other scholars have explored effects of late-night comedy on information seeking. In "Moments of Zen" (2009), Michael Xenos and Amy Becker use experimental studies to ascertain whether jokes about issues on *The Daily Show* lead less politically interested viewers to seek out additional information about the issues from other news sources. Results indicated that watching *The Daily Show* enhances time spent searching for additional information using Web-based news sources, and "that less politically interested comedy viewers may also more easily acquire information subsequently encountered in more traditional news media" (Xenos and Becker 2009, 329). This research suggests that some of the most significant learning impacts of *The Daily Show* may be related to searches for more information, post-viewing.

From these two studies, we see an expanded view of what it means to learn from late-night comedy, including impacts on information processing (Kim and Vishak 2008) and the motivation to learn more (Xenos and Becker 2009). We can also compare these findings to previous work which found that late-night comedy viewers are more likely to seek out more information from conventional news (Feldman and Young, 2008) and a focus group study which found that some participants see *The Daily Show* as motivating their interest in other forms of news (Rottinghaus, Bird, Ridout, and Self 2008). *The Daily Show* may be teaching, influencing, and motivating political information and political participation — effects that move beyond individuals' political attitudes.

Attitudes and Behaviors Toward Conventional News and Politics

Other research turns away from direct effects of *The Daily Show* and *The Colbert Report* to examine indirect effects, such as attitudes and behaviors toward other forms of news. In their study, "Primacy Effects of *The Daily Show* and National TV News Viewing" (2007), Lance Holbert and his colleagues examined whether watching *The Daily Show* lowered viewers' political gratifications met by watching conventional television news using experimental design and real-time broadcasts of Comedy Central's *The Daily Show* and CNN's *Headline News*. When students watched *The Daily Show* and then *Headline News*, viewers indicated the lowest levels of political gratifications met by the conventional news broadcast. As the researchers note, the primacy effect seems to explain *The Daily Show*'s effect when it was watched prior to *Headline News*. But their research also revealed that when students watched *Headline News* first and then *The Daily Show*, their political gratifications from national news were lower than when not watching *The Daily Show* at all (the control group). Holbert and his colleagues found similar results with the inverse of this order: watching *Headline News* prior to *The Daily Show* lowered the gratifications met by watching *The Daily Show*. Primacy effects for *The Daily Show* were limited to those with lower political self-efficacy: "Watching *The Daily Show* prior to CNN leads those individuals with lower internal political self-efficacy to think less of national television news as a source for political information" (Holbert, Lambde, Dudo, and Carlton 2007, 32). Holbert and his colleagues' research expands the scope of assessing late-night comedy effects beyond attitudes and political behavioral intentions to look at effects on other types of political information gathering. Such research paints a more dynamic, expansive conceptualization of late-night political comedy effects.

But watching *The Daily Show* affects more than how much viewers value conventional news. It can also affect how much cynicism viewers have toward news media. In "*The Daily Show* and Attitudes Toward the News Media" (2008), Jonathan Morris and Jody Baumgartner turned to experimental and survey data to reveal a connection between watching *The Daily Show* and viewers' trust in news media. Watching *The Daily Show* does not seem to cause viewers to think that news media covers politics with a liberal bias. But, there is a causal connection between the *The Daily Show* and cynicism toward the news media for young viewers age eighteen to thirty, a finding consistent with Baumgartner and Morris (2006). Cynicism caused by *The Daily Show* toward other media contrast with the effects of watching other types of late-night political humor — *The Tonight Show* and *Late Show* — where we find negative correlations with cynicism (Morris and Baumgartner 2008).

Effects on efficacy showcase the complexity of assessing effects of late-night television comedy. Jody Baumgartner and Jonathan Morris found that watching *The Colbert Report* decreases viewers' perceptions of their political efficacy: "Colbert's satire seems to confuse some young viewers" (Baumgartner and Morris 2008b, 634). But on the other hand, Baumgartner and Morris (2006) found that watching *The Daily Show* increases young viewers' perceptions of their political efficacy.

These studies remind us that effects of late-night television comedy, or more particularly, *The Daily Show* and *The Colbert Report*, extend beyond issues of learning and candidate evaluations. *The Daily Show* affects what viewers think they are getting from conventional news (Holbert, Lambde, Dudo, and Carlton 2007) and increases some young viewers' cynicism toward the news media (Morris and Baumgartner 2008), but it also increases viewers' perceptions of their political efficacy (Morris and Baumgartner 2006). *The Colbert Report*, on the other hand, appears to decrease viewers' perceptions of their political efficacy (Baumgartner and Morris 2008b).

Political Ideology and Political Parties

Does ideology matter when it comes to effects of *The Daily Show* and *The Colbert Report*? Brandon Rottinghaus, Kenton Bird, Travis Ridout, and Rebecca Self conducted a series of focus groups of *The Daily Show* viewers. One participant argued that ideology does not matter: "As long as it makes it funny, it's good" (Rottinghaus, Bird, Ridout, and Self 2008, 286). Is extant effects research consistent with this perception? The short answer is yes. But for an expanded picture, we can, in turn, examine research exploring viewers' ideology, perceived television program ideology, and differences in effects on targets of humor based on political party.

Kevin Coe and his colleagues explored ideology impacts in their study, "Hostile News" (2008). They based their study on the hostile media phenomenon, where ideology impacts perceived media bias (see Vallone, Ross, and Lepper, 1985). Their research, which also explored perceptions of FOX News' *The O'Reilly Factor* and CNN evening news, revealed that *The Daily Show* is perceived as more biased than *The O'Reilly Factor* and CNN evening news. Coe and colleagues also found that liberals feel more interested and informed after watching *The Daily Show* than conservative viewers, but that "almost uniformly, partisans of both stripes considered *The Daily Show* content to be less interesting and informative" than CNN evening news or Fox News' *The O'Reilly Factor* (Coe et al. 2008, 215).

Viewer ideology affects perceptions of television program ideology. But does political party matter in terms of the targets of late-night humor? According to Baumgartner and Morris (2006), for younger viewers, the 2004 presidential candidates from both parties were negatively affected by mockery from *The Daily Show*.

But during the 2004 party conventions, we find a difference in effects between the two parties. Jonathan Morris' investigation reveals viewers' more negative perceptions of Republicans. In his study, "*The Daily Show* with Jon Stewart and Audience Attitude Change During the 2004 Party Conventions" (2009), Morris reveals that attitudes toward President Bush and Vice-President Cheney worsened while watching *The Daily Show*'s coverage of the Republican Convention, but watching *The Daily Show*'s coverage of the Democratic Convention had little impact on perceptions of presidential candidate John Kerry or his running mate, John Edwards. "This relationship held even when several demographic and attitudinal factors were controlled, and the effect was not limited to partisan Democrats" (Morris 2009, 99). Morris suggests that these differences may be explained by the differing tones of jokes between the two conventions. Much of the humor on *The Daily Show* that was aimed at Democrats targeted the candidates' physical appearance, whereas the ridicule of Republicans was often based on policies and perceived candidate character (Morris 2009).

We also find that ideology matters with *The Colbert Report* effects. In their work, "The Irony of Satire" (2009), Heather LaMarre, Kristen Landreville, and Michael Beam found that liberal or conservative, viewers found Colbert funny. But conservative viewers were more likely to think that Colbert only pretends to be joking: he actually means what he says but cloaks his dislike of liberalism in humor. Liberal viewers think Colbert's humor is satire. As they (2009, 226) note, "results indicate that the ambiguous deadpan satire offered by Stephen Colbert in *The Colbert Report* is interpreted by audiences in a manner that best fits with their individual political beliefs." LaMarre and her colleagues wonder if this biased interpretation leads to a polarizing effect of political satire, with each "side" strengthening their positions after viewing the same message.

Jody Baumgartner and Jonathan Morris looked at effects of Stephen Colbert's *The Colbert Report* on young viewers' political attitudes and their perceived political efficacy (2008b). The results revealed that *The Colbert Report* affects political attitudes, but the influence was unexpected. As they (2008b, 634) explain:

> Instead of giving viewers pause to ponder the legitimacy of Colbert's implicit criticisms of the far right, this experiment found that exposure to Colbert increases support for President Bush, Republicans in Congress, and Republican policies on the economy and the War on Terror.

Instead of honing in on the implicit arguments of *The Colbert Report*, some viewers seemed to take the satire at face value. Quite simply, they didn't get the joke.

Summary of *The Daily Show* and *The Colbert Report* Scholarship Findings

The Daily Show and *The Colbert Report* affect viewers; in many instances, these effects challenge conventional wisdom. Some *Daily Show* viewers think more negatively about television news (Holbert, Lambe, Dudo, and Carlton 2007; Morris & Baumgartner 2008) and more negatively about some politicians (Morris 2009), but they're also learning some political information (Kim and Vishak 2009). *The Colbert Report* may be enhancing instead of derogating perceptions of a common target of its satire — the right wing (Baumgartner and Morris 2008b) — and lowering viewers' perceptions of their political efficacy (Baumgartner and Morris 2008b). But, with *The Colbert Report*, when it comes to effects, it also seems to matter who's watching — that is, the political ideology of the viewer can factor into the effects of *The Colbert Report* humor (LaMarre, Landreville, and Beam 2009).

Two studies explored effects of *The Daily Show* in relation to perceptions of other news media sources. Watching *The Daily Show* makes viewers think of conventional news less in terms of gratification (Holbert, Lambde, Dudo, and Carlton 2007) and this lowers younger viewers' trust in conventional news (Morris and Baumgartner 2008).

The two studies that teased out effects of *The Colbert Report* found these effects to be complementary. Many conservative viewers don't think Colbert is simply cracking jokes — he secretly means what he is saying (LaMarre, Landreville, and Beam 2009, 226). Viewers in general have more positive perceptions of Republicans after watching Colbert (Baumgartner and Morris 2008b).

Some of these effects are consistent with effects of other forms of late-night television political humor. For example, viewers with lower levels of political knowledge are most affected by late-night political humor when it is packaged with network late-night shows (e.g., Young 2004b, 2006) and cable shows such as *The Daily Show* (e.g., Holbert, Lambde, Dudo, and Carlton 2007; Morris and Baumgartner 2008). But, there are also differences between effects of *The Daily Show* and network late-night comedy. Watching *The Daily Show* appears to make some viewers more cynical, whereas watching network late-night comedy lowers cynicism (Morris and Baumgartner 2008). But we also see some differences emerge with effects of *The Daily Show* and

The Colbert Report. For example, we have some evidence that *The Daily Show* is more damaging to Republicans than Democrats (Morris 2009), but *The Colbert Report* seems to boost Republicans' image (Baumgartner and Morris 2008b).

Future Directions for Research

Scholarly attention to Comedy Central's *The Daily Show* and *The Colbert Report* has produced nuanced explanations for what it means to laugh with, and at, politicians. Future research of late-night television political humor in general, and *The Daily Show* and *The Colbert Report* in particular, will continue to clarify effects of political humor.

Scholars have pointed out that late-night comedy is not monolithic (Baumgartner and Morris 2008b; Young and Tissinger 2006). *The Daily Show* and *The Colbert Report* humor is not monolithic either. Consider, for example, the 2004 Democratic and Republican Conventions. While both party conventions were mocked on *The Daily Show*, a content analysis reveals that the humor directed at the Republicans was harder hitting and more substantive (Morris 2009). Furthermore, portions of the programs use different humorous techniques. Scholars using qualitative approaches have isolated specific segments of the shows (Baym 2007), and LaMarre, Landreville, and Beam's empirical effects research used a three-minute clip of an interview on *The Colbert Report* (LaMarre, Landreville, and Beam 2009). Yet our current understanding of effects of interviews on *The Daily Show* and *The Colbert Report* is limited, and future research should take a closer look (Compton 2008). Future scholarship should also explore recurring segments, such as the health news segment on *The Colbert Report*. Other recurring segments warrant effects scholarship, such as *The Daily Show*'s recurring religious news segment. Might these unique segments on *The Daily Show* and *The Colbert Report* have unique effects? Would we find different effects from watching the segments in the context of the entire program compared with watching the segments on their own in, for example, an online clip?

Types of humor differ on *The Daily Show* and *The Colbert Report* (Baumgartner and Morris 2008b; Druick 2009; Waisenen 2009). While some have pointed out that *The Daily Show* humor is more complex than other late-night offerings, such as Jay Leno's monologue (Jones 2005; Young and Tisinger 2006), there are moments of simple humor on *The Daily Show*. In a pilot study, Ya Hui Michelle See, Richard Petty, and Lisa Evans (2009) discovered that people found it more difficult to follow conventional political news forums (panel discussion and debates) than political humor (cartoons and, in their study, *The Daily Show*). Scholars could take an even more specific view of political humor by looking at specific types of humor, from extended satire to the occasional one-liner.

Future research should also explore effects of failed humor, or statements that elicit a backlash. Research into other forms of political humor — for example, Bippus' (2007) study about jokes told during political debates — suggests that the perceived quality of the humor matters in terms of effects. Failed humor in a radio broadcast annoys listeners (Duncan and Nelson 1985, 38), and failed humor during interpersonal conversations is often followed by such responses as silence (Hay 2001) or laughter (Bell 2009). But what happens when humor fails on late-night television comedy? Does failed humor on *The Daily Show* and *The Colbert Report* have a unique effect?

Some viewers are exposed to *The Daily Show* and *The Colbert Report* without watching the actual television programs and, instead, catch content in other venues. For example, late-night television political humor is often rebroadcast during conventional news programs (Compton 2008). We have reasons to believe these clips also have effects. Other types of late night comedy, such as *Saturday Night Live* and late-night television monologues shown at the conclusion of a news broadcast, can reduce viewers' worries and decrease their perceptions of the severity of the issues raised during the preceding news stories (Zillmann, Gibson, Ordman, and Aust 1994).

Additionally, viewers talk about late-night comedy with their friends, colleagues and family members (Schaefer and Avery, 1993). Research suggests that humor can affect and sometimes mitigate conflict during conversations (Norrick and Spitz 2008). Would political humor — Comedy Central political humor particularly — have similar mitigating effects? If so, perhaps word-of-mouth transmission of late-night political comedy content could help people approach potentially contentious topics with less chance of disruptive conflict.

Some theoretical approaches seem particularly well-suited for future late night comedy research. For example, scholars have wondered about a sleeper effect (see Hovland, Lumsdaine, and Sheffield, 1949) with late night political humor, where content lingers longer than recollection of the original source of the content (e.g., Compton 2006; LaMarre, Landreville, and Beam 2009). Inoculation theory offers another rich area for theoretical exploration (see Compton and Pfau 2005). Inoculation scholars find that weakened counterarguments motivate a process of resistance that leads to rejection of subsequent persuasive influences, working much the same way as a medical inoculation injecting a weakened version of an offending agent to bolster resistance against disease (see McGuire, 1964, for an overview of early research, and Compton and Pfau, 2005, for the most recent overview of subsequent scholarship). Can jokes function as weakened versions of persuasive attacks? If so, the humor on *The Daily Show* and *The Colbert Report* could be functioning as an inoculation.

Conclusion

Television political humor effects scholarship is on a path of increasing specificity. Our earliest findings of television political humor effects come from research on the larger genre of soft news. Scholars in pursuit of a more nuanced understanding of soft news effects turned to late night comedy shows in particular, then turned to specific comedy programs such as *The Daily Show* and *The Colbert Report*. Certainly, we will gain more precise understandings of political humor effects as scholars continue to examine specific types of humor and specific segments on *The Daily Show* and *The Colbert Report*. We can't help but wonder what's next. Will *The Daily Show* and *The Colbert Report* inspire other programs using similar types of late-night political humor, prompting scholars to study these programs as a new genre of late-night comedy? Or, will future research continue to find unique differences among late-night comedy television programs? The merging of news, politics, and entertainment has been profound, with "the line between entertainment and news ... blurred, if not completely eradicated" (Mutz 2004, 34). Perhaps no other programs reflect the merge better than *The Daily Show* and *The Colbert Report*.

References

Baek, Young Min, and Magdalena E. Wojcieszak. 2009. "Don't expect too much! Learning from late-night comedy and knowledge item difficulty." *Communication Research* 36, no. 6: 783–809.

Banerjee, Smita C., Kathryn Greene, Marina Krcmar, and Zhanna Bagdasarov. 2009. "Who watches verbally aggressive shows? An examination of personality and other individual difference factors in predicting viewership." *Journal of Media Psychology* 21, no. 1: 1–14.

Baum, Matthew A. 2002. "Sex, lies, and war: How soft news brings foreign policy to the inattentive public." *The American Political Science Review* 96, no. 1: 91–109.

_____. 2003. "Soft news and political knowledge: Evidence of absence or absence of evidence?" *Political Communication* 20, no. 2: 173–90.

_____. 2004. Circling the wagons: Soft news and isolationalism in American public opinion. *International Studies Quarterly* 48, no. 2: 313–38.

Baumgartner, Jody C., and Jonathan S. Morris. 2006. "*The Daily Show* effect: Candidate evaluations, efficacy, and American youth." *American Politics Research* 34, no. 3: 341–367.

_____. 2008a. *Laughing matters: Humor and American politics in the media age.* New York: Routledge.

_____. 2008b. "One 'nation,' under Stephen? The effects of *The Colbert Report* on American youth." *Journal of Broadcasting & Electronic Media* 52, no. 4: 622–43.

Baym, Geoffrey. 2005. "*The Daily Show*: Discursive integration and the reinvention of political journalism." *Political Communication* 22, no. 3: 259–276.

_____. 2007. "Representation and the politics of play: Stephen Colbert's *Better Know a District*." *Political Communication* 24, no. 4: 359–376.

Bell, Nancy D. 2009. "Responses to failed humor." *Journal of Pragmatics* 41, no. 9: 1825–1836.

Bippus, Amy. 2007. "Factors predicting the perceived effectiveness of politician's use of humor during a debate." *Humor* 20, no. 2: 105–121.

Brewer, Paul R., and Emily Marquardt. 2007. "Mock news and democracy: Analyzing *The Daily Show*." *Atlantic Journal of Communication* 15, no. 4: 249–267.

Brewer, Paul R., and Xiaoxia Cao. 2006. "Candidate appearances on soft news shows and public knowledge about primary campaigns." *Journal of Broadcasting & Electronic Media* 50, no. 1: 18–35.

_____. 2008. "Late night television shows as news sources." In *Laughing matters: Humor and American politics in the media age*, ed. Jody C Baumgartner and Jonathan S. Morris, 263–277. New York: Routledge..

Cao, Xiaoxia. 2008. "Political comedy shows and knowledge about primary campaigns: The moderating effects of age and education." *Mass Communication & Society* 11, no. 1: 43–61.

_____, & Paul R. Brewer. 2008. "Political comedy shows and public participation in politics." *International Journal of Public Opinion Research* 20, no. 1: 90–99.

Chaffee, Steve H., Xinshu Zhao, and Glenn Leshner. 1994. "Political knowledge and the campaign media of 1992." *Communication Research* 21, no. 3: 305–24.

Coe, Kevin, David Tewksbury, Bradley J. Bond, Kristin L. Drogos, Robert W. Porter, Ashely Yahn, and Yuanyuan Zhang. 2008. "Hostile news: Partisan use and perceptions of cable news programming." *Journal of Communication* 58, no. 2: 201–19.

Colletta, Lisa. 2009. "Political satire and postmodern irony in the age of Stephen Colbert and Jon Stewart." *The Journal of Popular Culture* 42, no. 5: 856–874.

Compton, Josh. 2006. "Serious as a heart attack: Health-related content of late-night comedy television." *Health Communication* 19, no. 2, 143–51.

_____. 2008. "More than laughing? Survey of political humor effects research." In *Laughing matters: Humor and American politics in the media age*, ed. Jody C Baumgartner and Jonathan S. Morris, 39–63. New York: Routledge.

_____, and Michael Pfau. 2005. "Inoculation theory of resistance to influence at maturity: Recent progress in theory development and application and suggestions for future research." In *Communication yearbook 29*, ed. Pamela J. Kalbfleish, 97–146. New York: Erlbaum.

Davis, Richard, and Diana Owen. 1998. *New media and American politics*. New York: Oxford University Press.

Druick, Zoe. 2009. "Dialogic absurdity: TV news parody as a critique of genre." *Television & New Media* 10, no. 3: 294–308.

Duncan, Calvin P., and James E. Nelson. 1985. "Effects of humor in a radio advertising experiment." *Journal of Advertising* 14, no. 2: 33–64.

Feldman, Lauren. 2007. "The news about comedy: Young audiences, *The Daily Show*, and evolving notions of journalism." *Journalism* 8, no. 4: 406–427.

_____, and Dannagal Goldthwaite Young. 2008. "Late-night comedy as a gateway to traditional news: An analysis of time trends in news attention among late-night comedy viewers during the 2004 presidential primaries." *Political Communication* 25, no. 4: 401–22.

Fox, Julia R., Glory Koloen, and Volkan Sahin. 2007. "No joke: A comparison of substance in *The Daily Show with Jon Stewart* and broadcast network television coverage of the 2004 presidential election campaign." *Journal of Broadcasting & Electronic Media* 51, no. 2: 213–27.

Hay, Jennifer. 2001. "The pragmatics of humor support." *Humor* 14, no. 1: 55–82.

Hoffman, Lindsay H., and Tiffany Thomson. 2009. "The effect of television viewing on adolescents' civic participation: Political efficacy as a mediating mechanism." *Journal of Broadcasting & Electronic Media* 53, no. 1: 3–21.

Holbert, R. Lance. 2005. "A typology for the study of entertainment television and politics." *American Behavioral Scientist* 49, no. 3: 436–453.

_____, Jennifer L. Lambe, Anthony D. Dudo, and Kristin A. Carlton. 2007. "Primacy effects of *The Daily Show* and national TV news viewing: Young viewers, political gratifications, and internal political self-efficacy." *Journal of Broadcasting & Electronic Media* 51, no. 1: 20–38.

Hollander, Barry. 2005. "Late-night learning: Do entertainment programs increase political campaign knowledge for young viewers?" *Journal of Broadcasting & Electronic Media* 49, no. 4: 402–15.

Hovland, Carl I., Arthur A. Lumsdaine, and Fred D. Sheffield. 1949. *Experiments on mass communication*. Princeton, NJ: Princeton University Press.

Jones, Jeffrey P. 2005. *Entertaining politics: New political television and civic culture*. New York: Rowman & Littlefield.

Kim, Young Mie, and John Vishak. 2008. "Just laugh! You don't need to remember: The effects of entertainment media on political information acquisition and information processing in political judgment." *Journal of Communication* 58, no. 2: 338–60.

LaMarre, Heather L., Kristen D. Landreville, and Michael A. Beam. 2009. "The irony of satire: Political ideology and the motivation to see what you want to see in *The Colbert Report*." *The International Journal of Press/Politics* 14, no. 2: 212–31.

McGuire, William J. 1964. "Inducing resistance to persuasion: Some contemporary approaches." In *Advances in experimental social psychology*, ed. Leonard Berkowitz, 191–229. New York: Academic Press.

McLeod, Jack M., Zhongshi Guo, Katie Daily, Catherine A. Steele, Huiping Huang, Edward Horowitz, and Huailin Chen. 1996. "The impact of traditional and nontraditional media forms in the 1992 presidential election." *Journalism & Mass Communication Quarterly* 73, no. 2: 401–426.

Morris, Jonathan S. 2009. "*The Daily Show* with Jon Stewart and audience attitude change during the 2004 party conventions." *Political Behavior* 31, no. 1: 79–102.

_____, and Jody C. Baumgartner. 2008. "*The Daily Show* and attitudes toward the news media." In *Laughing matters: Humor and American politics in the media age*, ed. Jody C Baumgartner and Jonathan S. Morris, 315–31. New York: Routledge.

Moy, Patricia, Michael Pfau, and LeeAnn Kahlor. 1999. "Media use and public confidence in democratic institutions." *Journal of Broadcasting & Electronic Media* 43, no 2: 137–158.

Moy, Patricia, Michael A. Xenos, and Verena K. Hess. 2005. "Communication and citizenship: Mapping the political effects of 'infotainment.'" *Mass Communication & Society* 8, no. 2: 111–31.

Mutz, Diana. 2004. "Leading horses to water: Confessions of a *Daily Show* junkie." *Journalism and Mass Communication Educator* 59, no. 1: 31–35.

Norrick, Neal R., and Alice Spitz. 2008. "Humor as a resource for mitigating conflict in interaction." *Journal of Pragmatics* 40, no. 10: 1661–1686.

Pfau, Michael, Jaeho Cho, and Kristen Chong. 2001. "Impact of communication forms in presidential campaigns: Influences on candidate perceptions and democratic process." *The Harvard International Journal of Press/Politics* 6, no. 4: 88–105.

Pfau, Michael, and William P. Eveland, Jr., 1996. "Influence of traditional and non-traditional news media in the 1992 election campaign." *Western Journal of Communication* 60, no. 3: 214–32.

Pfau, Michael, J. Brian Houston, and Shane M. Semmler. 2005. "Presidential election campaigns and American democracy: The relationship between communication use and normative outcomes." *American Behavioral Scientist* 49, no. 1: 48–62.

Prior, Markus. 2003. "Any good news in soft news? The impact of soft news preference on political knowledge." *Political Communication* 20, no. 2: 149–71.

Rottinghaus, B., Bird, K., Ridout, T., and Self, R. 2008. "'It's better than being informed': College-aged viewers of *The Daily Show*." In J. C Baumgartner & J. S. Morris (Eds.), *Laughing matters: Humor and American politics in the media age* (pp. 279–294). Routledge: New York.

Schaefer, Richard R., and Robert K. Avery. 1993. "Audience conceptualizations of *Late Night with David Letterman*." *Journal of Broadcasting & Electronic Media* 37, no. 3: 253–273.

See, Ya Hui Michelle, Richard E. Petty, and Lisa M. Evans. 2009. "The impact of perceived message complexity and need for cognition on information processing and attitudes." *Journal of Research in Personality* 43, no. 5: 880–889.

Vallone, Robert P., Lee Ross, and Mark R. Lepper. 1985. "The hostile media phenomenon: Bias perception and perceptions of media bias in coverage of the Beirut massacre." *Journal of Personality and Social Psychology* 49, no. 3: 577–585.

Waisanen, Don J. 2009. "A citizen's guide to democracy inaction: Jon Stewart and Stephen Colbert's comic rhetorical criticism." *Southern Communication Journal* 74, no. 2: 119–140.

Xenos, Michael A., and Amy B. Becker. 2009. "Moments of Zen: Effects of *The Daily Show* on information seeking and political learning." *Political Communication* 26, no. 3: 317–332.

Young, Dannagal Goldthwaite. 2004a. Daily Show *viewers knowledgeable about presidential campaign,* National Annenberg Election Survey *shows*. Philadelphia: Annenberg Public Policy Center.

_____. 2004b. "Late-night comedy in Election 2000: Its influence on candidate trait ratings and the moderating effects of political knowledge and partisanship." *Journal of Broadcasting & Electronic Media* 48, no. 1: 1–22.

_____. 2006. "Late-night comedy and the salience of the candidates' caricatured traits in the 2000 election." *Mass Communication & Society* 9, no. 3: 339–66.

_____, and Russell M. Tisinger. 2006. "Dispelling late-night myths: News consumption among late-night comedy viewers and the predictors of exposure to various late-night shows." *The Harvard International Journal of Press/Politics* 11, no. 3: 113–134.

Zillmann, Dolf, Rhonda Gibson, Virginia L. Ordman, and Charles F. Aust. 1994. "Effects of upbeat stories in broadcast news." *Journal of Broadcasting & Electronic Media* 65, no. 1: 65–78.

The Science of Satire

The Daily Show *and* The Colbert Report *as Sources of Public Attention to Science and the Environment*

LAUREN FELDMAN, ANTHONY LEISEROWITZ, *and* EDWARD MAIBACH

On April 8, 2010, Stephen Colbert devoted more than half of *The Colbert Report*'s 30-minute satirical news show to deriding President Obama's plan to scale back NASA's manned space program, first during a four-minute segment called "The Final Final Frontier" and then during a seven-minute interview with astrophysicist Neil deGrasse Tyson. In his interview with Colbert, Tyson argued that astronauts are vital not only to the science of space exploration but also as science's celebrities, inspiring children to grow up and become scientists themselves. In a rare departure from his ironic, often confrontational interview style, Colbert appeared at a loss for words and then lamented "we're going to lose ... we're going to lose that as Americans." A week later, when President Obama exhibited an apparent change of heart, reaffirming his commitment to human space exploration during an address at the Kennedy Space Center in Florida, Colbert responded by triumphantly declaring "I saved the space program!"

While perhaps Stephen Colbert cannot fairly lay claim to saving NASA's space program, there appear to be real public relations benefits conferred by his program. The "Colbert bump" is a term coined by Colbert to refer to the boost in popularity that guests — political candidates, in particular — achieve by appearing on his show. Lending credibility to the "Colbert bump," Fowler (2008) found that Democratic congressional candidates who appeared on *The Colbert Report*'s "Better Know a District" segment in fact went on to significantly out-fundraise their peers who were similarly matched in terms of political party, incumbency, and prior donations but who had not appeared on the show. In late 2009, Colbert extended the "Colbert bump" to the U.S. speed-skating team, signing on his fan club "ColbertNation" as the team's sponsor when its prior sponsor, Dutch bank DSB, went bankrupt, leaving the team with a $300,000 budget deficit in the lead-up to the 2010 Winter Olympics. According to *Sports Illustrated,* more than $200,000 were raised in the first week after Colbert announced the sponsorship on his show and, with two months left to go until the Olympics, traffic on the United States Speedskating website had doubled and skaters were receiving unprecedented amounts of media attention (Bechtel and Cannella 2009). Stephen Colbert himself, sporting full speedskating gear, appeared on the December 21, 2009, cover of *Sports Illustrated* beside the tagline "Stephen Colbert and his Nation Save the Olympics."

Could, then, *The Colbert Report* and its "fake news" predecessor *The Daily Show with Jon Stewart,* by shining a light on science and scientists, be providing them with a "bump" in terms of increased public attention and engagement? According to a recent *USA Today* article, Comedy Central — the home of *The Colbert Report* and *The Daily Show*—has become *the* place for science on television (Vergano 2010). Indeed, Sean Carroll, a physicist who appeared on *The Colbert Report* in March 2010, was quoted as saying "Comedy Central is it, as far as science goes" (Vergano 2010). It is perhaps no coincidence, then, that when Neil deGrasse Tyson was interviewed on *The Colbert Report* in April 2010, it was his seventh appearance on the show — the record for any guest (Vergano 2010). The astrophysicist has also appeared on *The Daily Show* four times. An informal scan of past episodes of *The Colbert Report* and *The Daily Show* on Comedy Central's website revealed that, between October 2005 and April 2010, the two shows have together hosted more than three dozen scientists, discussing everything from particle physics to evolution to global warming. Both shows have also featured public figures and advocates discussing science and environmental policy issues, including former Vice President Al Gore, who has become a major voice on the issue of climate change, and Ron Reagan, Jr., who has spoken out in support of stem cell research.

Moreover, *The Daily Show*'s and *Colbert Report*'s attention to science and the environment extends beyond their selection of interview guests. Both shows frequently include news segments dealing with such issues as global warming, energy, stem-cell research, astronomy, genetics, and evolution. For example, *The Daily Show* aired a week-long series on evolution in September 2005 ("Evolution Schmevolution"); *The Colbert Report* explored the science of genetics and DNA in an August 2007 episode; and in 2009, both programs covered news about the Large Hadron Collider, the world's largest and highest-energy particle accelerator. More systematic evidence for the attention paid to science on Comedy Central comes from a content analysis conducted by the Project for Excellence in Journalism (2008), which found that, in 2007, *The Daily Show* devoted a greater percentage of its news to science/technology and environmental stories than did the mainstream news media. Global warming, specifically, received twice as much coverage on *The Daily Show* than it did in the mainstream press; in fact, in 2007, global warming ranked among the top five most-covered stories on *The Daily Show*. Thus, not only does *The Daily Show* appear to rival traditional news outlets in terms of the substance and quantity of its political coverage (Fox, Koloen, and Sahin 2007), it also does so when it comes to issues of science, technology, and the environment.

However, while the hybridization of comedy and politics and its implications for political engagement have been the subject of much recent scholarly inquiry, little — if any — systematic attention has been devoted to the science-comedy crossover that is also characteristic of *The Colbert Report* and *The Daily Show*. Prior research on the political effects of late-night comedy programs has demonstrated that by piggy-backing political content on entertainment fare, such programs provide a "gateway" to increased audience attention to news and public affairs (Baum 2003; Cao 2010; Feldman and Young 2008). This essay considers whether a similar process could be at work relative to public attention to science and the environment. In addressing this question, we use nationally representative survey data to evaluate the relationship between watching *The Daily Show* and *The Colbert Report* and attention to science and environmental issues, specifically global warming. Findings suggest that just as exposure to late-night comedy correlates with increased audience attention to politics, so too does exposure to *The Daily Show* and *The Colbert Report* go hand-in-hand with attention paid to science and the environment. Before turning to a detailed explanation of these results, the essay first considers the challenge of science engagement in the U.S., and then offers a theoretical account of how a couple of satirical news programs could help to improve science engagement among their audiences.

The Challenge of Science Engagement

Science and technology pervade all aspects of American life. A basic understanding of science and technology informs our decision-making in the workplace, in the marketplace, in the doctor's office, and at the dinner table. Without such an understanding, we would be ill-equipped to make a computer purchase, for example, or comprehend a medical diagnosis. Science literacy is also critical to our competency as citizens. Awareness of threats to public health and to the environment allows us to act in ways that benefit not only our personal but also our collective well-being. Moreover, the intensity of public engagement with scientific and technological issues impacts government funding and policymaking related to such topics as climate change, nanotechnology, and stem cell research.

Despite the central role that science and technology play in the lives of American citizens, public engagement with science and technology is low, particularly relative to other issues. Although, in 2008, more than 80 percent of Americans reported that they are interested in new scientific discoveries, a figure that has remained relatively stable over the last decade (National Science Board 2010), only 13 percent of Americans reported that they follow news about science and technology "very closely," down from 22 percent a decade earlier (Pew Research Center, cited in National Science Board 2010, Table 7–1). Using this criterion, science and technology ranked 13th among 18 different news topics in 2008, which represents a lower ranking than in prior years (Pew Research Center 2008).

Environmental news fares a bit better: In 2008, 21 percent of Americans said they follow environmental news "very closely," the same percentage who said they follow political news "very closely" (Pew Research Center 2008). However, when asked to name the top problem facing the country, just 1 percent of Americans mention the environment (Jones 2009). Further, in March 2010, Gallup reported that Americans were less worried about a host of environmental problems, ranging from air and water pollution to the extinction of plant and animal species, than at any point in the past twenty years (Jones 2010).

And, even as the scientific evidence for global warming accumulates (IPCC, 2007), public concern about this issue, as measured on a number of indicators, is in decline (Newport 2010). Moreover, of eight environmental problems polled by Gallup, global warming ranked last in terms of public concern (Jones 2010). Just 28 percent of Americans said that they worried about global warming "a great deal," relative to 50 percent who worried about the pollution of drinking water. Maibach, Roser-Renouf, and Lesierowitz (2009) found that, in the fall of 2008, 12 percent of Americans were completely disengaged on the issue of global warming, meaning that they had hardly thought about global warming at all, did not consider it personally important, and tended not to worry about it. Another 18 percent was either doubtful or dismissive of the reality of global warming. By January 2010, while the proportion of disengaged Americans had dropped to 6 percent, the proportion who were doubtful or dismissive had grown to 29 percent (Leiserowitz, Maibach and Roser-Renouf 2010).

Running parallel to this downward trend in public engagement, coverage of science, space, and technology on the major television news networks (i.e., ABC, NBC, CBS) has decreased since 2003, based on tracking by the Tyndall Report (cited in National Science Board 2010, Figure 7–6). In 2008, of approximately 15,000 minutes of annual nightly weekday newscast coverage on the networks, coverage of science, space and technology occupied just 200 minutes, down from a record high of 752 minutes in 1999. The environment garnered 422 minutes of coverage; of that time, just 15 minutes were spent discussing global warming (Tyndall Report 2008).

Given that the news media serve as agenda-setters for the public (McCombs and Shaw 1972), it is perhaps, then, no surprise that science, technology, and the environment don't register as high sources of attention or concern among Americans. Moreover, many non-news approaches to science and the environment, like PBS's *NOVA*, reach only a small audience of already informed science enthusiasts, thereby failing to engage a wider, more diverse public (Nisbet and Scheufele 2009). Complicating this trend, public views on science are strongly confounded with religion, leading some Americans to be dismissive of evolutionary biology, for one (Pew Research Center 2009a). The politicization of scientific issues like climate change further serves to polarize public opinion; for example, Republicans and Democrats are deeply divided in their beliefs about the reality and causes of global warming (Pew Research Center 2009a; 2009b). Scientists themselves have recently come under attack, particularly relative to climate change. The 2009 "Climategate affair" — referring to leaked emails from leading climate scientists allegedly revealing that they had manipulated climate data — and controversy surrounding errors in the 2007 IPCC (Intergovernmental Panel on Climate Change) report have fueled the rancor of climate skeptics and become fodder for conservative media personalities like Fox News' Glenn Beck and Sean Hannity. During this time, confusion over intense winters, the economic recession, and a preoccupation with the debate over health care reform also may have attenuated Americans' concern for and attention to global warming (Nisbet 2010).

Science communication scholars Nisbet and Scheufele (2009) argue that public engagement with science does not necessarily turn on the availability of higher quality information and news coverage, or even on increased science literacy. Engaging the public is, instead, a matter of strategic communication. Rather than conforming to a "transmission" model, whereby scientific "facts are assumed to speak for themselves" (p. 1767), scientists must serve as translators, communicating science in ways that make it more accessible and relevant to ordinary Americans. Part of this strategy includes the utilization of non-traditional science venues, such as entertainment programming, to promote incidental exposure to scientific information among otherwise inattentive publics.

Comedy as a Gateway to Science

Information seeking, ultimately, is governed by cost-benefit calculations (Popkin 1994). Due to the finite resources that individuals have available for cognitive processing, the perceived benefits or utility of new information must outweigh the perceived costs, in terms of time and energy, of acquiring that information. Because prior knowledge of an issue is critical for the accumulation of new knowledge, the "entry-costs" for learning about specialized scientific topics like climate change are high for non-experts — in other words, becoming informed about science is both time-consuming and challenging (Ungar 2000). Consistent with this expectation, Nisbet et al. (2002) found an education gap in science-related media use, such that individuals with higher levels of formal education were more likely to watch science-related television programming and read science magazines than those with less education; more education was also correlated with superior knowledge of and fewer reservations concerning science.

Compounding the costs of acquiring scientific information is the "attention economy" in which science must compete against the all-encompassing popular culture (Ungar 2000). According to Ungar, representations of popular culture provide "the connective threads of information and conversation that tie us together" (p. 302). So, while scientific information may hold value from a practical standpoint or from the perspective of good citizenship, its perceived social or conversational utility is often trumped by entertainment stories and celebrity facts. Because there is seen to be relatively little return, socially or conversationally, for being scientifically informed, the motivation to withstand the high costs of acquiring scientific knowledge remains low.

This offers a compelling argument for how making science part of the popular culture could increase public attentiveness and engagement. When science is discussed on *The Daily Show* or *The Colbert Report* it becomes complementary to, instead of in competition with, popular culture and entertainment (see Baym 2005, for a similar argument relative to entertainment and politics on *The Daily Show*). This increases the benefits of engagement (making it worthy of "water-cooler" conversations) while decreasing the costs (attaching it to information people *already* want to pay attention to). Indeed, political scientists (e.g., Downs 1957; Popkin 1994) have long theorized that individuals, in order to preserve their limited cognitive resources, often acquire "high-cost" political information derivatively during non-political pursuits. In other words, just by going about their daily lives, without any dedication of effort, people can glean relevant political content. They pick it up in conversation, when passing by newspaper stands or, as Baum (2003) has demonstrated, while consuming entertainment. Specifically, Baum (2003) has found that coverage of politics in entertainment-oriented news sources like *Access Hollywood* or *Oprah*—what he calls "soft news"—can increase attentiveness to politics, especially among typically apolitical audiences. In this way, soft news serves to close traditional gaps in political attentiveness between those with high and low levels of interest in politics. Thus, just as the acquisition of political information becomes "a free bonus, or an incidental by-product" of entertainment consumption (Baum 2003, 30), audiences of *The Daily Show* and *Colbert Report* might likewise attend to and potentially learn about science inadvertently, as a consequence of their attention to entertainment.

Piggy-backing science content on entertainment fare might not only help to ensure some minimal exposure to science content among the otherwise unengaged, it could also promote subsequent attention to scientific topics in other outlets, whether the traditional news media or popular science programming like *NOVA*. In the political realm, Baum's (2003) "gateway" hypothesis suggests that the treatment of political topics in entertainment-oriented programs helps make political information more cognitively accessible, or top of mind, to entertainment audiences. At the same time, it provides a basic level of understanding about politics, or a knowledge schema, which aids in the assimilation and interpretation of new political information. Once people have some baseline familiarity and cursory knowledge of a political topic due to its coverage on soft news programs, it becomes easier and less costly to pay attention to information about the same topic when it is later encountered in more traditional news programs.

In support of his hypothesis, Baum found that watching entertainment-oriented news programs and talk shows — which tend to cover news of war and foreign policy crises, even if only in the context of celebrity involvement — increased viewers' attention to crisis-related information in traditional news venues. This gateway effect was true, however, primarily among those who reported low levels of political interest. Individuals with high levels of political interest have already determined that political news is worth their time and effort and thus pay attention to politics regardless of their exposure to coverage of these topics in soft news outlets. Subsequent research has focused more narrowly on the gateway effects of late-night comedy (Feldman and Young 2008) and *The Daily Show* specifically (Cao 2010), finding in both cases that exposure leads to increased attentiveness to traditional political news.

Communication has long been understood to spur further communication (Chaffee and McLeod 1972) and, in fact, Baum's gateway hypothesis is conceptually similar to several other frameworks applied to the study of media effects. For example, Holbert (2005) has argued for the study of intramedia mediation, the phenomenon by which one type of media use influences another and they then jointly affect outcomes like learning and attitude change. Likewise, the reinforcing spirals model (Slater 2007) proposes that the cognitive or behavioral outcomes of media use influence subsequent information-seeking, and, in fact, this model has been used to understand the reciprocal dynamics involved in individuals' media use and their global warming perceptions (Zhao 2009). While the reinforcing spirals model contends that exposure to media content can pique interest in the subject of that content, prompting further information-seeking from the media, selection of the initial content is governed by individual predispositions and interests (Slater 2007). This is consistent with the expectation that an interest in entertainment and perhaps politics, but not science, drives people to *The Daily Show* and *The Colbert Report*. The gateway effect would occur precisely because audiences are not especially interested in scientific information initially but acquire it as a byproduct of their entertainment consumption, thereby increasing its accessibility and reducing costs of further scientific information seeking.

Following from this logic, the appearance of scientists on *The Colbert Report* and *The Daily Show*, along with these programs' sustained coverage of science and environmental topics more generally, are apt to increase the public's motivation to pay attention to science and the environment by decreasing the transaction costs and increasing the perceived benefits associated with engaging with a fairly specialized domain of knowledge. We thus hypothesize that people who watch *The Colbert Report* and *The Daily Show* will exhibit greater attention to news about science and the environment than those who don't watch these programs. Further, we expect this relationship to be particularly pronounced among those for whom the initial costs of engaging with scientific and environmental topics are higher. To this end, given previous research (Nisbet et al. 2002) that has identified formal education as a correlate of science information-seeking, we examine whether the strength of the relationship between *Daily Show* and *Colbert Report* viewing and attention to science and the environment is stronger among those with less formal education. Data consistent with this hypothesis would show that exposure to *The Daily Show* and *The Colbert Report* helps to narrow traditional education gaps in science attentiveness.

Method

Data for this study come from a survey covering a range of topics related to global warming and the environment. The survey was fielded in September and October 2008 by Knowledge Networks, using its nationally representative online panel. The Knowledge Networks panel consists of about 50,000 U.S. residents, age 18 and older, recruited through probability sampling and using published sampling frames that cover 99 percent of the U.S. population. The within-panel completion rate for the survey was 54 percent. The final sample included 2,164 respondents.

Measurement of Dependent Variables

The analysis focuses on three different dependent variables. The first two dependent variables capture how closely respondents follow news about science and technology and news about the environment, respectively, on a scale from (1) "not at all" to (4) "very closely." Nineteen percent of respondents said that they follow science and technology news "not at all." Forty-seven percent reported following "a little," which was the median response. About a quarter (26 percent) said that they followed news about science and technology "somewhat closely," and just 8 percent said that they followed "very closely." When it came to news about the environment, 17 percent of respondents reported following "not at all." Forty-eight percent reported following "a little," which was again the median response. Twenty-nine percent said that they followed environmental news "somewhat closely," and 7 percent said that they followed "very closely." The third dependent variable reflects respondents' attentiveness to the specific environmental issue of global warming. Respondents were asked to indicate how much attention they pay to information about global warming from 1 "none" to 4 "a lot." Eighteen percent of respondents said that they paid no attention to global warming. Thirty-nine percent said that they paid "a little" attention, which was the median response, and 30 percent paid "some attention." Fourteen percent of respondents reported paying "a lot" of attention to information about global warming.

Measurement of Independent and Control Variables

Using a response scale from (1) "never" to (4) "often," respondents were asked to report how frequently they watch *The Colbert Report* and *The Daily Show with Jon Stewart*, respectively. A full 70 percent of respondents said that they "never" watched *The Daily Show*. Fifteen percent watched "hardly ever," 10 percent watched "sometimes," and 5 percent watched "often." Similarly, 73 percent of respondents said that they "never" watched *The Colbert Report*, 13 percent watched "hardly ever," 10 percent watched "sometimes," and 5 percent watched "often." Because the correlation between the two items was substantial ($r = .77$, $p < .001$), responses were averaged to form a single, combined measure of satirical news use ($M = 1.5$, $SD = 0.8$; *Median* = 1 "never"). This avoids problems with multicollinearity, whereby when two (or more) predictor variables in a regression equation are highly correlated, their standard errors become artificially inflated and, as a consequence, it becomes increasingly difficult to obtain distinct, reliable estimates of their effects on the dependent variable (Allison 1999). Due to its skewed distribution, the combined measure was further collapsed into a three-level ordinal variable for use in analysis: Sixty-five percent of respondents "never" watched satirical news (i.e., scored 1 on the combined scale); 23 percent were "occasional" viewers (i.e., scored above 1 but below 3 on the combined scale), and 11 percent were "regular" viewers (i.e., scored 3 or higher).

Formal education was measured by asking respondents to report the highest level of education that they had completed. More than a third (39 percent) reported having a high school diploma or less; 29 percent completed some college, and 32 percent had earned a bachelor's degree or higher.

All analyses also controlled for demographic variables (age, gender, race/ethnicity, income), other news media use (print news, online news, national network news, cable news, National Public Radio), as well as relevant values and predispositions (political party identification, political ideology, church attendance, environmentalism, attitudes toward modern science). Measurement of the control variables is described in Appendix A.

Results

To examine the relationship between satirical news use and attentiveness to science, the environment and global warming, respectively, each of the three dependent measures was regressed on frequency of satirical news viewing, along with an extensive set of controls. Due to the ordinal measurement of the dependent variables, ordered logit was used to estimate the regression models. The results of these analyses are presented in Table 1. In interpreting the results, it is important to keep in mind that the cross-sectional nature of the data only permits a test of correlation between variables, not causation — a limitation that is taken up in more detail in the essay's discussion section.

The results from the first, third, and fifth models in Table 1 indicate that for all three dependent variables, satirical news use is positively associated with attentiveness at levels of statistical significance ($p < .05$). Thus, consistent with expectations, as exposure to *The Daily Show* and *The Colbert Report* increases so too do attentiveness to science news (Model 1), environmental news (Model 3), and information about global warming (Model 5). Several other predictors also demonstrated consistently positive and statistically significant relationships with all three dependent variables. These include education (although this relationship was only marginally significant in the case of global warming attentiveness), online news use, national network television news viewing, National Public Radio (NPR) listening, environmentalism, and positive attitudes toward modern science. Importantly, the extensive battery of controls included in the regression models rule out the possibility that the observed relationships between satirical news use and attentiveness can be explained by third variables such as demographics, political orientation, other forms of news use, or predispositions toward science and the environment.

The logit coefficients presented in these models can be translated into predicted probabilities, making it easier to interpret the magnitude of the relationship between satirical news use and attentiveness. As satirical news use increases from never to regularly, the corresponding probabilities of following science and technology news, environmental news, and information about global warming "somewhat closely" increase by 8 (from .24 to .32), 8 (from .26 to .34), and 7 (from .31 to .38) percentage points, respectively. Notably, in its ability to draw attention to science and environmental topics, satirical television news appears to be on par with or even exceed its traditional television news counterparts. An increase in CNN/MSNBC viewing corresponds to an increase in the probability of following science and technology news, environmental news, and information about global warming "somewhat closely" by just 1 (from .25 to .26), 7 (from .25 to .32), and 8 (from .30 to .38) percentage points, respectively. As a result of watching more Fox News, the corresponding shifts in the probability of following science and technology news, environmental news, and information about global warming "somewhat closely" are 9 (from .22 to .31), 6 (from .25 to .31), and -.03 (from .330 to .327) percentage points, respectively. An increase in national network television use is associated with a 6 percentage point increase (from .22 to .28) in the probability of following science and technology news "somewhat closely," which is slightly lower than the 8 percentage point jump in probability associated with increased satirical news use. Watching more national network news, however, is associated with a somewhat greater increase in the probability of attending to the environment (14 percentage points, from .20 to .34) and global warming (16 percentage points, from .24 to .40) than is an increase in satirical news use.

Turning again to Table 1, models two, four, and six test the interaction between satirical news use and education for each dependent variable. This test permits us to examine whether the relationship between satirical news use and attentiveness is stronger among those with less formal education, i.e., those for whom the initial costs of paying attention to information about science and the environment are likely to be higher.[1] The results support this

Table 1. Ordered Logit Analyses of Attentiveness

	Science and Technology News		Environmental News		Global Warming Information	
	Model 1	Model 2	Model 1	Model 2	Model 1	Model 2
Demographics						
Age	0.0008 (.003)	0.007 (.003)	-0.005 (.003)	-0.005 (.003)	0.0008 (.003)	0.008 (.003)
Gender (Male)	0.58 (.09)***	0.57 (.09)***	-0.16 (.09)+	-0.16 (.09)+	-0.29 (.09)**	-0.30 (.09)**
Race (White)	-0.05 (.12)	-0.05 (.11)	-0.09 (.12)	-0.09 (.11)	-0.11 (.11)	-0.11 (.11)
Education	0.38 (.06)***	0.48 (.07)***	0.16 (.06)**	0.22 (.07)**	0.10 (.06)+	0.19 (.07)**
Income	0.008 (.03)	0.008 (.03)	-0.003 (.03)	-0.002 (.03)	-0.01 (.03)	-0.01 (.03)
Media Use						
Satire	0.24 (.07)**	0.68 (.18)***	0.22 (.07)**	0.50 (.17)**	0.22 (.07)**	0.62 (.17)***
Print news	0.04 (.02)*	0.04 (.02)*	0.09 (.02)***	0.09 (.02)***	0.02 (.02)	0.02 (.02)
Online news	0.17 (.02)***	0.17 (.02)***	0.13 (.02)***	0.13 (.02)***	0.10 (.02)***	0.10 (.02)***
Network TV news	0.13 (.05)**	0.13 (.05)**	0.27 (.05)***	0.27 (.05)***	0.32 (.05)***	0.31 (.05)***
Fox News	0.17 (.05)***	0.17 (.04)***	0.11 (.05)*	0.10 (.05)**	-0.009 (.04)	-0.01 (.04)
CNN / MSNBC	0.01 (.06)	0.007 (.06)	0.13 (.06)*	0.13 (.06)*	0.17 (.06)**	0.16 (.06)**
National Public Radio	0.26 (.05)***	0.27 (.05)***	0.32 (.05)***	0.32 (.05)***	0.17 (.05)***	0.18 (.05)***
Values and Predispositions						
Political Party Identification (Republican)	0.01 (.03)	0.01 (.03)	-0.05 (.03)	-0.05 (.03)	-0.10 (.04)**	-0.10 (.03)**
Political Ideology (Conservative)	-0.02 (.05)	-0.02 (.05)	-0.13 (.05)*	-0.13 (.05)*	-0.12 (.05)*	-0.12 (.05)*
Church attendance	-0.01 (.03)	-0.02 (.03)	0.006 (.03)	0.005 (.03)	-0.03 (.03)	-0.04 (.03)
Environmentalism	0.55 (.06)***	0.55 (.06)***	1.04 (.07)***	1.04 (.07)***	1.12 (.06)***	1.12 (.06)***
Positive attitudes toward modern science	0.35 (.06)***	0.35 (.06)***	0.19 (.06)**	0.18 (.06)**	0.27 (.06)***	0.26 (.06)***
Satire x Education Interaction	—	-0.21 (.08)**	—	-.13 (.08)+	—	-0.19 (.07)*
Constant 1	3.80 (.35)	3.93 (.36)	3.25 (.36)	3.33 (.36)	2.86 (.35)	2.98 (.35)
Constant 2	6.49 (.38)	6.64 (.38)	6.23 (.38)	6.33 (.38)	5.31 (.36)	5.44 (.36)
Constant 3	8.65 (.40)	8.79 (.40)	8.72 (.40)	8.81 (.41)	7.39 (.38)	7.52 (.38)
Pseudo R^2	0.13	0.13	0.18	0.18	0.17	0.17
N	2023	2023	2013	2013	2024	2024

Note. Table entries are ordered logit coefficients; standard errors are in parentheses.

$^+p < .10.$ $^*p < .05.$ $^{**}p < .01.$ $^{***}p < .001.$

expectation. For each of the three dependent variables, the coefficient for the interaction term (i.e., "Satire x Education Interaction") is negative, indicating that the strength of the relationship between satirical news use and attentiveness to science and technology (Model 2), the environment (Model 4), and global warming (Model 6), respectively, increases as one's level of education decreases. The interaction is statistically significant ($p < .05$) in the case of both science and technology news and global warming information attentiveness; the interaction is marginally significant ($p < .10$) in the case of environmental news attentiveness.[2]

The three graphs in Figure 1 illustrate the predicted probability of following each type of news *more* than "a little" as a function of varying levels of education and satirical news use, with all control variables held constant at their mean values. As can be seen in each graph, for those respondents with at least a Bachelor's degree, attentiveness to news about science and technology, the environment, and global warming, respectively, varies little as a function of satirical news use. Indeed, as exposure to satirical news among those with a Bachelor's degree or higher increases from "never" to "regularly," the probability of following news about science and technology, news about the environment, and information about global warming increases just 2 (from .39 to .42), 6 (from .33 to .39), and 8 (from .42 to .50) percentage points, respectively — all non-significant increases. On the other hand, among those with a high school diploma or less, attentiveness increases significantly with rising levels of satirical news use. As this group's satirical news use increases from "never" to "regularly," the probability of following news about science and technology, news about the environment, and information about global warming jumps 18 (from .20 to .38), 17 (from .25 to .42), and 23 (from .33 to .56) percentage points, respectively.[3]

These patterns not only confirm that *The Daily Show* and *The Colbert Report* serve as a source of attention to news about science and the environment primarily among those with less formal education, they also suggest that satirical news can help to equalize and even reverse educational gaps in attention to these issues. At the lowest level of satirical news use, attention to science and technology news is characterized by large disparities favoring those with higher levels of education. With regular satirical news use, however, these gaps all but disappear. Likewise, while the educational gaps in attention to the environment and global warming at the lowest levels of satirical news use are somewhat less pronounced than that seen with science and technology news attention, these gaps are minimized with just moderate increases in satirical news consumption. And, at the maximum level of satirical news use, those with lower levels of education pay *more* attention to these topics than those with higher levels of education.

Figure 1. Probability of Following News More Than "A Little," as Satirical News Use and Education Vary

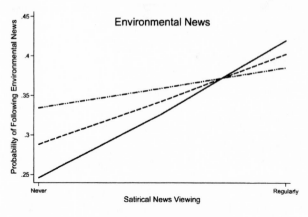

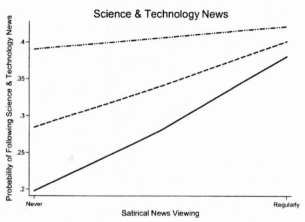

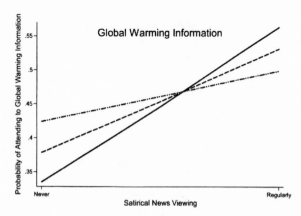

Highest Level of Education Completed

——— High school diploma or less   ----- Some college   --·--· Bachelor's Degree or higher

Discussion

Both anecdotal observations in the popular press (Vergano 2010) and systematic evaluations of program content (Project for Excellence in Journalism 2008) have identified Comedy Central's *The Daily Show* and *The Colbert Report* as dishing up a relatively heavy dose of science and the environment along with their comedy and political satire. This study goes a step further, establishing these programs as sources of public attention to science and the environment: The more people watch *The Daily Show* and *The Colbert Report*, the more attention they pay to news about science and technology, news about the environment, and information about global warming, respectively. These relationships emerge despite robust controls for demographics, other media use, and relevant values and predispositions. Moreover, the relationship between satirical news use and attentiveness is most pronounced among those with the least amount of formal education. This is ostensibly because those with less education find it more challenging and time-consuming to acquire information about science and the environment than those with more education, and are thus less motivated to seek it out on their own; however, by piggybacking such information on entertainment content, attention to science and the environment becomes an inadvertent consequence of entertainment consumption.

These findings extend prior research which has demonstrated that exposure to political content in entertainment and comedy programs is associated with increased attentiveness to politics, particularly among those who are initially less politically engaged (Baum 2003; Cao 2010; Feldman and Young 2008). The pattern of results is likewise consistent with Baum's (2003) "gateway" hypothesis, which suggests that by making information about politics — or, in the present case, information about science and the environment — more cognitively accessible to viewers, entertainment programs can promote *subsequent* attention to news about these topics. However, without the benefit of longitudinal or experimental data, it is not possible to make firm assertions about the direction of causality. That is, we don't know for certain that exposure to *The Daily Show* and *The Colbert Report* actually *leads* people to pay attention to science and the environment in the news. It is possible that those who closely follow science and the environment in the news are driven to *The Daily Show* and *The Colbert Report* explicitly in search of science and environmental content. This, however, would fail to explain the especially strong relationships between satirical news exposure and attention among those with low levels of education, who are assumed to lack the intrinsic motivation to follow traditionally packaged news about science and the environment. We can thus be reasonably confident that, at least among this group, the causal arrow runs from satirical news exposure to science and environmental attentiveness. Still another possibility is that there is some unmeasured third variable, such as a personality characteristic, that explains *both* exposure to satirical news and attention to science and the environment. An additional limitation is that without measures of media-specific news attention, it is not clear which sources audiences are using to follow news about science and the environment. It could be that what we are seeing are contemporaneous effects whereby viewers of *The Daily Show* and *The Colbert Report* are paying more attention to these topics as they encounter them in *The Daily Show* and *The Colbert Report* as opposed to in other, more traditional sources of science and environmental news.

Even with these ambiguities, there is clear evidence that attention to news about science and the environment goes hand-in-hand with exposure to *The Daily Show* and *The Colbert Report*. Moreover, education appears to be a weaker determinant of science and environmental attentiveness among avid viewers of satirical news: Satirical news is an attention equalizer, reducing traditional gaps in attentiveness between those with low and high levels of education. In this way, satirical news helps information about science and the environment reach a broader swath of the American public than would ordinarily seek out such information. Although "attentiveness" reflects a fairly cursory level of engagement and is not necessarily indicative of an issue's personal salience — nor does it guarantee knowledge or opinion-holding about an issue — it is an important precursor to these phenomena (Baum 2003). One needs to pay attention to an issue in order to gain knowledge or form an opinion about it. Indeed, studies of public opinion have demonstrated that attention to or awareness of an issue increases one's willingness to offer an opinion on that issue (Page and Shapiro 1983; Zaller 1991). At the same time, research has found that attention to news content is associated with greater factual knowledge of that content (Chaffee and Schleuder 1986). Evidence for the link between issue attentiveness and knowledge and opinion-holding has also been found in the specific context of global warming (e.g., Kahlor and Rosenthal 2009; Krosnick et al. 2006). To the extent, then, that attentiveness ultimately translates into knowledge and opinion-holding, the present findings indicate not only the possibility of a more scientifically informed and active public, but also that knowledge and engagement, at least among satirical news viewers, will not be concentrated solely among those with high levels of education. This suggests a more equitable distribution of the scientific information citizens need to make critical decisions related to their personal and collective wellbeing and, particularly as policy-making focuses on such scientific concerns as climate change, carries important normative implications for democratic politics as well.

Still, future research will want to verify the causal direction of the observed relationships and provide a true test of the gateway effect using either longitudinal or experimental methods. Subsequent studies should also examine what exactly people take away from their exposure to science and environmental content in satirical news, in terms of knowledge and opinions. Specifically, studies should look more carefully at *how* scientific and environmental issues are depicted on *The Daily Show* and *The Colbert Report* and at the effects of these depictions on audience understanding and perceptions. For example, LaMarre, Landreville, and Beam (2009) found that politically conservative viewers of *The Colbert Report* took Colbert's satire at face-value, believing him to be sincere. It is thus important to consider whether the satirical tenor of *The Daily Show* and *The Colbert Report* detracts from the perceived importance or seriousness of the scientific and environmental issues that they cover, while at the same time increasing attentiveness to these issues. Likewise, understanding the intramedia mediation processes (Holbert 2005) potentially at work here, whereby satirical news exposure spawns further exposure to science content from other media sources, which then influences knowledge and opinion, is an important endeavor for future research.

When interviewed by *USA Today*, physicist Sean Carroll said, "It is a very bad thing for the country that Comedy Central is the go-to place for hearing scientists talk about their recent work" (Vergano 2010). While perhaps true to the extent that this suggests other media outlets are less friendly to science and scientists, we argue for a silver lining. Comedy Central, by showcasing science and scientists, is serving as a source of public attention to science and the environment, particularly among those who might otherwise lack the resources or motivation to pay attention to these topics. As media choice proliferates and audiences fragment across information outlets and content domains, simply broadcasting a message cannot guarantee widespread public attention. It has become all too easy for audiences to tune out issues and information in which they are not inherently interested (Prior 2005). Many politicians have accepted this reality of our current media environment, reaching out to apolitical audiences by appearing as interview guests on entertainment talk shows, with some success (Baum 2005). Indeed, President Obama appeared on *The Tonight Show with Jay Leno* in March 2009 to promote his economic recovery plan, making him the first sitting president ever to be interviewed on a late-night comedy program. Our findings suggest that scientists are well-advised to follow suit, as their interviews on *The Daily Show* and *The Colbert Report*, along with these programs' topical coverage of scientific and environmental issues, are helping to raise the profile of science and the environment among harder to reach audiences.

So, is Comedy Central saving science? Given the relatively modest-sized audiences of *The Daily Show* and *The Colbert Report* (i.e., in April 2010, each show attracted a nightly viewership in the vicinity of 1—1.5 million people; Seidman 2010), Comedy Central is unlikely to kindle Americans' engagement with science all on its own. Still, satirical news programs appear to be important outlets for broadening public attention to science and the environment. Thus, in the language of Colbert, science and the environment are indeed benefiting from an attentiveness "bump" at the hands of Comedy Central. In addition to its practical implications for scientists seeking to promote their trade, this research suggests that the same theoretical models used to understand the political effects of late-night comedy can be used to understand effects in other contexts, in this case science. Hopefully, this study will serve as a call for future research in this vein, so that we can more fully understand the implications of comedy and satire for how people learn about and engage with science.

Notes

1. It is important to point out that although education and satirical news viewing are moderately and positively correlated ($r = .18$), those with a high school education or less comprise a full 25 percent of the regular audience of satirical news, which is roughly equivalent to the proportion of the regular audience who completed some college. The remaining 45 percent of regular satirical news viewers have a Bachelor's degree or higher. In other words, while the likelihood of watching satirical news increases somewhat with higher levels of education, satirical news still attracts a substantial audience among those at the lower end of the education spectrum and thus holds the potential to draw this group's attention toward science and the environment.

2. While education was suggested by prior research (e.g., Nisbet et al. 2002) to be the best indicator of respondents' intrinsic interest in or motivation to follow news about science and the environment, environmentalism and attitudes toward modern science could also serve as appropriate proxies for such motivation. Accordingly, we would expect that the interactions between satirical news use and these variables would also be negative and significant, such that those respondents with less positive attitudes toward modern science and environmentalism — and thus less inherent interest in these topics — would demonstrate the most pronounced relationships between satirical news use and attentiveness. Indeed, for all three dependent variables, there was a significant, negative interaction (all $p < .01$) between satirical news use and attitudes toward modern science. In a pattern similar to that seen with satirical news use and education, the relationship between satirical news use and science, environmental, and global warming attentiveness was stronger among those who agree with the statement that modern science does more harm than good than among those who disagree with this statement. This pattern was not upheld when examining the interaction between environmentalism and satire. Here, the interaction terms were non-significant for environmental news and global warming information, though marginally significant and *positive* in the case of science and technology news ($p < .07$). Thus, when it comes to their attention to the environment and global warming, environmentalists and non-environmentalists do not differ as a function of their satirical news use — that is, the relationship is uniformly positive. That attention to the environment and global warming increases among non-environmentalists as a function of satirical news use is consistent with expectations. On the other hand, the attention of environmentalists increases at comparable levels. This could be because those passionate about the environment are especially activated by related content in satirical news, or, because they are more attuned to these issues at baseline,

they may even watch *The Daily Show* and *The Colbert* explicitly to see content related to the environment. Longitudinal data would be needed to better sort out these effects. The finding that the positive relationship between satirical news use and attention to science and technology is marginally more pronounced among environmentalists than among non-environmentalists is somewhat more difficult to explain. Future research may want to probe why non-environmentalists are relatively unresponsive to satirical news as a source of science and technology news. Nonetheless, the fact that the expected pattern of relationships held for two out of three possible moderating variables (education and attitudes toward modern science) lends credence to our theoretical expectations.

3. The confidence intervals around these probability estimates were computed using the simulation procedure developed by Tomz, Wittenberg, and King (2001; see also King, Tomz, and Wittenberg 2000). For all three dependent variables, attentiveness among those with no more than a high school education increased significantly at the .05 level as a function of satirical news use: The 95 percent confidence interval (CI) around the probability of attending to science and technology news at the lowest levels of satirical news viewing was .17-.23; at the highest levels of satirical news viewing, it was .30-.47. The 95 percent CI around the probability of attending to environmental news at the lowest levels of satirical news viewing was .21-.28; at the highest levels of satirical news viewing, it was .33-.51. The 95 percent CI around the probability of attending to global warming information at the lowest levels of satirical news viewing was .30-.37; at the highest levels of satirical news viewing, it was .46-.66. On the other hand, increases in attentiveness among those with a Bachelor's degree or higher were not statistically significant: The 95 percent CI around the probability of attending to science and technology news at the lowest levels of satirical news viewing was .34-.44; at the highest levels of satirical news viewing, it was .34-.51. The 95 percent CI around the probability of attending to environmental news at the lowest levels of satirical news viewing was .29-.38; at the highest levels of satirical news viewing, it was .31-.47. The 95 percent CI around the probability of attending to global warming information at the lowest levels of satirical news viewing was .37-.47; at the highest levels of satirical news viewing, it was .41-.58.

References

Allison, Paul. 1999. *Multiple Regression: A Primer.* Thousand Oaks, CA: Sage.
Bechtel, Mark, and Stephen Cannella. 2009. 5th Annual: The Year in Sports Media. *Sports Illustrated*, December 21. http://sportsillustrated.cnn.com/vault/article/magazine/MAG 1163994/index.htm.
Baum, Matt. A. 2003. *Soft News Goes to War.* Princeton, NJ: Princeton University Press.
_____. 2005. "Talking the Vote: Why Presidential Candidates Hit the Talk Show Circuit." *American Journal of Political Science* 49: 213-234.
Baym, Geoffrey. 2005. "Discursive Integration and the Reinvention of Political Journalism." *Political Communication* 22: 259-276.
Cao, Xiaoxia. 2010. "Hearing It from Jon Stewart: The Impact of *The Daily Show* on Public Attentiveness to Politics." *International Journal of Public Opinion Research* 22: 26-46.
Chaffee, Steven H., and Jack M. McLeod. 1973. "Individual vs. Social Predictors of Information Seeking." *Journalism Quarterly* 50: 237-245.
Chaffee, Steven, and Joan Schleuder. 1986. "Measurement and Effects of Attention to News Media." *Human Communication Research* 13: 76-107.
Colbert Report. 2010, April 8. New York: Comedy Central.
_____. 2010, April 15. New York: Comedy Central.
Downs, Anthony. 1957. *An Economic Theory of Democracy.* New York, NY: Harper Collins.
Feldman, Lauren, and Dannagal G. Young. 2008. "Late Night Comedy as a Gateway to Traditional News: An Analysis of Time Trends in News Attention Among Late-Night Comedy Viewers During the 2004 Presidential Primaries." *Political Communication* 25: 401-422.

Fowler, James H. 2008. "The Colbert Bump in Campaign Donations: More Truthful Than Truthy." *PS: Political Science and Politics* 41: 533–539.

Fox, Julia R., Glory Koloen, and Volkan Sahin. 2007. "No Joke: A Comparison of Substance in the Daily Show with Jon Stewart and Broadcast Network Television Coverage of the 2004 Presidential Election Campaign." *Journal of Broadcasting & Electronic Media* 51: 213–227.

Holbert, R. Lance. 2005. "Intramedia Mediation: The Cumulative and Complementary Effects of News Media Use." *Political Communication* 22: 447–462.

Intergovernmental Panel on Climate Change. 2007. "Summary for Policymakers." In *Climate Change 2007: The Physical Science Basis. Contribution of Working Group I to the Fourth Assessment Report of the Intergovernmental Panel on Climate Change*, edited by S. Solomon, D. Qin, M. Manning, Z. Chen, M. Marquis, K.B. Averyt, M. Tignor, and H.L. Miller. Cambridge: Cambridge University Press.

Jones, Jeffrey M. 2009. "Economy, Healthcare Top 'Most Important Problem' List." The Gallup Organization, September 9. http://www.gallup.com/poll/122885/Economy-Healthcare–Top-Important-Problem-List.aspx (accessed March 30, 2010).

_____. 2010. "In U.S., Many Environmental Issues at 20-Year-Low Concern." The Gallup Organization, March 16. http://www.gallup.com/poll/126716/environmental-issues-year-low-concern.aspx (accessed March 30, 2010).

Kahlor, LeeAnn, and Sonny Rosenthal. 2009. "If We Seek, Do We Learn? Predicting Knowledge of Global Warming." *Science Communication* 30: 380–414.

King, Gary, Michael Tomz, and Jason Wittenberg. 2000. "Making the Most of Statistical Analyses: Improving Interpretation and Presentation." *American Journal of Political Science* 44: 347–61.

Krosnick, Jon A., Allyson L. Holbrook, Laura Lowe, and Penny S. Visser. 2006. "The Origins and Consequences of Democratic Citizens' Policy Agendas: A Study of Popular Concern About Global Warming." *Climatic Change* 77: 7–43.

Leiserowitz, Anthony, Edward Maibach, and Connie Roser-Renouf. 2010. *Global Warming's Six Americas, January 2010*. Yale University and George Mason University. New Haven, CT: Yale Project on Climate Change. http://environment.yale.edu/uploads/SixAmericas-Jan2010.pdf

Maibach, Edward, Connie Roser-Renouf, and Anthony Leiserowitz. 2009. *Global Warming's Six Americas: An Audience Segmentation Analysis*. Yale University and George Mason University. New Haven, CT: Yale Project on Climate Change. http://www.climatechangecom-munication.org/images/files/GlobalWarmingsSixAmericas2009c.pdf

McCombs, Maxwell E., and Donald L. Shaw. (1972). "The Agenda-Setting Function of the Press." *Public Opinion Quarterly* 36: 176–187.

Newport, Frank. 2010. "Americans' Global Warming Concerns Continue to Drop." The Gallup Organization, March 11. http://www.gallup.com/poll/126560/Americans-Global-Warming-Concerns-Continue-Drop.aspx

National Science Board (NSB). 2010. *Science and Engineering Indicators 2010*. NSB 10–01. Arlington, VA: National Science Foundation. http://www.nsf.gov/statistics/seind10/

Nisbet, Matthew. 2010. "Chill Out: Climate Scientists Are Getting a Little Too Angry for Their Own Good." *Slate*, March 18. http://www.slate.com/id/2248236/pagenum/all

_____, and Dietram Scheufele. 2009. What's Next for Science Communication? Promising Directions and Lingering Distractions. *American Journal of Botany* 96: 1767–1778.

_____, et al. 2002. "Knowledge, Reservations, or Promise? A Media Effects Model for Public Perceptions of Science and Technology." *Communication Research* 29: 584–608.

Page, Benjamin I, and Robert Y. Shapiro. 1983. "Effects of Public Opinion on Policy." *American Political Science Review* 77: 175–190.

Pew Research Center for the People and the Press. 2008. *Key News Audiences Now Blend Online and Traditional Sources*. Pew Research Center, August 17. http://people-press.org/report/444/news-media

_____. 2009a. *Public Praises Science; Scientists Fault Public, Media*. Pew Research Center, July 29. http://people-press.org/report/528/

_____. 2009b. Fewer Americans See Solid Evidence for Global Warming. Pew Research Center, October 22. http://people-press.org/report/556/global-warming

Popkin, Samuel L. 1994. *The Reasoning Voter: Communication And Persuasion in Presidential Campaigns*. Chicago, IL: University of Chicago Press.

Prior, Markus. 2005. "News v. Entertainment: How Increasing Media Choice Widens Gaps in Political Knowledge And Turnout." *American Journal of Political Science* 49: 594–609.

Project for Excellence in Journalism. 2008. *Journalism, Satire or Just Laughs? "The Daily Show with Jon Stewart," Examined*. Project for Excellence in Journalism, May 8. http://www.journalism.org/node/10953

Seidman, Robert. 2010. "'The Tonight Show with Jay Leno' and 'Late Night with Jimmy Fallon' score April 26–30 late-night wins." *TV by the Numbers*, May 6. http://tvbythenumbers.com/2010/05/06/the-tonight-show-with-jay-leno-and-late-night-with-jimmy-fallon-score-april-26-30-late-night-wins/50759

Slater, Michael. 2007. "Reinforcing Spirals: The Mutual Influence of Media Selectivity and Media Effects and Their Impact on Individual Behavior and Social Identity." *Communication Theory* 17: 281–303.

Tomz, Michael, James Wittenberg, and Gary King. 2001. CLARIFY: Software for Interpreting and Presenting Statistical Results, Version 2.0. Cambridge, MA: Harvard University. http://gking.harvard.edu

Tyndall Report. 2008. "Year in Review 2008." http://tyndallreport.com/yearinreview2008/

Ungar, Sheldon. 2000. "Knowledge, Ignorance, and the Popular Culture: Climate Change Versus the Ozone Hole." *Public Understanding of Science* 9: 297–312.

Vergano, Dan. 2010. "Best Science on TV: Comedy Central's Stewart, Colbert?" *USA Today*, March 2. http://www.usatoday.com/tech/science/2010-03-02-sciencecomedy02_ST_N.htm

Zaller, John. 1991. "Information, Values, and Opinion." *American Political Science Review* 85: 1215–1237.

Zhao, Xiaoquan. (2009). "Media Use and Global Warming Perceptions: A Snapshot of the Reinforcing Spirals." *Communication Research* 36: 698–723.

Appendix A: Control Variables

Demographics

- Age in years (M = 49.70, SD = 16.41)
- Gender (50.1 percent male)
- Race (79.2 percent white)
- Income (*Range* = 1 "less $25,000" to 5 "$100,000 or more;" *Median* = 4 "$50,000-$74,999")

Media Use

- Days per week read a printed newspaper (M = 4.03, SD = 2.85)
- Days per week read news online (M = 3.90, SD = 2.73)
- Network TV news use (*Range* = 1 "never" to 4 "often;" *Median* = 3 "sometimes")
- Fox News use (*Range* = 1 "never" to 4 "often;" *Median* = 2 "hardly ever")

- CNN / MSNBC use (average of two items, r = .65; *Range* = 1 "never" to 4 "often;" *Median* = 2 "hardly ever")
- NPR use (*Range* = 1 "never" to 4 "often;" *Median* = 1 "never")

Values and Predispositions

- Political party identification (*Range* = 1 "strong Democrat" to 3 "Independent" to 5 "strong Republican;" *Median* = 3 "Independent)
- Political ideology (*Range* = 1 "strong liberal" to 3 "moderate" to 5 "strong conservative;" *Median* = 3 "moderate")
- Frequency of religious service attendance *(Range* = 1 "never" to 6 "more than once a week;" *Median* = 3 "a few times a year")
- Attitudes toward modern science (Agreement with statement "Overall, modern science does more harm than good;" *Range* = 1 "strongly agree" to 4 "strongly disagree;" *Median* = 3 "somewhat disagree")
- Environmentalism (Agreement with statement "I consider myself an environmentalist;" *Range* = 1 "strongly disagree" to 4 "strongly agree;" *Median* = 3 "somewhat agree")

Making Sense of *The Daily Show*

Understanding the Role of Partisan Heuristics in Political Comedy Effects

MICHAEL A. XENOS, PATRICIA MOY, *and* AMY B. BECKER

Communications scholarship exploring the effects of exposure to political humor is at a critical juncture. To date, researchers have explored how exposure to political comedy or entertainment programming affects political awareness and learning (Baum, 2003; Brewer and Cao, 2006; Hollander, 2005; Kim and Vishak, 2008), attitudes and opinions (Baum and Jamison, 2006; Baumgartner and Morris, 2006; Moy, Xenos, and Hess, 2006; Nabi, Moyer-Gusee, and Byrne, 2007; Young, 2004), and political engagement (Cao and Brewer, 2008; Moy, Xenos, and Hess, 2005). Amidst these studies on the persuasive effects of comedy (Nabi et al., 2007), some have called for greater focus on the cognitive implications of comedy for information processing, which would enable researchers to treat humorous content as "more than just another input variable in a media effects equation" (Young, 2008, p. 133). In addition, attention to the breadth of political entertainment outlets available to television audiences can help identify appropriate theoretical approaches to understanding the effects of political humor, based on both differences in programming and how particular shows are perceived by viewers (Holbert, 2005).

This essay extends these currents in the literature on the persuasive effects of political humor. Specifically, we explore how the influence of comedy shows, given their reputations and audience characteristics, may be best explained as a result of processing aided by partisan or ideological heuristics. As simple "rules of thumb" or "cognitive shortcuts," heuristics allow individuals to form attitudes and opinions without taking the trouble to study all aspects of an issue, such as when one adopts an opinion espoused by a trusted source on the logic that a more thorough cognitive process would very likely lead to the same outcome. Because certain comedy programs (or comedy figures) are sufficiently associated with a particular set of political opinions, viewers can rely on a source cue to simplify the processing of messages from them, much as they might when dealing with political messages associated with more traditional political figures (Mondak, 1993). We begin by reviewing the relevant literature from which we derive specific hypotheses. Namely, we seek to examine whether watching political comedy can generate message-consistent persuasive effects, and whether these effects are moderated by viewers' partisan identification. Our experiment-based results reveal how viewers' reliance on partisan or ideological heuristics can influence the processing of humorous messages. We then discuss the implications of our study for research on how political comedy shapes not only attitudes and opinions, but also political knowledge and learning.

The Impact of Political Comedy on Attitudes

Ample research illustrates the influence of political comedy on global opinions and attitudes, suggesting that comedy has a direct effect on viewers. Driven by normative concerns about whether political comedy programs such as *The Daily Show* promote a "culture of cynicism" (Hart and Hartelius, 2007) by routinely lambasting prominent political figures and traditional media outlets, this research has documented a generally negative influence of exposure to political comedy on attitudes toward the political system. For example, exposing research participants to clips from *The Daily Show* and the *CBS Evening News*, Baumgartner and Morris (2006) found that viewing comedy content depressed not only attitudes toward the political figures depicted in the clips, but also participants' faith in the electoral system and their trust in the news media to provide fair and accurate coverage of political events. In another experiment, Holbert, Lambe, Dudo and Carlton (2007) found that viewing *The Daily Show* concurrently with similar content from CNN decreased participants' assessment of traditional television news. Moreover, this effect was even stronger among participants with lower levels of political efficacy. Corroborating data also have emerged from non-experimental research; based on survey data collected regarding media effects in presidential elections, Pfau et al. (2007) identified some evidence of "corrosive" effects stemming from exposure to political comedy.

Unlike the consistent negative effects of political comedy on global political attitudes, the effects of political humor on specific partisan or ideological judgments are weaker and more mixed. For example, whereas Pfau, Cho, and Chong (2001) found a significant relationship between viewing late-night comedy and attitudes toward Al Gore, they did not find similar effects for attitudes toward George W. Bush. Conversely, in another study of candidate appearances during the 2000 presidential race, Moy, Xenos and Hess (2005) showed that Bush's appearance on *The Late-Show with David Letterman* primed voters to weight a character consideration more heavily in subsequent evaluations of him. However, they did not find a similar effect for opinions toward Gore. In exploring impacts of exposure to interviews with political figures and jokes on trait ratings of the candidates, Young (2004, 2008) reported no direct effects of such exposure on partisan opinions.

In contrast with the literature on the effects of comedy exposure on learning and knowledge, studies of direct partisan or ideological persuasion resulting from comedy display a markedly less consistent pattern of findings. Some of the differences in these two sets of findings can be attributed to differences in conceptualization and/or methodology and analyses. It is beyond the scope of this paper to reconcile such issues. However, to offer greater theoretical clarity to research on the effects of political comedy, we turn to the role that ideological heuristics can play in shaping such effects.

Ideological Heuristics and Political Comedy

For over three decades, the notion that individuals often seek to simplify complex judgment tasks by relying on heuristic devices — "cognitive shortcuts" or simple "rules of thumb" — has proven useful to scholars of political cognition (Lau, 2003). In the realm of partisan politics, source cues have proven particularly relevant to understanding patterns of both individual and mass opinion (Mondak, 1993). When faced with unfamiliar or complicated political issues or questions, individuals often are able to form judgments by simply applying accessible information (such as their feelings toward or perceptions of a more familiar political figure) to the opinion object in question. A number of considerations suggest that a fruitful approach to understanding how exposure to political comedy programs such as *The Daily Show* influences attitudes concerns the extent to which viewers may use the show (or others like it) as an instrument of cognitive efficiency.

First, researchers who study the cognitive processes involved in the reception (and enjoyment) of political humor have found that 'getting the joke' systematically steers comedy viewers away from complex political judgment processes (Young, 2008). Recent experimental work has suggested that in comparison to traditional newscasts, comedy tends to stimulate less-taxing online processing of information as opposed to more effortful memory-based processing (Kim and Vishak, 2008). Although some of this work implicates

viewers' motivation as well as ability for systematic or central-route information processing, we focus primarily on the latter.

In building her counterargument disruption model of the effects of political comedy, Young (2008) relies on theories of humor from linguistics and
neuroscience to argue that at its core, humor involves creating and resolving
narrative incongruities. Given these incongruities, a joke's recipient needs to
mentally shift from an initial frame of reference to another one using the
punch-line as a bridge. Understanding and appreciating political humor thus
requires a significant expenditure of cognitive effort as the premises of the
joke are processed and re-processed in working memory, often requiring the
recall of other considerations from long-term memory in order to fully appreciate the joke. Since cognitive resources are finite, energy directed at 'getting
the joke' is rendered unavailable for other purposes, such as critical scrutiny
of message elements that may be in conflict with one's underlying predispositions.

Within the larger framework of dual-process persuasion models assumed
by this approach (Eagly and Chaiken, 1993; Petty and Cacioppo, 1986), individuals who choose not to scrutinize arguments are considered to be engaging
in peripheral or heuristic processing. In other words, the same forces that
reduce the likelihood of cognitive elaboration or systematic information processing also make individuals more likely to use source cues (through heuristic
processing) to make sense of the issues addressed in political humor. Taxed
by the cognitive activities associated with processing humorous content, individuals should be more likely to pursue a shortcut in further comprehending
the broader context and significance of the message. But we should not expect
comedy viewers to avail themselves of a heuristic strategy in all instances.
According to one classic account of political heuristics, such a processing strategy requires the message (comedic or otherwise) arrive with both a relevant
and accessible source cue, and the use of heuristics is more likely as the relative
difficulty of the processing task increases (Mondak, 1993). Under such conditions, it is certainly plausible that opinions formed on the basis of exposure
to humorous political content would be marked by evidence of processing
aided by heuristics or source cues.

Indeed, there are many indications that such conditions exist in political
comedy, and manifest themselves in a particular way with respect to *The Daily
Show*. In his work on soft news, for example, Baum (2003) argues that political
entertainment can facilitate awareness and understanding of political issues
(especially among those with lower levels of political interest) by providing
simplified caricatures that rely on highly accessible partisan and ideological
stereotypes and groupings. Although not specifically exploring the operation
of *ideological* heuristics, Baum and Jamison (2006) document a significant

relationship between viewing daytime talk shows during the 2000 presidential campaign season and casting votes consistent with underlying predispositions among those with low levels of political awareness. They argue that such patterns demonstrate how entertainment programming can help facilitate low-information rationality. By considering general tendencies of a particular political comedy show, we contend that it is possible to identify ways in which the ideological and partisan narratives commonly offered by its host might provide cues enabling a clear and predictable pattern of heuristic processing effects.

In the case of *The Daily Show* and its host Jon Stewart, scholarly investigations suggest that the most likely scenario for source cues involves Stewart operating in a role akin to a left-leaning political pundit. To be sure, Stewart's fame is in part derived from a widely viewed appearance on CNN's *Crossfire* in which he candidly criticized political pundits of all stripes. Additionally, scholars such as Baym (2005) have identified critical differences between Stewart's program and cable offerings similar to *Crossfire*. However, if one considers the nature of Stewart's opening newscasts alongside the relative frequency with which they focus on the foibles of conservative targets, such an assumption begins to find support. Consider, for example, that whereas its companion program *The Colbert Report* offers unalloyed, ambiguous, deadpan satire, *The Daily Show* supplements its satire with contextual cues and interpretations (LaMarre, Landreville, and Beam, 2009). Indeed, analysis of the show and interviews with Stewart concerning his approach has highlighted his explicit and implicit rejection of the traditional journalism norm of objectivity. This perspective is further articulated in Baym's (2005) detailed rhetorical analysis of *The Daily Show*, which sharply differentiates between the dispassionate objectivity to which traditional news aspires, and Stewart's "subjective interrogation" of news content through rhetorical and comedic strategies like juxtaposition and "dialogic confrontation" (pp. 265–266).

The second corpus of literature upon which we base our study of heuristics focuses on selective exposure, or the idea that "people expose themselves primarily to information that conforms to their political perspectives and other predispositions" (Best, Chmielewski, and Krueger, 2005, p. 55; see also Zillmann and Bryant, 1985). For example, Stroud (2007a) showed that selective exposure to politically consistent media can reinforce and even strengthen pre-existing political attitudes. Similar work has revealed that the influence of selective exposure may become more relevant given habitual or long-term exposure to the same partisan-oriented news content (Stroud, 2007b). Additionally, individual-level evaluations of the slant and ideological orientation of mainstream media outlets (i.e., Fox News, CNN) can act as heuristics in the processing of a wide range of media content (Baum and Gussin, 2008;

Iyengar and Hahn, 2009). In fact, these heuristic judgments have been shown to influence the processing of both hard and soft news content and may prove to be particularly important for individuals trying to make sense of media content tackling unfamiliar political issues or featuring unknown political actors (Iyengar and Hahn, 2009). With respect to selective exposure vis-à-vis political entertainment, Young and Tisinger (2006) found that an individual's liberal ideological orientation was a significant predictor in their selection of *The Daily Show* as the "most often viewed" late night comedy program.

In light of these considerations, we explore the possibility that exposure to the political comedy of *The Daily Show* produces patterns of opinion formation consistent with heuristic processing of message content aided by cues stemming from Stewart's association with left-leaning ideological beliefs. Similar patterns have been glimpsed in this literature before, for example, in Young's (2004) finding that effects of exposure to jokes about Bush and Gore made by Letterman and Leno were moderated by partisanship. If opinion formation patterns of this kind are more likely responses to *The Daily Show*, given its unambiguous subjective positioning, message-consistent effects between self-identified Democrats and Republicans should differ systematically. We formalize this expectation in the following hypothesis.

H1: Message-consistent effects of exposure to *The Daily Show* will be moderated by partisan identification.

As noted earlier, however, the application of heuristics is not uniform. Even in situations where suitable cues are both accessible and relevant, there is variation in the degree to which individuals are likely to rely on information shortcuts in reaching political judgments. By their very nature, information shortcuts are more likely to be used when individuals face greater difficulty in reaching a judgment through complex deliberation, such as when the opinion object in question is less familiar, or when individuals possess less information specific to the object (Mondak, 1993; Baum and Jamison, 2006). We thus look for additional evidence of heuristic processing in responses to content from *The Daily Show* by testing the following hypothesis.

H2: Moderation of message-consistent persuasive effects flowing from *The Daily Show* content will be more pronounced when the subjects of such content are less familiar to viewers.

Method

The data used to test these hypotheses were collected in a laboratory experiment conducted at a large Midwestern university using the MediaLab software platform. A total of 332 undergraduates were recruited from lower- and upper-level communications courses and participated in the experiment between February 23, 2007 and March 9, 2007. Students received a small amount of extra credit in return for their participation. Participants were provided a standard consent form, which described the study as an investigation of "news formats," and those who agreed to participate were randomly assigned to one of four conditions by the software program. Three conditions received a video clip: the hard news condition (n = 96), the comedy condition (n = 76), and the mixed clip condition (n = 83). The fourth condition (n = 77) served as the control group and did not receive any video stimulus material. The first two conditions enable contrasts that speak directly to the differences between hard news and comedy, while the third simulates a mixed diet of news and comedy inspired by the findings of Young and Tisinger (2006) concerning the media habits of younger viewers.

Stimulus materials were drawn from television content that aired shortly after the U.S. House of Representatives passed a non-binding resolution against the Bush administration's proposed troop surge in Iraq. The hard news clip was edited from evening news broadcasts that aired on NBC and ABC in early February 2007 to produce a news stimulus that was approximately five minutes in length. The comedy clip was created by capturing and editing content from the "Dance, Dance Resolution" segment aired on *The Daily Show* during the same period. The comedy stimulus was also approximately 5 minutes in length and featured much of the same footage presented by NBC and ABC in the hard news clip. Indeed, both stimuli featured many of the same shots of House members participating in floor debate and presented similar footage of the final vote.

Consistent with the analysis of *Daily Show* content conducted by Baym (2005) and Baum's (2003) notion that comedy narratives tend to simplify stories through partisan stereotypes, the humorous clip heightened the partisan dimensions of the story. Stewart engaged in a strong subjective critique of the Democrats, and House Speaker Nancy Pelosi in particular, for offering what seemed an ineffectual and symbolic form of political action. The mixed-video stimulus was the same length as the other two, and combined content from both the hard news and comedy clips.

Together, the two clips provide stimuli similar to those used in traditional studies of heuristics and source cue effects outside of the late-night comedy literature. Stimuli in these studies typically range from a simple wording shift in a questionnaire item or brief textual description, such as in the work of Mondak (1993) or Cohen (2003), to the approximately six-minute video clips used by Rahn (1993) in her work on partisan stereotypes in candidate evaluation. Like the messages used in these studies, ours offer a similar amount of informational content, but differ in the extent to which they feature a relatively unambiguous ideological or partisan reference point, in this case the host of *The Daily Show*, Jon Stewart. To be sure, this manipulation also differs from traditional cueing studies in that it is impossible to disconnect the cue (Stewart) from the comedic message within the context of a video stimulus. However, this difference does not prevent us from testing our basic hypotheses related to how partisanship might moderate the effects of exposure to the comedy clip.

Regarding the events from which our political comedy content was derived, it is worth noting that Congresswoman Nancy Pelosi's appointment as Speaker of the House received considerable media attention in late 2006 and into early 2007. Initially, Pelosi was viewed fairly favorably by the American public, with 51 percent of Americans indicating approval for the way she was handling her job as Speaker of the House in a January 2007 CNN poll (CNN, 2007). By the spring of 2007, public approval for Pelosi waned, with only 36 percent of Americans approving of Pelosi's job as Speaker in a late May/early June 2007 Pew Research Center poll (Pew, 2007). Part of this slide in public support for the Speaker was in direct response to the Democrats' failure to act decisively on the Iraq War issue, including the passage of a nonbinding, primarily symbolic resolution against President Bush's planned troop surge (Hulse and Pear, 2007).

At the start of the study, subjects completed a pre-test questionnaire that included measures of our moderator variable, partisan identification, as well as other items. Following the pre-test, participants viewed one of the video clips (or in the case of participants in the fourth condition, no clip). Participants were subsequently exposed to a simulated Internet news portal for a limited time. This further served to embed the stimulus clips within a broader media environment that included other sources of information about the troop surge resolution, as well as other news stories of that time period. Finally, participants concluded by answering a series of questions, including items asking for their attitudes toward major political figures mentioned in both the network news and *The Daily Show* clips.

Key Measures

Partisan Identification

Subjects were asked to indicate their partisan identification, namely whether they were Democrat, Republican, Independent, or "something else/none of these." The final sample was 56.6 percent Democrat and 26.2

percent Republican, and 9.0 percent Independent. Eight percent of subjects did not indicate a preference for a particular political party.

Political Interest

Interest in following matters related to politics and government (M = 1.73, SD = .73) was measured on a four-point scale (1 = "Most of the time," 2 = "Some of the time," 3 = "Hardly at all," and 4 = "Never"). The item was reverse-coded and participants who indicated that they were never interested in matters related to politics and government were recoded as "0" in the dataset.

Media Use

Subjects were asked to assess the frequency (0 = "Never" to 7 = "Seven days a week") with which they followed news about politics and public affairs in the past week across a wide range of media outlets. The measures examined viewing patterns for "national network news program, such as *ABC World News with Charles Gibson*, *NBC Nightly News with Brian Williams,* or the *CBS Evening News with Katie Couric*," (M = 1.29, SD = 1.34), and "late-night comedy programs, such as *The Daily Show with Jon Stewart*, or *The Tonight Show with Jay Leno*" (M = 1.28, SD = 1.66).

Feelings Toward Politicians/Groups

A series of questions asked subjects to indicate their general attitude or feelings toward politicians and political parties central to the Iraq resolution debate using the standard 0-to-100 feeling thermometer scale employed by the American National Election Studies. Specifically, the Democrats in Congress (M = 64.41, SD = 21.57) and Speaker of the House Nancy Pelosi (M = 57.03, SD = 22.41) received the warmest ratings, while President George W. Bush (M = 37.30, SD = 25.68) and the Congressional Republicans (M = 41.97, SD = 25.58) were viewed less favorably.

Demographics

Finally, a few demographic items were included in the study to account for any variation that might exist in the subject pool. Key measures used in the analyses presented in this paper include gender (0 = "Male," 1 = "Female") and year in school (as a proxy for age and experience). The final subject pool was 75.6 percent female and 24.4 percent male. Additionally, on average, subjects had already completed two or more years of college (M = 2.22, SD = 1.06; 1 = "Freshman" to 5 = "Fifth-year senior").

Results

Before we turn to whether our experimental data supported our hypotheses, we present survey data that support our assumption regarding selective exposure and the partisan nature of viewership of *The Daily Show*. Table 1 presents the results of a national telephone survey conducted by the Pew Research Center two months before our experimental data were collected. Given the lack of a direct measure of exposure to political comedy, we regressed the extent to which respondents reported learning about the presidential campaign or candidates from comedy shows such as *Saturday Night Live* and *The Daily Show* (1 = "Regularly," 2 = "Sometimes," 3 = "Hardly ever," 4 = "Never"; reverse-coded) on key demographic variables. As shown in Table 1, males, younger adults, and less affluent respondents were more likely to report having learned political information from political comedy. Most pertinent to our argument is the finding that self-identified Republicans were less likely — and Democrats more likely — to report learning from this genre.

Table 1. Predicting Learning from Political Comedy

Learning from Political Comedy

Demographics	
Sex (Female)	-.13**
Age	-.21**
Education	.10**
Income	-.08*
Race (White)	-.01
Republican	-.09**
Democrat	.08*
R^2 (%)	8.0**
Adjusted R^2 (%)	7.4**

NOTES: All coefficients are standardized coefficients from hierarchical regression analyses. Data come from a national telephone sample of 1,500 adults; fieldwork was conducted 19 December 2007 to 2 January 2008. # p < .10; * p < .05; ** p < .01

Analysis of our experimental data began with an initial search for any direct message-consistent persuasive effects of the comedy stimulus materials, which were critical of both Congressional Democrats and Nancy Pelosi; we examined participants' feelings toward 'Democrats in Congress' as well as the House Speaker. This took the form of a simple comparison of means by condition. These preliminary results faintly echoed those from other studies focusing on the direct persuasive influences of political comedy. Specifically, participants in the comedy-only condition registered mean thermometer ratings of 60.53 for Democrats in general (S.D. 21.55) and 52.04 for Speaker Pelosi (S.D. 19.69), whereas comparable means for the subjects in the other conditions were 65.56 (S.D. 21.49) and 58.56 (S.D. 23.03) respectively. Based on a two-tailed test, these differences were marginally significant (for both comparisons, p = .08), and provide only weak support for a simple message-consistent effect flowing from the *Daily Show's* humorous and slightly uncharitable portrayal of the House Democrats' symbolic action against the Bush Administration.

Hypothesis Testing

To test our hypotheses concerning the possibility that partisan cue-taking may provide a better explanation for the potential influence of *The Daily Show*, we specified a number of OLS regressions in which the feeling thermometer measures for Democrats and Speaker Pelosi served as the outcome variables. Specifically, one pair of models regressed feeling thermometer ratings for each opinion object on the stimulus variables, while controlling for demographics, chronic media exposure and other variables. A second pair of models included interaction terms to test for partisan differences in the effects of the stimuli. The results of these analyses are summarized in Table 2.

Table 2. OLS Analysis of Pelosi and Democrats Feeling Thermometers

	Model 1 (Stimulus only)		Model 2 (Stimulus × Party ID)	
	Democrats	Pelosi	Democrats	Pelosi
Gender	.10*	.12	.10*	.12#
Year in school	.04	-.13#	.04	-.13#
Political interest	-.04	.06	-.04	.03
Party identification (R)	-.66**	-.26**	-.69**	-.49**
Network news exposure	.12*	-.08	.12**	-.10
Late night comedy exposure	.02	.10	.02	.12
News Stimulus	-.05	-.00	-.07	-.00
Mixed Stimulus	-.08	.00	-.08	-.08
Comedy Stimulus	-.09#	-.09	-.10	-.20*
Party ID × News			.03	.03
Party ID × Mixed			.02	.20#
Party ID × Comedy			.02	.27*
Adjusted R²	.44	.09	.43	.11
n	323	201	323	201

NOTES: Cell entries are standardized OLS regression coefficients. # p < .10; * p < .05; ** p< .01

Hypotheses 1 and 2 predicted that message-consistent persuasive effects would be moderated by partisanship, especially with regard to the Speaker, who is undoubtedly a less familiar object of opinion for our research participants. On the whole, the analyses shown in Table 2 provided support for both hypotheses. The results presented in Model 1 suggest that partisan predispositions most strongly drive attitudes toward the Democrats in Congress and the Speaker, and provide almost no evidence of direct persuasive effects from exposure to the comedy clip. Specifically, the results in the first column illustrate how, as expected, Republicans were significantly cooler toward the Democratic Party, and the comedy stimulus exerted a marginally significant negative main effect on the same feelings. With respect to attitudes toward Pelosi, partisan identification has a weaker effect, and no significant stimulus effects emerge. When accounting for partisan differences in receiving the comedy stimulus (Model 2), the data produce a model in which the partisan identification-comedy stimulus interaction term is associated with a significant positive effect ($B = 22.40$ $SE B = 10.58$, $p = .04$), and the corresponding interaction term for the mixed stimulus produces a marginally significant positive effect ($B = 20.23$, $SE B = 11.03$, $p = .07$). Put another way, consistent with the notion that Stewart is perceived as left-leaning, these results indicate that after seeing Stewart criticize Pelosi and her party, Democrats and Independents noticeably cooled in their overall evaluation of the Speaker. Conversely, upon exposure to Stewart's humorous critique of Pelosi and her colleagues, Republican participants actually warmed toward the Speaker, as compared to their fellow partisans in other conditions. Proverbially, the comedy-only condition

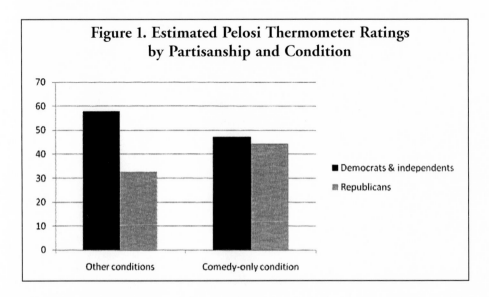

Figure 1. Estimated Pelosi Thermometer Ratings by Partisanship and Condition

thus appears to have led Democrats and Independents to interpret Pelosi as an "enemy of my friend," while simultaneously leading Republican participants in the same condition to view her as an "enemy of my enemy." This dynamic can be seen more clearly in Figure 1, which plots expected values for feelings toward Nancy Pelosi based on unstandardized coefficients derived from the regression analysis summarized in Table 2.

Discussion

In summarizing the research literature on the effects of exposure to political comedy programs, it is often useful to erect a partition between studies examining political humor's effects on knowledge or political awareness and those focused on its potential to affect attitudes and opinions (whether global or more specific). In the first instance, researchers have explored the degree to which comedy can serve as a "gateway" to greater knowledge or understanding of political events (Baum, 2003). In the latter vein, researchers have tested hypotheses that implicate humor in persuasion, perhaps through its tendency to sap our ability and motivation for mentally arguing against political zingers that are inconsistent with our core beliefs (Young, 2008). This essay bridges these two sub-domains of research while advancing a theoretical and empirical understanding of the roles played by comedy programs in contemporary politics.

In many ways, the results reported here bring to light the possibility of a hybrid (learning and opinion) effect. Ostensibly, the hypotheses tested in this paper posit weak prospects for persuasion via humor, suggesting that participants might decode Jon Stewart's humorous messages through mental reference to his association with a left-leaning perspective on American politics, thus blunting his persuasive power. Our results lend a modicum of support to these expectations, revealing an almost knee-jerk response to his criticism of Nancy Pelosi among self-identified Republicans (who displayed a response *inconsistent* with the text of Stewart's segment), as well as Democrats and Independents (whose evaluations of Pelosi moved in the direction of Stewart's subjective critique). Consistent with the literature on partisan heuristics and political opinions, this dynamic was observed clearly with respect to the less-familiar opinion object (Speaker of the House), though not for the more familiar object (Democrats in Congress).

However, our results can also be read as a positive effect on political awareness, precisely because the moderating effect of partisanship observed in our data appears to be most evident for political objects or symbols that are less clear in the minds of those exposed to political humor. Similar to

Baum and Jamison (2006), who found that exposure to political content on *Oprah* is associated with holding opinions more consistent with underlying predispositions (often a mark of opinion quality), our results suggest that perhaps due to Stewart's widely perceived left-of-center ideological positioning, exposure to *The Daily Show* may be enabling those Neuman (1986) might label "marginally attentive" to form opinions and make sense of the political world in ways they otherwise might not. Although one could argue that the heuristic explored here is also an example of how information shortcuts are not always entirely accurate (in that fully rational or informed Republicans likely would *not* warm to Pelosi under these circumstances), our findings suggest that both Democrats and Republicans may be able to find some guidance from Stewart's musings, particularly when they deal with issues with which they may not be entirely familiar.

In order to avoid attaching undue significance to these findings, it is necessary to temper these conclusions with a brief consideration of study limitations. Like many experiments, this one relies on a convenience sample of college students. Though national survey data suggest that younger viewers make up a substantial portion of the late-night comedy audience, these individuals do not represent all viewers in terms of age, ideology, or levels of political sophistication. Additionally, characteristics of the particular issue and television clips investigated here must also be kept in mind as a check on overgeneralization. For example, few issues on the national political agenda are as familiar or polarizing as the war in Iraq. Thus, while our design did enable us to test effects on a more — versus a less — familiar opinion object, it does not permit us to examine for similar patterns with respect to more — versus less-familiar issues. Perhaps most notably, our stimulus material from *The Daily Show* is unusual in the sense that it offers a rare example of Stewart criticizing the Democratic Party. Technically, the clip is certainly consistent with Stewart's ideological positioning and subjective critique, which sometimes includes criticism of Democrats for a lack of stridency in their opposition to the Bush administration (Baym, 2005; Young, 2004). Nevertheless, a more representative example may have included a more straightforward direct criticism of the sitting administration itself.

These limitations notwithstanding, we contend that the present study identifies an important area in which research on the effects of political humor can benefit from more attention to both the particular qualities of certain comedy outlets, as well as the applicability of theoretical frameworks originally developed outside of the comedy literature. If future examinations of these dynamics can further develop this perspective, perhaps with a broader range of cases and examples, it is possible that our scholarly understanding of political humor's effects may yet keep pace with increases in its prevalence within political media content.

References

Baum, M. A., 2003. *Soft News Goes to War: Public Opinion and American Foreign Policy in the New Media Age*. Princeton, N.J.: Princeton University Press.

_____, and Gussin, P. 2008. "In the Eye of the Beholder: How Information Shortcuts Shape Individual Perceptions of Bias in the Media." *Quarterly Journal of Political Science, 3*(1), 1–38.

Baum, M. A., and Jamison, A. S. 2006. "The Oprah Effect: How Soft News Helps Inattentive Citizens Vote Consistently." *Journal of Politics*, 68(4), 946–959.

Baumgartner, J., and Morris, J. S. 2006. "The Daily Show Effect: Candidate Evaluations, Efficacy, and American Youth." *American Politics Research, 34*(3), 341–367.

Baym, G. 2005. "The Daily Show: Discursive Integration and the Reinvention of Political Journalism." *Political Communication, 22*(3), 259–276.

Best, S. J., Chmielewski, B., and Krueger, B. S. 2005. "Selective Exposure to Online Foreign News During the Conflict with Iraq." *The Harvard International Journal of Press/Politics, 10*(4), 52.

Brewer, P. R., and Cao, X. X. 2006. "Candidate Appearances on Soft News Shows and Public Knowledge About Primary Campaigns." *Journal of Broadcasting & Electronic Media, 50*(1), 18–35.

Cao, X. X., and Brewer, P. R. 2008. "Political Comedy Shows and Public Participation in Politics." *International Journal of Public Opinion Research*. 20(1), pp. 90–99.

CNN/Opinion Research Corporation Poll, January, 11, 2007. Retrieved on July 10, 2008, from http://www.pollingreport.com.

Cohen, G. 2003. "Party over policy: The Dominating Impact of Group Influence on Political Beliefs." *Journal of Personality and Social Psychology, 85*(5), 808–822.

Eagly, A. H., and Chaiken, S. 1993. *The Psychology of Attitudes*. Fort Worth, TX: Harcourt Brace Jovanovich College Publishers.

Hart, R. P., and Hartelius, J. 2007. "The Political Sins of Jon Stewart." *Critical Studies in Media Communication, 24*(3), 263–272.

Holbert, R. L. 2005. "A Typology for the Study of Entertainment Television and Politics." *American Behavioral Scientist, 49*(3), 436–453.

_____, Lambe, J. L., Dudo, A. D., and Carlton, K. A. 2007. "Primacy Effects of the Daily Show and National TV News Viewing: Young Viewers, Political Gratifications, and Internal Political Self-Efficacy." *Journal of Broadcasting & Electronic Media, 51*(1), 20–38.

Hollander, B. A. 2005. "Late-Night Learning: Do Entertainment Programs Increase Political Campaign Knowledge for Young Viewers?" *Journal of Broadcasting & Electronic Media, 49*(4), 402–415.

Hulse, C., and Pear, R. 2007. "Republican Unity Trumps Democratic Momentum." *The New York Times*. Retrieved on July 17, 2008, from: http://www.nytimes.com/2007/12/21/washington/21cong.html

Iyengar, S., and Hahn, K. S. 2009. "Red Media, Blue Media: Evidence of Ideological Selectivity in Media Use." *Journal of Communication, 59*(1), 19–39.

Kim, Y. M., and Vishak, J. 2008. "Just Laugh! You Don't Need to Remember: The Effects of Entertainment Media on Political Information Acquisition and Information Processing in Political Judgment." *Journal of Communication, 58*(2), 338–360.

LaMarre, H. L., Beam, M., and Landreville, K. D. 2009. "The Irony of Satire: Political Ideology and the Motivation to See What You Want to See." *International Journal of Press/Politics, 14*(2), 212–231.

Lau, R.R. 2003. "Models of Decision Making." In *Oxford handbook of political psychology*, D. O. Sears, L. Huddy, and R. Jervis (Eds.), (pp. 19–59). New York: Oxford University Press.

Mondak, J. J. 1993. "Public opinion and heuristic processing of source cues." *Political Behavior, 15*(1), 167–192.

Moy, P., Xenos, M. A., and Hess, V. K. 2005. "Communication and Citizenship: Mapping the political effects of infotainment." *Mass Communication and Society, 8*(2), 111–131.

_____, _____, and _____. 2006. "Priming Effects of Late-Night Comedy." *International Journal of Public Opinion Research, 18*(2), 198–210.

Nabi, R. L., Moyer-Guseé, E., and Byrne, S. 2007. "All Joking Aside: A Serious Investigation into the Persuasive Effect of Funny Social Issue Messages." *Communication Monographs, 74*(1), 29–54.

Neuman, W. R. 1986. *The Paradox of Mass Politics: Knowledge and Opinion in the Mass Electorate.* Cambridge, MA: Harvard University Press.

Petty, R. E., and Cacioppo, J. T. 1986. *Communication and Persuasion: Central and Peripheral Routes to Attitude Change*: New York: Springer-Verlag.

Pew Research Center for the People & the Press Poll, May 30–June 3, 2007. Retrieved on July 10, 2007, from http://www.pollingreport.com.

Pfau, M., Cho, J. H., and Chong, K. 2001. "Communication Forms in U.S. Presidential Campaigns: Influences on Candidate Perceptions and the Democratic Process." *Harvard International Journal of Press-Politics, 6*(4), 88–105.

Pfau, M., Houston, J. B., and Semmler, S. M. 2007. *Mediating the Vote: The Changing Media Landscape in U.S. Presidential Campaigns.* Lanham, MD: Rowman & Littlefield.

Rahn, W. 1993. "The Role of Partisan Stereotypes in Information Processing About Political Candidates." *American Journal of Political Science, 37*(2), 472–496.

Stroud, N. J. 2007a. "Media Effects, Selective Exposure, and Fahrenheit 9/11." *Political Communication, 24*(4), 415–432.

_____. 2007b. "Media Use and Political Predispositions: Revisiting the Concept of Selective Exposure." *Political Behavior, 30*(3), 341–366.

Young, D. G. 2004. "Late-Night Comedy in election 2000: Its Influence on Candidate Trait Ratings and the Moderating Effects of Political Knowledge and Partisanship." *Journal of Broadcasting & Electronic Media, 48*(1), 1–22.

_____. 2008. "The Privileged Role of the Late-Night Joke: Exploring Humor's Role in Disrupting Argument Scrutiny." *Media Psychology, 11*(1), 119–142.

_____, and Tisinger, R. A. 2006. "Dispelling Late-Night Myths: News Consumption Among Late-Night Comedy Viewers and the Predictors of Exposure to various Late-Night Shows." *Harvard International Journal of Press-Politics, 11*(3), 113–134.

Zillmann, D., and Bryant, J. 1985. *Selective Exposure to Communication.* Mahwah, NJ: Lawrence Erlbaum Associates.

Stoned Slackers or Super Citizens?

The Daily Show *Viewing and Political Engagement of Young Adults*

Jody C. Baumgartner *and* Jonathan S. Morris

Those who question Jon Stewart's social or political relevance risk being perceived as completely out of touch. In fact it is somewhat risky to challenge Stewart at all, if only because he is particularly skilled at skewering other public figures. Stewart appeared on CNN's long-running debate program "Crossfire" in October of 2004, sharply criticizing the show's format and it's hosts for their hyper-charged political discourse. Video of the appearance went viral on the Internet, attracting over four million views (as of November 2009) on "ifilm" and over three million more on Youtube.com. Not long after the infamous encounter, it was announced "Crossfire" would be cancelled, ending its 23 year run. The decision was at least in part because of Stewart's criticism. Announcing the cancellation, Jonathan Klein (the President of CNN) stated "I agree wholeheartedly with Jon [Stewart]" (Carter 2005).

In the spring of 2009 Jim Cramer of CNBC's "Mad Money" became embroiled in a public, cross-network feud with Stewart (Fisher 2009). As with the "Crossfire" altercation, Stewart fired the first shot, criticizing Cramer's investment advice, particularly regarding the recently-collapsed Bear-Sterns financial firm. When Cramer suggested that Stewart had taken his comments out of context, Stewart responded with more criticism and video evidence that this was not the case. The feud escalated further, but ended in a clear victory for Stewart when a contrite and apologetic Cramer appeared on *The Daily Show*. In the months that followed the altercation, ratings for "Mad Money," and CNBC as a whole, plummeted by double digits (Clark 2009).

Both the "Crossfire" and "Mad Money" incidents made *Time* magazine's June 2009 list of "Top 10 TV Feuds," (Top 10 TV Feuds 2009) and implicit in most of the media coverage of both was that Stewart's criticisms were timely, accurate, and appropriate. In the past decade Stewart has been elevated in popular culture to the status of a modern day Mark Twain or Will Rogers. He is seen as social critic, political seer, pundit *extraordinaire*, and creator of a new form of politically and socially significant news that brings a needed and refreshing change.

Much of the praise lavished on the program (and it's spin-off, *The Colbert Report*) has focused, at least implicitly, on it's ability to engage chronically disinterested young people in the political process. Most notably, a 2004 study from The University of Pennsylvania contended that *The Daily Show's* audience was more knowledgeable about the 2004 presidential campaign than those who rely only exclusively on television news or newspapers (Daily Show Viewers 2004). These findings were surprising to many at the time, particularly talk show host Bill O'Reilly, who had publicly called TDS watchers "stoned slackers." (Long 2004) However, recent years have seen a building admiration of the political intelligence of Jon Stewart's audience.

This essay disputes this notion. Using survey data collected during the 2008 presidential elections, we argue that exposure to TDS does not correlate with increased political knowledge or activity among young adults. In short, we contend that the contributions of TDS to the political engagement of young adults are negligible. Our argument is grounded in the idea that the measurement of TDS's audience has been oversimplified. We focus on those individuals who follow TDS *more* than any other traditional form of news. When we look at these individuals, there is little evidence that they comport with the popular assumption that TDS is creating new legions of super-citizens among young adults.

In fact we go further, suggesting that exposure to TDS may have potential negative effects on heavy viewers. First, we find that those who rely on TDS more than other sources of news may have a over-inflated sense of political intelligence. Second, we show that exposure to TDS may engender more cynical perspectives on politics and government by constantly emphasizing its negative aspects. Of course, there is nothing wrong with highlighting the shortcomings of elected officials, candidates, and political institutions. However Stewart goes far beyond highlighting the negative by focusing exclusively on the political bad apples. This approach may lead viewers to believe that the system comprises *only* of bad apples and that it is poisoned beyond repair.

Jon Stewart as Political Seer

Since taking over from Craig Kilborn as host of TDS in 1999 Jon Stewart has received accolades from a wide range of sources. For example the show has been nominated for 32 Emmy Awards and won a total of 13, including Outstanding Variety, Music Or Comedy Series from 2003 to 2009 (Rowe 2009). Stewart was named *Entertainment Weekly*'s "Entertainer of the Year, 2004" (Harris N.D.); graced the cover of *Newsweek* magazine in 2004; and was listed among *Time* magazine's 2005 "Top 100 most influential entertainers in the world." In addition, the show received two Peabody Awards for its "Indecision 2000" and "Indecision 2004" election coverage (Segal 2005), and he, the program, and/or the writing staff, have won or been nominated for a number of other entertainment-related awards.

Journalists seem equally enamored of Stewart. NBC News anchor Brian Williams, for example, once claimed that "at our editorial meeting, we [often] talk about what "The Daily Show" did the night before" (McDonald 2009). In another interview Williams referred to Stewart as "a separate branch of government ... an essential part of modern media and society," and went on to suggest that if it came to a choice between watching traditional news or TDS, "By all means watch "The Daily Show"" (Weisman 2008). Tom Brokaw, former NBC News anchor, once called Stewart "the citizens' surrogate" (Kakutani 2008). A *New York Times* article from 2008 story led with a headline implying that Stewart might be "the most trusted man in America." The story cites a 2007 survey in which Stewart placed fourth behind Tom Brokaw, Dan Rather and Anderson Cooper as the most trusted journalist in America. The story references a 2008 study from Pew's Project for Excellence in Journalism that claimed TDS is "getting people to think critically about the public sphere" (Kakutani 2008).

Newsweek magazine once referred to TDS as "the coolest pit stop on television" (Kakutani 2008). One journalist suggested that "for old hands watching the deterioration of political analysis on TV, Stewart has been a source of renewed hope," calling the program a political "game-changer" and a "role model for what a hardcore news program should strive for." Praise even comes from Fox News (one of Stewart's most frequent targets), who praised him for covering the 2009 "climategate" scandal, a story the traditional networks largely ignored (Macedo 2009). Les Moonves, President and Chief Executive Officer of CBS, only half-jokingly suggested he might consider replacing Katie Couric with Stewart as anchor of the "CBS Evening News" (Fitzgerald 2009). A recent scholarly review of discourse in the popular press confirms what these examples suggest: Stewart is taken very seriously by individuals in the news business as a serious cultural and "political force" (Feldman 2007).

Stewart is also taken seriously by politicians. In the interview portion of his show he has hosted scores of congressional representatives, Cabinet officials, presidential candidates, and foreign heads of state. During the 2008 presidential campaign, only Jay Leno had more candidate appearances on his program

(22) than did Stewart (21; see Associated Press 2008). Beyond appearing on TDS, political figures publicly lavish praise on Stewart. Most recently, White House Communications Director Anita Dunn praised TDS for it's high quality "fact-checking" and "investigative journalism" (Nichols 2009)

Given the attention paid to the program from entertainers, journalists, and politicians, it is no surprise that scholars from various disciplines have turned their attention to TDS in recent years. Several communications scholars, for example, have suggested that TDS programming is, or may be, a new journalistic style that eschews strict objectivity and incorporates newer forms of discourse (Baym 2005, 2007; Young 2007). In a 2003 interview with Stewart, Bill Moyers suggested as much, wondering if the host was practicing a "new form of journalism" (Trier 2008). One scholar claimed that Stewart's "influence on the state of contemporary journalism and emerging models of journalism is palpable" (Young 2007). Indeed, at least two studies have compared traditional news broadcasts with those of TDS, concluding that there is as much news content in the latter as in the former (Brewer and Marquardt 2007; Fox et al. 2007).

Many, while not crediting Stewart with practicing a "new form of journalism," suggest the program has other features which distinguish it from ordinary television. For example, one claims that the show is "the best critical media literacy program on television" (Trier 2008). Another suggests that because of Stewart's interviews of political leaders and other notables the program represents a "new communicative model" (Baym 2007). Others glowingly discuss the program's "dissident humor" and "narrative semiotics" (Warner 2007; Gaines 2007) or defend the host against charges that he produces a more cynical viewing audience (Hariman 2007; Bennett 2007). A professor of Kinesiology even went so far as to edit a collection of essays discussing the philosophy of the program as it relates to classical philosophy (Holt 2007).

Stewart's popularity is highest among young adults, many of whom not only tune into the program, but claim to get their news from it. In this regard, much of the praise lavished upon Stewart and TDS centers around the idea that the program contributes to the democratic process by engaging this younger cohort. In the past few decades youth are turning away from more traditional forms of news and tuning into alternatives like TDS and social networking websites for their news. Many people believe the program can stimulate political interest among this age group, which is typically less knowledgeable about (and less engaged in) politics (Wattenberg 2007).

We challenge this assumption. While many TDS viewers are more politically knowledgeable and interested than some other media audiences, there is little evidence to support the idea that viewership of the program is associated with major increases in political knowledge and/or political participation. We suggest that TDS' impact on young adults and their engagement in the democratic process has been over-dramatized in American popular culture. In the next section we begin to present the case that supports this assertion.

The Daily Show Audience and Perceived Learning

To begin, we should confirm that TDS appeals to young adults. According to data from the Pew Research Center's 2008 Media Consumption Study, 14 percent of 18–24 year-olds watch TDS on a regular basis (Pew Research Center 2008a). By contrast, only 4 percent of those 25 years of age or older do so. Table 1 outlines viewing habits by age group for TDS, as well as several other programs that are typically counted as sources of news and information. TDS is clearly the most popular of these sources among young adults. In addition to the 14 percent that watch TDS regularly, another 28 percent of this age group report watching TDS "sometimes." Again, these numbers compare favorably with other programs that cover public affairs. Among young adults, no other single news program has a larger following than TDS.

Table 1. Viewership/Listenership of Selected Public Affairs Programming, by Age Group

Percent who regularly watch/listen to...	18–24 year-olds	25 years or older
The Daily Show	14%	4%
CBS Evening News	2	10
ABC World News Tonight	7	14
NBC World News Tonight	5	16
Larry King Live	7	7
Countdown w/Keith Olbermann	2	3
Hannity	2	9
Rush Limbaugh	5	6
Hardball w/Chris Matthews	0	4
O'Reilly Factor	4	13

Source: Pew Research Center, "April 2008 Media Survey," August 17, 2008.

As we have noted, praise directed toward TDS goes beyond the fact that they have a significant following among young adults. The contention, at least implicitly, is that the program contributes to the democratic process by informing young adults about political issues, events, and perspectives that they might otherwise have ignored. In other words, the belief is that young adults learn about politics from watching TDS. Here again, data suggest that this may be the case. A 2007 Pew Research Center study asked individuals to rate how often they learned about the presidential primary campaigns from various sources of news (Pew Research Center 2008b). Unfortunately, subjects were not asked about learning specifically from TDS, but rather how often they learned from "Comedy shows such as *Saturday Night Live* and *The Daily Show*." The trend line in Figure 1 shows the percentage of individuals who claimed they learned about the 2008 presidential primary campaigns from these sources "regularly" or "sometimes," by age group.

Figure 1. Perceived Political Learning from Comedy Programming, by Age Group

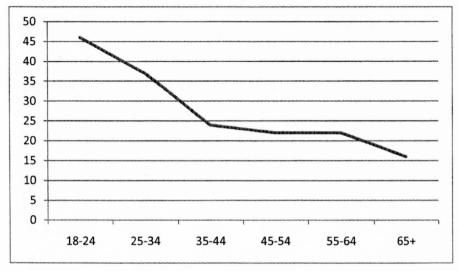

Source: Pew Research Center, "Late December 2007 Political Communications Study," January 11, 2008.

As the figure shows, young adults (18–24 years old) reported higher frequencies of learning than did any other age group. Almost half (46 percent) said they learned from comedy shows such as TDS "regularly" or "sometimes." This figure falls to 37 percent for the next-youngest group (25–34) and plummets further for those over the age of 35. Overall, these findings confirm that young adults not only watch TDS frequently, but believe they are learning about politics as the result. But are they actually learning? We return to this question later, after describing the data used in this study and introducing several types of TDS viewer.

Varieties of TDS Viewers

In order to analyze the political knowledge and behavior of young adults who follow TDS, data were collected from an email survey of college students in December of 2007. To obtain our sample, we selected 10 universities from each state. We then sent the registrar of each university a letter requesting a directory of undergraduate student email addresses. We included a description of the research, a copy of the survey, and the institutional review board approval from our university. We received directories from institutions in 48 different states, as well as the District of Columbia.

Throughout 2007 we sent emails to these undergraduate students inviting them to participate in a six-wave panel study about the political attitudes and behavior of college students. We informed them that their participation was voluntary and that the surveys would take from 10–20 minutes to complete. As an incentive, we also told them that if they completed all six surveys, their name would be entered into a drawing (held in December of 2008) for a top prize of $2,500, and a second prize of $1,000. In all, 10,343 people signed up to participate.

This sampling strategy has several advantages that answer common concerns about external validity. First, while our subjects are college students, this age group corresponds to the target population (18–24 year old youth). Thus, the results of the research are more generalizable than many studies that use college-aged students (Sears 1986). A second advantage is that this particular age group is becoming increasingly difficult to contact via telephone (Pew Research Center 2006). Of those who responded to the survey, only a small percentage reported they had land line telephones in their residence, meaning that a traditional telephone survey would likely have reached a non-representative sample. Finally, the sample was drawn from public universities located in all regions of the country and, as such, is fairly representative of the larger population of university students.

The present study relies on data from the first survey of the six-wave project only. The survey began on December 15, 2007. Reminders were sent on December 19 and 21, and the survey was closed on December 23, 2007. In all we received of 3,577 responses (response rate, 37.9 percent).

A primary problem associated with measuring media habits is overlap. Few Americans rely exclusively on one media source for their information. It is difficult to gauge reliance on a particular program based on asking about the viewing habits of that program alone. For our purposes the question becomes, how to classify or categorize TDS viewers? For example, we could say that one-third of the American public are TDS viewers, but this approach is far too broad, considering that a significant number of viewers report they "hardly ever" watch the program. Furthermore, even a claim that one watches TDS frequently does not imply relying on the program for news or learning from it.

We define three types of TDS viewers, based on the viewing habits of the program relative to other media sources. Particularly, we asked respondents how many days per week they watched various media sources that contained public affairs information in a "typical" week. Table 2 shows the programming type, followed by the average number of days followed for each.

Table 2. Average Number of Days Viewing/ Listening to Various Sources of News

During a typical week, can you tell us about how many days do you:	*Mean number of days in a week (0–7 scale)*
Watch news on the Cable News Channel (CNN)?	1.47
Watch news on the Fox News Channel?	1.39
Watch news on MSNBC?	1.16
Listen to news on the radio?	1.84
Watch or read news on the Internet?	4.01
Read news in a printed newspaper?	2.08
Watch "The Daily Show with Jon Stewart"?	1.31

It should be noted that TDS is the only specific program we are examining. All other sources are broader categories, such as television networks, radio news, newspaper, or Internet news. Thus, we are comparing exposure to a single program that airs for one-half hour a night — four days per week — to larger programming groups, most of which are available throughout the week, many of which can be seen around the clock. This said, we can see that the average level of exposure to TDS is comparable to each of the other, more encompassing, sources of news. Only "Internet" news ranks significantly higher, which is not surprising given the broad nature of the medium and the age demographic of our sample.

Based on these average values, we divided respondents into one of three distinct types of TDS viewer. Our first type consists of those individuals who report watching TDS at least once in a "typical" week, but follow at least one other major source of news with more frequency. We refer to these viewers as "casual" viewers. They watch the program, but rely more heavily on some other media source. Fifteen percent of our sample falls into this category.

Our second type of viewer follows other major sources of news *as much as* TDS, but not more. These we refer to as "moderate" viewers. This category of viewer is the largest, because it includes those individuals who might watch TDS as often as every day of the week, but also follow at least one other major source of news with the same frequency. Twenty-three percent of the sample falls into this category. That is, these moderate viewers are those individuals who reported watching TDS the same number of days per week as some other source (or sources) of news.

Our third type of TDS viewers are those who watch the program more than any other major source of news. This is the highest level of TDS reliance. We refer to these viewers as "heavy" viewers, and they constitute six percent of our sample. This is not a surprisingly low number, since following any major source of news with any frequency precludes an individual from falling into this category. For instance, an individual who watches TDS on a daily basis would be excluded from this category if they also read a printed newspaper every day. However given the strict manner in which this category is defined, it's size is substantial. It is, for example, larger than comparable audiences for "late night comedy" (Leno, Letterman, and O'Brien), which is only two percent of the sample, or for the audience that relies on Oprah Winfrey more than other sources (three percent). In total, 44 percent of our sample can be categorized as one of these three types of TDS viewers, while 56 percent are identified as non-viewers. See Table 3.

Table 3. Types of TDS Viewer

Type of Viewer	Description	Percentage
Non-viewers	Do not watch TDS	56%
Casual	Watches TDS at least once a week, but follow at least one other major source of news with more frequency	15
Moderate	Follows other major sources of news *as much as* TDS, but not more	23
Heavy	Watches TDS more than any other major source of news	6

Breaking the TDS audience into three separate categories based on their reliance on TDS relative to other sources of news provides the opportunity to conduct a more thorough examination of how viewing TDS may or may not provide for higher levels of political knowledge and/or participation among young adults. This is because we can now make some reasonable inferences about their reliance on the program. Are there political engagement differences between the three types of viewers? We turn to that question next.

Political Knowledge and Participation of TDS Viewers

How do the various TDS audiences differ from one another — if at all — when it comes to political knowledge and participation? How do they differ from those who do not watch the program? Table 4 is a first step at examining these differences with regard to knowledge of the field of candidates seeking the Democratic and Republican Parties' nomination for president in late 2007. In the survey, subjects were asked to enter the names of as many presidential candidates as they could remember. Cell entries are the percentage of each type of viewer who listed a given candidate. As can be seen, the casual and moderate TDS viewers were the most knowledgeable about the field of candidates. For each candidate, these viewers were significantly more knowledgeable than those who never watched TDS. It might therefore be logical to infer that exposure to TDS is associated with a greater ability to identify political figures.

However, when we look at heavy TDS viewers we see that they did not differ significantly from those who do not watch the program at all in their ability to identify any of the presidential candidates. In the majority of cases, these heavy viewers appear to be slightly more knowledgeable than non-viewers, but these difference are not statistically significant.

Similarly, it appears that general civic knowledge among heavy viewers is not significantly different from that of non-viewers. Table 5 shows the percentage of each type of viewer who could identify certain facts and/or actors in American politics. It is apparent that casual and moderate viewers are significantly more knowledgeable than non–TDS viewers. This finding is consistent with other studies that suggest that TDS viewers are more knowledgeable than the average citizen (Young 2004). However, there appears to be little difference between non-viewers and heavy viewers.

Table 4. Knowledge of Presidential Candidates, by TDS Viewer Type

Percent able to recall candidate name:	*Casual Viewers*	*Moderate Viewers*	*Heavy Viewers*	*Non-TDS Viewers*
Hillary Clinton	96*	94*	92	90
Barack Obama	94*	93*	91	84
John Edwards	62*	53*	45	37
Rudy Giuliani	77*	73*	62	58
John McCain	55*	50*	41	38
Mitt Romney	53*	42*	29	28
Fred Thompson	30*	29*	16	18
Mike Huckabee	48*	40*	25	27

*Difference from non–TDS watchers is significantly different at $p<.05$ (Scheffe post-hoc test for multiple group comparison).

Table 5. General Civic Knowledge, by TDS Viewer Type

Percent able to identify...	*Casual Viewers*	*Moderate Viewers*	*Heavy Viewers*	*Non-TDS Viewers*
Speaker of House of Representatives	70*	66*	53	48
Majority Party in Congress	62*	58*	47	39

Percent able to identify ...	*Casual Viewers*	*Moderate Viewers*	*Heavy Viewers*	*Non-TDS Viewers*
Chief Justice of Supreme Court	22*	16	10	12
Political party that is generally more conservative	92*	92*	90	87
Percent of Congress necessary to override veto	86*	84*	78	79

*Difference from non–TDS watchers is significantly different at p<.05 (Scheffe post-hoc test for multiple group comparison).

The evidence presented in Tables 4 and 5 suggests that the more knowledgeable TDS viewers are those who rely on other major sources of news *as much as* or *more than* TDS. Perhaps surprisingly, those who rely on TDS more than any other major source of news are not more knowledgeable than non–TDS viewers. This uncovers an interesting aspect about the effects of TDS viewing on young viewers' political knowledge. We see little evidence that suggests exposure to TDS is the sole or direct cause of higher levels of political knowledge. If this were the case, heavy viewers would look more like TDS viewers who also follow other sources of news. Instead, those who rely heaviest on TDS for their news and information are not much more knowledgeable than those who never watch the program. Based on these results, we suspect that praise heaped on Stewart for helping create a more informed citizenry may be overblown. The knowledgeable portions of his audience are those who follow other major sources of news at least as much as TDS. While this is an indirect test only, the evidence suggests that viewers are not necessarily learning from TDS.

Interestingly, however, there is some evidence to suggest that those who rely on TDS for most of their news may, in fact, *think* they are more politically knowledgeable. Our survey asked respondents to agree or disagree with the statement that, "I feel that I have a pretty good understanding of the important political issues facing our country" (a 10 point-scale, where 1 = completely disagree; 5 = neither agree nor disagree; and 10 = completely agree). On average, casual and moderate viewers were most confident about their understanding of important political issues (casual viewers, average score, 7.1, moderate viewers, 6.4). These number seem to reflect actual relative knowledge levels presented above. Heavy TDS viewers have a lower level of confidence than casual and moderate viewers (average score, 6.1), which also reflects actual knowledge findings.

However, the interesting difference here is between the average confidence of heavy viewers and those who never watch TDS (average score, 5.6). That is, those who rely most on TDS for news are a full half-point more confident in their understanding of important political issues than those who never watch TDS, even though data in Tables 4 and 5 indicate no significant difference in actual levels of knowledge. This suggests the possibility that heavy reliance on TDS for political information gives an individual the impression of being more politically knowledgeable than they actually are.

We now turn to a different aspect of political engagement, namely, political participation. Table 6 shows the political activity of different types of TDS viewer. Here, respondents were asked to report whether or not they had engaged in one of the following activities in the previous 12 months: contacted a public official, attended a political rally, attended a town hall meeting, or tried to persuade another individual to change their mind on an issue or candidate, etc. The table illustrates significant differences across the different types of TDS viewers. Consistent with the findings about political knowledge, the most politically active viewers are those who watch the show as a supplement to other sources of news. Heavy viewers do not significantly differ from non-viewers in any of the political activities listed.

Table 6. Political Activity by Types of TDS Viewer

Percent who said they engaged in the following political activity in the last year...	Casual Viewers	Moderate Viewers	Heavy Viewers	Non-TDS Viewers
Written or called a politician	23*	17*	10	11
Attended a political speech/ rally/protest	22*	19*	9	9
Attended a public local town public meeting	23*	24*	15	15
Tried to persuade a person to support a political issue or candidate	56*	53*	43	36
Worked for a political party or campaign	6*	4*	2	2
Been an active member of an interest group	13*	11*	7	7

*Difference from non–TDS watchers is significantly different at $p<.05$ (Scheffe post-hoc test for multiple group comparison).

Of course, the most fundamental form of political participation in America is voting. This is a notoriously difficult activity to measure, because many non-voters are unwilling tell survey researchers they did not do so. With this limitation in mind we asked our survey participants to tell us how likely it was that they would vote in the 2008 general election. Not surprisingly, the estimated turnout (91 percent) far exceeded actual voter turnout (49 percent) among 18–24 year olds (United States Census Bureau 2009). Nevertheless, there was enough variation in our collective responses to examine it across the various types of TDS viewer.

While 95 percent of casual TDS viewers and 94 percent of moderate viewers reported they were likely to vote in the 2008 election, only 91 percent of heavy viewers did so. This is slightly higher than the 90 percent intended vote among non–TDS viewers, but the difference here was not statistically significant. This illustrates — again — a noticeable difference between those who heavily rely on TDS and those who include TDS in a larger array of sources.

The data presented above seem to substantiate our contention that the effect of exposure to TDS is more benign than some might suggest. Yes, some of his viewers are more knowledgeable and engaged than those who do not watch the program, but our data show that these young adults do not rely on TDS as a primary source of information. When we look at those who rely on TDS more than any other source of news, these differences disappear. If viewing the program had a significant positive impact on political knowledge and participation, we would expect to see it in this group.

Discussion

We have thus far shown that heavy TDS viewers do not differ significantly from non–TDS viewers with respect to their levels of political knowledge and participation. Interestingly, the only major difference we found was in their perceived knowledge, which suggests a possible negative impact of exposure to TDS. In other words, heavy exposure does not necessarily make viewers more politically knowledgeable or active, and somewhat counter-intuitively, leaves them with the sense that they know more than they do about contemporary political issues.

There is, however, a second potentially negative effect on heavy TDS viewers, which is grounded in the idea that high levels of exposure to Stewart's sharp and pervasive cynicism may cause that cynicism to rub off. Laughs generated by TDS are almost exclusively at the expense of public officials, political candidates, and the political system as a whole. Primary reliance on TDS puts the viewer as witness to a constant barrage of comic criticism that paints a picture of a completely dysfunctional political system. A more cynical audience may be the result. Without debating the possible virtues or drawbacks of political cynicism, heavy TDS viewers may differ from non-viewers in this regard.

To test this, we included two statements in our survey and asked respondents to agree or disagree (on a 1 to 10 scale). The first stated: "Public officials don't care much what people like me think." A higher level of agreement with this statement would indicate a higher level of cynicism about public officials.

Heavy TDS viewers had the highest average level of agreement with this statement (5.9). Moderate and casual viewers (average scores of 5.5 and 5.7, respectively) were in slightly less agreement, and non–TDS viewers agreed least with the statement (5.5). These findings hint at the idea that those who heavily rely on TDS for information are slightly more cynical, although the differences in this case lack statistical significance.

The second measure of cynicism, lends more support to our idea. When asked to agree or disagree with the statement that, "I have faith in the U.S. electoral system" (1 to 10 scale), heavy viewers had less faith than any other group, showing the lowest level of agreement (average score, 4.4), followed by moderate (4.7) and casual viewers (4.5). All of these groups were significantly different from the non–TDS audience, which had an average agreement score of 5.1.

In both cases here the most cynical group was the heavy TDS viewers. This finding holds even when these viewers are compared to other subgroups of the non–TDS audience, including those who rely most on cable news, newspapers, online news, or the radio. In short, heavy TDS viewing seems to be associated with greater levels of political cynicism.

It should be noted again that in this analysis we measured the number of days that individuals reported watching TDS. In some respects this constitutes only an indirect test of the relationship between TDS viewing and political knowledge and participation. This is because claiming to watch the program is not necessarily the same as stating that one relies on the program for news and information. This caveat is particularly important with regard to the relationship between TDS viewing and political knowledge. The idea that viewership of the program may mobilize young adults to higher levels of political action is probably less affected by this distinction.

So what are we to make of this analysis? Does Jon Stewart provide a public good? Or in an ironic twist, is he guilty of what he accused the hosts of "Crossfire" of, namely, "hurting America?" This question is beyond the scope of this essay. The show is, undeniably, entertaining, and this by itself would seem to suggest that viewing may have some benefits. In particular, TDS may attract the attention of some people who otherwise might pay little or no attention to politics. While this may translate into some incidental learning about politics our analysis suggests that the amount of information acquired in this manner may be limited. This by itself may be a benign effect, but, the viewership of the program may give some viewers a false sense of being informed. In addition, any learning that may occur as the result of exposure to TDS does not seem to translate necessarily into more political participation on the part of viewers, and, may in fact engender greater feelings of political cynicism.

Are these two findings related? Does viewing TDS lead to greater levels of cynicism among young adults, which in turn makes it less likely that they will participate in politics? We cannot answer that question here. However, given the evidence presented in this essay, Stewart's popularity, and the fact that young adults are generally less likely to participate in politics than their older counterparts, it strikes us as a possibility that cannot be immediately ruled out. More research would help clarify this relationship, and given the substantive importance of the question, would seem to be justified. At minimum, this analysis suggests that we exercise some caution before concluding that Jon Stewart is the savior of democracy in the new millennium.

References

Associated Press. 2008. "Politicians Found Late-Night an Asset in 2008." December 29, 2008. Available at http://www.cmpa.com/news/12_29_2008.pdf.

2005 Time 100. 2009. *Time.* Available at http://www.time.com/time/2005/time100/ (accessed November 20, 2009).

Baym, Geoffrey. 2005. "*The Daily Show*: Discursive Integration and the Reinvention of Political Journalism." *Political Communication.* 22 (3): 259–76.

_____. 2007a. "Crafting New Communicative Models in the Televisual Sphere: Political Interviews on *The Daily Show*." *The Communication Review.* 10 (2):93–115.

_____. 2007b. "Serious Comedy: Exploring the Boundaries of Political Discourse." In *Laughing Matters: Humor and American Politics in the Media Age*, eds. Jonathan S. Morris, and Jody Baumgartner, 21–38. New York: Routledge.

Bennett, W. Lance. 2007. "Relief in Hard Times: A Defense of Jon Stewart's Comedy in an Age of Cynicism." *Critical Studies in Media Communication.* 24 (3): 278–83.

Brewer, Paul R., and Emily Marquardt. 2007. "Mock News and Democracy: Analyzing *The Daily Show*." *Atlantic Journal of Communication.* 15 (4): 249–67.

Carter, Bill. 2005. "CNN Will Cancel 'Crossfire' and Cut Ties to Commentator." *New York Times.* January 6, 2005. Available at http://www.nytimes.com/2005/01/06/business/media/06crossfire.html.

Clark, Andrew. 2009. "Viewers Switch off Business Channel." *New Zealand Herald.* August 10, 2009.

Feldman, Lauren. 2007. "The News About Comedy: Young Audiences, *The Daily Show*, and Evolving Notions of Journalism." *Journalism.* 8 (4): 406–27.

Fisher, Luchina. 2009. "Jon Stewart vs. Jim Cramer: Who Will Win Shoutdown?" *ABCNews.com.* March 12, 2009. Available at http://abcnews.go.com/Entertainment/Television/story?id=7070600&page=1.

Fitzgerald, Toni. 2009. "Seriously, Jon Stewart as Anchorman." *Media Life.* April 3, 2009. Available at http://www.medialifemagazine.com/artman2/publish/Dayparts_update_51/Seriously_Jon_Stewart_as_anchorman.asp.

Fox, Julia R., Glory Koloen, and Volkan Sahin. 2007. "No Joke: A Comparison of Substance in *The Daily Show* with Jon Stewart and Broadcast Network Television Coverage of the 2004 Presidential Election Campaign." *Journal of Broadcasting & Electronic Media.* 51 (2): 213–27.

Gaines, Elliot. 2007. "The Narrative Semiotics of *The Daily Show*." *Semiotica.* 166: 81–96.

Hariman, Robert. 2007. "In Defense of Jon Stewart." *Critical Studies in Media Communication.* 24 (3): 273–77.

Harris, Mark. Nd. Party Lines. *Entertainment Weekly.* Available at http://www.ew.com/ew/arti
cle/0,,767401__1011609,00.html, accessed November 20, 2009.

Holt, Jason, ed. 2007. *The Daily Show and Philosophy: Moments of Zen in the Art of Fake News.*
Malden, MA: Wiley-Blackwell.

Kakutani, Michiko. 2008. "The Most Trusted Man in America?" *New York Times.* August 17,
2008. P. AR1.

Macedo, Diane. 2009. "Comedy Central Scoops Network News on Climate-Gate Scandal."
Fox News. December 3, 2009. Available at http://www.foxnews.com/story/0,2933,
578990,00.html.

McDonald, Kathy A. 2009. "Mainstream Media Remains in on Joke." *Daily Variety.* January
22, 2009. Pp. A4–5.

Newsweek. 2003. Vol. 143, Issue 1 (December 29, 2003).

Nichols, Hans. 2009. "Obama Aide Dunn Renews Criticism of Fox, Hails Jon Stewart."
Bloomberg. November 14, 2009. Available at http://www.bloomberg.com/apps/news?pid=
20601070&sid=aBRJYGPAmOoo.

Pew Research Center. 2006. The Cell Phone Challenge to Survey Research. May 15, 2006.
Available at http://people-press.org/reports/display.php3?ReportID=276.

_____. 2008a. April 2008 Media Survey. Accessed 17 November 2009. 17 August 2008. Available
at: http://people-press.org/dataarchive/#2008

_____. 2008b. Late December 2007 Political Communication Study. 11 January 2008. Available
at: http://people-press.org/dataarchive/#2008

Rowe, Robin. 2009. "Two Emmys for Jon Stewart The Daily Show. *Hollywood Today.*" September 20, 2009. Available at http://www.hollywoodtoday.net/?p=10889.

Sears, David O. 1986. "College Sophomores in the Laboratory: Influence of a Narrow Data
Base on Social Psychology's View of Human Nature." *Journal of Personality and Social Psychology.* 51: 515–530.

Segal, David. 2005. "Anchors Comic And Serious Win Peabodys." *Washington Post.* May 17,
2005. Available at http://www.washingtonpost.com/wp-dyn/content/article/2005/05/16/
AR2005051601462.html.

"Top 10 TV Feuds." 2009. *Time.com.* June 12, 2009. Available at http://www.time.com/time/spe
cials/packages/article/0,28804,1884499_1884515_1904503,00.html

Trier, James. 2008. "*The Daily Show with Jon Stewart.*" *Journal of Adolescent & Adult Literacy,*
51 (5): 424–27.

United States Census Bureau. 2009. "Voter Turnout Increases by 5 Million in 2008 Presidential
Election." U.S. Census Bureau. July 20, 2009. Available at http://www.census.gov/Press-
Release/www/releases/archives/voting/013995.html.

Warner, Jamie. 2007. "Political Culture Jamming: The Dissident Humor of *The Daily Show
With Jon Stewart.*" *Popular Communication.* 5(1): 17–36.

Wattenberg, Martin P. 2007. *Is Voting for Young People?* New York: Pearson Longman.

Weisman, Jon. 2008. "The Ground Breakers: Television: Jon Stewart." *Daily Variety.* October
31, 2008. P. A18.

Winant, Gabriel. 2009. "Cramer Talks down Stewart Feud." *Salon.com.* March 12, 2009. Available at http://www.salon.com/politics/war_room/2009/03/12/cramer_stewart/print.html.

Young, Dannagal Goldthwaite. 2004. "Daily Show Viewers Knowledgeable About Presidential
Campaign." National Annenberg Election Survey (2004). September 21, 2004. Available
on-line at <http://www.naes04.org>.

_____. 2007. *The Daily Show* as New Journalism: In Their Own Words. In *Laughing Matters:
Humor and American Politics in the Media Age,* eds. Jonathan S. Morris, and Jody Baumgartner, 241–259. New York: Routeledge.

Is Fake News the Real News?

The Significance of Stewart and Colbert for Democratic Discourse, Politics, and Policy

MARK K. MCBETH *and* RANDY S. CLEMONS

Introduction

Studies of the impact of popular culture on political and social life have increased in the past decade (Foy 2010; Cantor 2003). Yet, even without the plethora of good social science studies (Fox, Koloen, Sahin 2007; Colletta 2009; Holbert and Geidner 2009 and Baumgartner and Morris 2008), showing that "fake" news shows have both content equally as meaningful as the "real" news shows and a significant impact on real world politics and political opinion; there was, and is, prima facie evidence that these two naming categories (real and fake) may no longer convey an accurate picture. Our two-pronged thesis is that these fake news shows are not only at least as real as the mainstream news, but also that they contribute more to the type of deliberative discourse essential to genuine democracy and public policy.

Some of the evidence about "realness" comes from the so-called real news. For example, these shows regularly replay political comedy segments, and in the fall of 2009 CNN fact-checked a *Saturday Night Live* (SNL) sketch about President Obama — promptly getting skewered by *The Daily Show* (TDS) for doing so. The news-opinion program *Crossfire* invited Jon Stewart on their show (and surely came to regret it), and there was the wide-spread coverage of his thrashing of MSNBC's Jim Kramer over the coverage the real news was providing of the economic collapse.

That level of acknowledgment — combined with Presidential and Vice-Presidential candidates appearing on the fake news shows, announcing their candidacy on them (Edwards, TDS, in 2003), thanking them for their popularity bump in the polls (Huckabee on *The Colbert Report*), and even using crucial time to appear on SNL the weekend before the Tuesday of the election (McCain) — speaks to a sense of legitimacy that made it unsurprising when a 2004 Pew Study showed that *The Daily Show*, when compared to traditional broadcast news, was an equally important source of campaign knowledge for young adults (Fox, Koloen, Sahin 2007, 215). From our perspective, it was more telling when a 2007 Pew Study revealed that those who got their knowledge from Stewart's and Colbert's shows were better informed than those who got their information from more traditional sources (Pew Research Center for the People & the Press 2007).

Typically, popular culture is viewed as fiction or satire mimicking political and social life. For example, when *Saturday Night Live* debuted in 1975 it heralded a new brand of comedy. Led by a cast of Vietnam era comedians, SNL was viewed as edgy, anti-establishment, and political. Dan Akroyd's portrayals of President Nixon and later President Carter, and Chevy Chase's bumbling President Ford imitation, satirized the politics of the day. The show also included "Weekend Update," a five to six minute fake news skit that made fun of politics and current events. Today, thirty-five years later, SNL is still popular, but two "fake" news shows have become integral parts of the political discourse of contemporary politics. *The Daily Show* and *The Colbert Report*, go far beyond SNL in their impact on modern politics. Why?

There are arguments today that much of what passes for serious coverage of political discourse in the United States has become a simulation of reality or, worse yet, theatre, comedy, and fictional. In the 2008 U.S. presidential election skits on SNL and a skipped appearance on Letterman's *Late Show* became news. In fact, as referenced above, John McCain hosted SNL the weekend before the 2008 election appearing in a skit with Tina Fey portraying McCain's vice-presidential choice Sarah Palin. While Fey's caricature of Palin is generally viewed as negatively impacting public opinion of her, McCain had no problem participating in a skit where Fey's Palin "goes rogue" during an infomercial and tries to sell "Palin in 2012" t-shirts. It was a surreal moment, a Republican candidate for president on a show with a simulated vice-presidential candidate making fun of his own ticket.

While SNL's "Weekend Update" segment was considered sharp political satire in the 1970s, much of what was done on that show is today done more sensationally in the real news programs on Fox News, MSNBC, and CNN. How could suave original anchor Chevy Chase compete with the likes of Lou Dobbs, Keith Olbermann, Glenn Beck, and Bill O'Reilly, and their highly postmodern mixing of entertainment, commentary, and news? Indeed, we ask if even Stewart or Colbert can "outfake" the outrageous and entertaining news commentators of 2010. Our answer is that they cannot.

Using a mixture of postmodern and other literature, and results from a survey experiment, we argue in this essay that much of American political coverage is inauthentic (fake) and that the programs of Jon Stewart and Stephen Colbert both represent authentic (real) discourse that breaks through the shell of the real (fake) news revealing layers of social construction, empty symbolism, and simulacra — thus positively affecting the traditional coverage and political discourse.

Politics as Catch-Phrases and Empty Symbols

In recent years critics have bemoaned the lack of substance in American political discourse. In a democracy citizens are sovereign, but today's political discourse is dominated by soft news, popular culture references, and moralistic fights on highly contrived events. American politics has become entertainment: professional wrestling in moral arenas with constructed villains, heroes, and victims.

Citizen opinion is considered the lynchpin of democracy. It is assumed that a better informed public, clear on their political preferences, is a positive situation. For example, Miller and Fox (2006) describe the "loop model" of democracy. The loop model asserts that the core of democracy is a sovereign citizen with political preferences. Political parties then form and put together various policy packages to meet these preferences. (The technical term for this is "interest aggregation.") Citizens vote for the parties and candidates that meet their preferences. Elected officials then pass legislation and citizens vote to retain these officials or to remove them. The key to the loop model is that there is a direct connection between citizens and elected officials.

As others also do, Miller and Fox (2006) argue that the loop model's accuracy has been severely undermined. In contemporary American politics, even at the local level, elected officials act more as "symbols" (noisy cymbals) raising campaign dollars, identifying and exploiting wedge issues. This produces interesting sound-bites that the media reports, usually uncritically and often exaggerating the importance.

Miller (2002, xi) convincingly argues that "the public discourse has taken a peculiar shape in the era of mass communication and mass marketing" and that "information has become a commodity much like fashion design." As Miller suggests, public policy making becomes little more than an exercise in marketing. Thus, in today's political environment, even decisions involving war, and therefore life and death, are marketed to citizens as "shock and awe," "mission accomplished," and the "the surge."

It has been widely noted for decades that much of network coverage of campaigns has focused on what is called horserace coverage. That is, they cover the race for the nominations and the election (Who's ahead? Who has momentum? Who's exceeding expectations? Who dropped way behind? Who raised how much money?), rather than exploring the issues in any depth, outlining the policy positions of the candidates, or meaningfully examining their qualifications. Even the coverage of the candidates tends to seem more similar to what we would expect from *Live With Regis and Kelly*, or *The View*, than from a hard news show. Exacerbated by campaigns that are intentionally vague and pitched to our emotions, for example featuring mom and apple-pie positions and pictures of candidates playing with children, the end result is candidates elected with little to no mandate regardless of the size of their victory.

For decades the impact of media was discounted because studies showed it was very difficult to alter party identification. Today though, with our greater reliance on and understanding of electronic, visual media, we have a more sophisticated understanding of the way in which media can impact public opinion. For example: framing — and its impact on how you perceive and think about an issue; priming, including subliminal affective priming — which relates to the accessibility of an issue and the criteria by which we evaluate that issue; and the question of which issues we are even evaluating, i.e. agenda setting. With all the research findings about the brain and emotion it is simply impossible to discount the importance of the media's coverage of politics.

For example, recent research in cognitive science has called into question how individuals form opinions about politics. While scholars traditionally have argued that individuals are rational and dispassionate, carefully weighing the costs and benefits of various actions or candidates for office, Westen (2008) argues that political decisions are significantly grounded in emotion. Moreover, our policy analysis approach (Clemons and McBeth 2009) is grounded in narrative analysis. That is, we view policy making as a battle of conflicting stories that play out in the media. These policy narratives have plots, characters, themes, and often use stark language or images to accomplish a variety of strategic policy goals including influencing public opinion, in part by expanding or containing issues. Indeed, the evidence of humor's affective effect, the quality of the stories both *The Daily Show* and *The Colbert Report* tell, and the reality that both real and fake news coverage consists of prototypical stories, suggests one should not expect much difference in terms of what people learn from them (except that perhaps the fake news asks tougher questions).

The work of scholars such as Edelman (1964), Stone (2002), and Lakoff (2004) have led studies in political communication, policy analysis, and electoral politics to focus on the use of symbols, metaphors, euphemisms, and statistics to frame issues, set the agenda, and persuade. However, while the earlier focus was on cognitive based rational actor models, the new models stress our affective domain. This is not completely new — for example, Murray Edelman noted that metaphors can evoke on both the rational and emotional level. Yet, the work of Lakoff on framing, Loftus (1997) on creating false memories, Westen (2008) on fighting political fights at the gut level, and authors such as Gigerenzer (2007) and Gladwell (2005) on unconscious decision making, is starting to impact all of the social sciences. While some of this research is particularly related to the topic of this book (e.g. the role of humor in priming and framing), for our purposes here, it is enough to note that both the cognitive and affective pathways of learning can affect, if not effect, political views.

While the real news includes cognitive inputs, it is also a form of entertainment with its sound bites, symbols, and heroes and villains; and this emotive aspects impacts the political views of its audiences. The fake news is funny and certainly emotive but it also includes cognitive elements, possibly more. Thus, certainly fake news has an impact on politics. The questions are, does it have more of an impact, or as much impact, as the real news; and, is that impact perhaps more positive for democracy and policy?

We will test our thesis that the fake news is actually the real news by examining the 2008 United States' presidential election campaign. We first review existing literature on *The Daily Show* and *The Colbert Report*, as well as literature asserting that American politics has become little more than empty symbolism and entertainment. Second, we (de)construct some of the major narratives and symbols emanating from that election cycle as reported in the "real" media. Then we provide an analysis of how both the TDS and the TCR altered these narratives and ultimately punctured the empty symbols. This sets the stage for our extended case study on one of the symbols, the detailing of a survey experiment, the reporting of our results, and, finally, concluding thoughts about the topic of the fake news versus the real news.

Review of the Literature

An impressive body of literature on fake news, particularly focusing on the TDS and the TCR has developed in recent years. Holbert, Lamb, Dudo, and Carlton (2007) study the priming effects of viewing *The Daily Show* and find that individuals with lower political efficacy are particularly attracted to the message of Stewart. Colletta (2009) discusses both Stewart and Colbert in the context of "political satire and postmodern irony." Colletta (2009, 856) argues that postmodern irony is different from our traditional view of irony.

Postmodern irony is based in the notion that there is no external or objective reality but rather simply constructions of reality and it is self-referential in that "(a) postmodern audience is made conscious of the constructed nature of meaning and of its own participation in the appearance of things." Colletta views the television viewer as "in on the joke" in that the viewer knows that they are watching a construction of reality. She (2009, 856) states that while Colbert (fake news) uses absurdity in his parody of Bill O'Reilly, O'Reilly himself (the "real" news) uses similar strategies, thus "blurring the distinction between absurdity and politics as usual." Later, she questions whether it is possible to satirize shows such as this, and then argues that Jon Stewart's famous *Crossfire* appearance was ultimately more effective than the satire regularly displayed on the TDS. Finally, in a study that also explored the satire of Colbert along with the effect of political ideology on viewer perceptions, LaMarre, Landreville, Beam (2009) found that while conservatives believed that Colbert was actually conservative, liberals were more likely to view his act as satire.

Following this reasoning, Baumgartner and Morris (2008) conducted an experimental study showing that while *The Colbert Report* (TCR) has an impact on viewer attitudes it is not in the direction that Colbert may want, in that exposure to Colbert led to increases in support for President Bush and Republican policies for casual viewers (i.e. not his regular audience). An earlier study by Fox, Koloen, and Sahin (2007) found that while the TDS's coverage of the 2004 U.S. presidential election was mostly about humor, they were still equal in substance with the network news in terms of addressing the issues and candidate qualifications. While the literature provides evidence that the fake news might really be the real news (Colletta 2009; Baumgartner and Morris 2008; and Fox, Koloen and Sahin 2007), an alternative interpretation of the literature is that it also suggests the real news is the fake news.

Definitions

One task that must be addressed before continuing is to define the terms real and fake. The word real is a powerful word and, with apologies to the great definition in the children's classic *The Velveteen Rabbit*, in terms of the news, two components — content and impact — would seem most relevant. Real news would cover serious and important topics (more on the deficit, less on Tiger Woods or Anna Nicole Smith), in greater quantity than fake news. This coverage would reveal meaningful policy differences, puncture the false balloons, peel back layers, and hold themselves and others accountable (e.g. by showing viewers their earlier statements, votes, and actions). It would be more than an easily manipulated echo chamber eviscerated by repeated claims about bias and guilty of just repeating, over and over again, the standard story-line others tell. The distracting bread and circus coverage that dominates the news sometimes makes it seem as if the old carnival fraud of *Wizard of Oz* fame is back there behind the curtain using smoke and flames, flashing lights, computer altered images, and other special effects — not to mention a frighteningly loud and intimidating voice.

On a continuum between real and fake, the impact of real news should be such that it impacts public opinion and other media coverage, strengthens democracy, matters to key political players, informs the policy debate, and creates a discourse where alternative views are engaged (rather than people talking past each other or being allowed to make unsupported claims). Its impact would also ideally include an educational function, teaching citizens not what to think, but how to think; providing a lens through which the media's consumers would recognize the use of moral fables, false simulacra, distracting highly controversial events of little significance, and rhetoric that frames issues as a Hobson's Choice, or on the basis of sacrosanct — and therefore non debatable — grounds.

Thus defined, relative to both content and impact, the terms real and fake in the context of the media, can be evaluated by not only the authors, but also by the reader. Next, we begin our analysis.

The 2008 Election: The Stories of the Mainstream Media

The 2008 U.S. Presidential election campaign can profitably be used by narrative analysts to explore the use of empty symbols, villains, victims, and heroes. The election was historic with the early front runner for the Democratic nomination a woman (Hilary Clinton), an eventual nominee who was African-American (Barack Obama) and the second female vice president nominee in U.S. history (Sarah Palin). The United States was involved in an unpopular and increasingly difficult war in Iraq, the economy collapsed in the fall of 2008, and the stage was set for a historic moment in American politics. Yet, the narrative of the 2008 election did not necessarily hone in on America's role in the world, the relationship between democratic government and capitalism, or the exciting possibility that the American power structure was to fully include both African-Americans and women in the competition for the most powerful office in the world.

While these issues were certainly debated and discussed, the masses were exposed to a litany of marketing exercises, catch phrases, and name calling, as well as thoroughly introduced to various characters in the professional (mud) wrestling of 2008 U.S. politics. In order to set up our analysis of how TDS and TCR contributed to the political discourse of the election, we will focus on issues (or entertainment events) that dominated the 2008 election. First, we will discuss and report media coverage data on four major symbols of the 2008 election: Joe the Plumber, William Ayers, ACORN, and Jeremiah Wright.

Table 1: News Stories from Google News

Symbols and All News Sources

"Jeremiah Wright" — Google News stories for 2008: 16,600
"Joe the plumber" — Google News stories for 2008: 8,250
"William Ayers" and "Obama" — Google News stories for 2008: 6,390
"ACORN" — Google News stories for 2008: 14,300

Substantive Policy Issues

"Health Care Reform" — Google News stories for 2008: 10,100
"Iraq War" — Google News stories for 2008: 54,800
"Recession" — Google New stories for 2008: 275,000

Symbols and Cable News (Google News)

Cable News	Wright	Joe	Ayers	ACORN
Fox News	1,260	230	291	269
MSNBC	449	123	129	114
CNN	1,380	238	236	225

Source: Google News Search for 2008

Joe the Plumber

Using Google News, we found 6,360 stories about Joe the Plumber in the year 2008. This included 230 stories on Fox News, 238 stories on CNN, and 123 on MSNBC (see Table 1). On October 12, 2008, Joseph Wurzelbacher asked Barack Obama a question about his tax proposals during a campaign stop in Ohio. Wurzelbacher told him that he was about to buy a plumbing business and asked Obama whether his tax policies would lead to higher taxes on his future business (Rueters 2008). This was three days before the final presidential debate and the McCain campaign quickly knighted Wurzelbacher with the name "Joe the Plumber." Thus dubbed, Wurzelbacher became a media celebrity and McCain repeatedly mentioned Joe the Plumber in the 15 October 2008 presidential debate. Eventually he campaigned with McCain despite the news media discovering that Joe wasn't really a plumber. Nonetheless, he became an important symbol for McCain's framing of Obama as out of touch with the average American (Joe) in the waning days of the 2008 campaign.

Joe the Plumber was a classic synecdoche and part of a larger "strategic problem definition" (Stone 2002, 155). He was a single individual meant to represent a larger whole; in this case, a working man who had pulled himself up by his boot straps and was about to purchase his own small business. Standing in the way of McCain's supposed everyman hero was Senator Barack Obama whose tax policies, according to the McCain campaign, were going to crush the dreams of the victimized plumber.

On 16 October 2008, Jon Stewart covered the Joe the Plumber phenomena with reporter John Oliver providing a review of the excessive news exposure given to the man, claiming the media was "trying to destroy his life." During the same episode, they covered the many references by both Obama and McCain to Joe. Stewart engaged in typical sophomoric humor before launching into how the fascinated media had facilely fixated on Joe, showing clip after clip of media attention. Stewart seemed to be indicating that Obama had fallen for the trap, and that by giving Joe so much attention he was making this fictional plumber a real entity. Much of Stewart's attention was on how easily the media fell in love with the Joe the Plumber storyline, showing that at a time of war and financial crisis a fictional plumber's false scenario dominated media discourse. It is rather clear that he is pulling back the curtain to reveal both an empty symbol and the media's complicity or incompetency.

Colbert covered this story on 22 October 2008, referencing McCain's Joe multiple references and a stereotype of an overweight blue collar worker's waistline ("I am afraid he is addicted to crack"). He noted that McCain and Palin built upon the concept by giving others identities too (e.g., Wendy the Waitress and Molly the dental hygienist), arguing that these ordinary Americans needed "tax cuts and off-shore drilling, not universal health care and last names."

Colbert, in essence, deconstructs McCain's reification of Joe the Plumber by refocusing our attention from the McCain campaign's focus on these fictional characters to the few substantive, and traction-less policies that the McCain/Palin ticket was promoting at the time (drilling and across the board tax cuts). On the face of it, Colbert's comedy on Joe the Plumber seems light-hearted and even at times non-political, yet his redirecting of the debate from a fictional plumber to real issues either being promoted or ignored by McCain and Palin is piercing. But it would take his regular Colbert Nation audience to understand Colbert's clever deconstruction, and even they would be unlikely to consciously recognize how deftly he punctured both the false symbol of the campaign and the legitimacy of the media's coverage.

William Ayers

William Ayers was a member of the subversive 1960s anti–Vietnam War group the Weathermen. Ayers engaged in several bombings in the 1960s and much later he became a professor at the University of Illinois where in the 1990s he served on a committee with Barack Obama. He subsequently hosted a fund-raiser that Obama, then running for the Illinois state legislature, attended (Shane 2008). The media, led by the McCain campaign jumped on the association, linking Obama to Ayers — once again trying to call into question Obama's fundamental character. We found 6,390 stories about Ayers (a Google News search for 2008) including 291 stories on Fox. The Ayers theme furthered the McCain campaign's narrative by asking "who is the real Barack Obama" as they tried to solidify their construct of Obama as dangerous, different, and not a typical American.

Such construction of opponents as the "other" is a typical narrative tactic and they hoped to find fertile ground tapping into the culture of fear that had permeated post 9-11 America. Approximately 40 years after Ayers' crimes, by labeling Ayers a terrorist (language not used at the time of his crimes), they tried to tie events from the 60s to today. In the McCain campaign narrative, Ayers is the villain and by default Obama, despite very tenuous, slight ties to Ayers, is also constructed as a villain for associating with Ayers ("pal"ing around with a terrorist). Both McCain and Palin positioned themselves as heroes trying to save the American public from the "real" Barack Obama.

The Daily Show (7 October 2008) dealt with Ayers by directing attention toward Sarah Palin. Stewart shows a clip of Palin stating, "it's time that we find out who the real Barack Obama is." Stewart then retorts to Palin, "Excuse me woman that we met six weeks ago, we want to find out more about you, is your husband a crazy secessionist? Did you fire that guy for not firing the guy that you wanted him to fire?" Stewart thus redirects the audience toward the fact that Palin was even more of a political unknown than Obama, who had just weathered a long and grueling national campaign. Interestingly, Colbert only dealt with Ayers in short segments. Colbert's most sustained treatment of Ayers (9 October 2008) was in a clip that included conservative complaints about McCain's failure to raise Ayers in the most recent debate. This pattern on both shows — of peeling back the layers to reveal, with silliness, the silliness of the supposedly important issue, and then moving on — is both a hallmark of their mode of operation and testimony to their success.

ACORN

The low-income lobbyist group, the Association of Community Organizations for Reform Now (ACORN) more easily became a symbol of the 2008 presidential election because Barack Obama and others had, in 1995, represented the group in a lawsuit over voting rights And, additionally, the Obama campaign supposedly gave money to ACORN (Strom 2008). All of this was controversial because several local chapters of ACORN were in legal trouble for allegations of voter fraud and embezzlement (Strom 2008).

Because Obama had been a community organizer, ACORN provided a way for critics to negatively portray his past occupation. John McCain raised Obama's relationship to ACORN in the 15 October 2008 presidential debate (New York Times 2008). This issue was very successfully sold to the media. In fact, in 2008, there were over 14,000 news stories found via Google News dedicated to ACORN — more than were dedicated to health care reform during the campaign year. Among cable news, Fox News led the way with 269 stories about ACORN.

In a show (30 October 2008), the week before the 2008 general election, TDS correspondent John Oliver narrated a story about what community organizers do. After showing video of Sarah Palin and Rudy Gulianni making fun of Obama's work as an organizer, Oliver interviews a conservative think tank representative who argues that Osama Bin Laden too is a community organizer. Oliver concludes with interviews of ACORN employees, as well as a conservative organizer who works with children in poverty and who says she is voting for Obama. Then Oliver returns to the conservative think tank advocate who contends, without offering any evidence, that community organizers exchange crack cocaine for votes.

Colbert too focused on ACORN on 21 October 2008. After typical TCR humor involving the group's name, Colbert launched into his "The Word" segment with the theme "Fantasyland." After explaining that ACORN had been accused of registering Donald Duck and Mickey Mouse to vote, Colbert launches into a fiery argument to convince the audience that cartoon figures should not vote; thus revealing the absurdity of the claim that this somehow constituted voter fraud. Colbert then raises the issue of the Help America Vote Act, discussing how it allows the government to disqualify voters due to typos and other irregularities on government records. Finally, Colbert concludes with John McCain speaking to ACORN in 2006, allowing viewers to see McCain praising ACORN.

Jeremiah Wright

Our Google News search found 16,600 stories on "Jeremiah Wright" for 2008 (see Table 1). Wright was a perfect villain for the Republicans. An African-American preacher and a proponent of black liberation theology, Wright had made controversial remarks both in public and in his pulpit. His "God Damn America" sermon chastised the United States, holding the government at least partially deserving of the 9/11 attacks (Knowlton and Cantor

2008). These remarks and others from the pastor who had married Barack and Michelle Obama, baptized their children, and whose phrase, "the audacity of hope," was used as the title of an Obama book (Knowlton and Cantor 2008), set off a feeding frenzy among television news journalists and commentators. As seen in Table 1, CNN had 169 stories on Wright during March 2008 alone and 1380 stories for all of 2008. Fox News had 129 stories during the first month of the controversy and 1260 for the year, whereas the more liberal MSNBC had "only" 95 stories in March 2008 and 449 for the year.

In-depth Case Study: Jeremiah Wright

The media fascination with Wright led to our choosing Wright as our symbol to use in an experiment. Wright received more media coverage than health care reform and coverage of him totaled fully one-third of the coverage afforded to the Iraq War (see Table 1). To accomplish our goals, we first analyzed a sampling of mainstream media coverage of Wright along with an analysis of how both the TDS and the TCR covered Obama's controversial pastor. Then, we designed a survey experiment where students answered questions after watching clips from the mainstream media, from *The Daily Show*, and from *The Colbert Report*.

We selected a 13 March 2008 story from ABC's *Good Morning America* (ABC News, 2008) as representative of mainstream media coverage of Wright. This segment (that runs 3:24) juxtaposes images of Wright's fiery, angry, and controversial remarks at the pulpit with a calm Obama who is not interviewed for the clip, but rather has his words taken out of context to set up ABC's story. For example, Obama is shown saying that "I don't think that my church is particularly controversial," and then Obama is shown talking about Wright's work on South Africa. These remarks are then used to setup an ABC News review of Wright's statements including calling the U.S. the KKK, attacks on Republicans, and the 9-11 themed comments about the U.S. supporting state terrorism ("America's chickens coming home to roost"). Then, two of Wright's church members are interviewed and they defend Wright. Finally, the clip closes with a statement that Senator Obama views Wright as an old uncle, who sometimes says things that he doesn't agree with.

The piece typifies modern mainstream journalism. Reporter Brian Ross first accurately states that Obama has been a member of Wright's church for 20 years, that Wright had performed the marriage ceremony for Obama and his wife Michelle, baptized Obama's children, and was the inspiration for Obama's book *The Audacity of Hope*. Then we see the "God Damn America" clip ending with the statement by Ross, "it is not known whether Senator

Obama was in church on this day." Then instead of waiting for an interview with Obama on Wright's controversial statements, ABC and Ross serve up decontextualized statements from Obama defending Wright, creating an almost imaginary conversation with Obama on the subject. Ross then uses Obama's comment about South Africa as a lead-in to a litany of Wright's angry outbursts on a variety of subjects.

The video is a classic political story with a villain (Wright) and a theme of guilt by association. There are no efforts to deal with the complexities of race relations or to try and view the world from an African-American's perspective (other than one short interview with an African-American woman that, in context of the Wright clips, seems insincere). Obama is portrayed more as a villain himself than a victim, in that Obama's decontextualized quotes consistently defend Wright, not for the remarks that ABC has just shown, but for other much less incendiary comments made by Wright. The whole piece is stitched together like a postmodern circus with short clips, quick editing, and the construction of a reality (guilt by association) that — upon logical examination — has little to do with electing a president to office.

The Daily Show's and *The Colbert Report's* Treatment of Wright

The Daily Show focused on Wright on 18 March 2008 in a 5:50 segment. After showing the "God Damn America" video while Stewart makes funny faces at the harshness of Wright's statement, Stewart plays clips from cable news pundits who all suggest that this is the end of Obama's run for the presidency. Introducing Obama's Philadelphia speech on the topic, Stewart introduces Obama as a prize fighter, mocking the very serious speech. Taking parts of Obama's speech out of context, Stewart sets up a joke about Obama and his mixed racial heritage. When Obama starts discussing black anger, Stewart auto locks the imaginary doors on his desk. As Obama then moves into a discussion of white anger, Stewart unlocks the doors. After a Klu Klux Klan joke, Stewart allows Obama to speak in length and then concludes that "a prominent politician spoke to Americans about race as though they were adults."

Later in the show, Stewart engages in a discussion with *The Daily Show's* "Senior Black Correspondent" Larry Wilmore. In an awkward and sometimes tense exchange, Stewart and Wilmore discuss black and white relations in the context of music, car stereos, and more serious topics like profiling. During one exchange Stewart auto locks his "auto" desk again. In the end, Stewart and Wilmore ultimately find consensus in their view of the Hutch character from the 1970s TV show *Starsky and Hutch*, suggesting that we have more in common than we have to fear.

Though much of the nearly 10 minutes devoted to Obama and Wright is comical, these clips ultimately portray Obama as a man of mixed race, intelligently and sensitively struggling with the complexity of race relations, an important issue that has long vexed our country. The exchange with Wilmore, while humorous and often light, is ultimately powerful as the two get into a discussion of America as a land of opportunity versus America as a former slave nation that still struggles with race. Remarkably, we found no real news show that similarly devoted 10 solid minutes to Obama's speech and Wright's remarks.

Colbert's first response to the Wright ordeal was also on 18 March 2008, in a segment titled "Yes we Can." After playing Wright's infamous quote, Colbert is shocked, mostly that Wright called America "she." Taking Obama's speech out of context (by backing up Obama's faux call for voters to flock to McCain), Colbert states that he will play Wright's speech everyday before the election. The next night, Colbert, in "The Word" segment, defined media reviews of Obama's speech as mixed (then reads the glowing reviews from the mainstream media), references his own church's "sanctioning" of child abuse, and uses video footage of Jerry Falwell and Pat Robertson blaming 9-11 on U.S. immorality. He then uses a video quote of McCain refusing to agree that Falwell is "an agent of intolerance."

Survey Experiment

In order to test our hypothesis that the fake news is, in fact, more real than the real news and that it thus contributes to an authentic discourse and democracy better than the real news, we designed an experiment around the Jeremiah Wright story. Students in introductory American Government courses in Idaho and Pennsylvania were given a survey and pre-tested on their partisan and ideological views. The students watched the ABC *Good Morning America* clip, then they were shown two *Daily Show* clips discussed above, and then finally they saw the 19 March TCR clip. After viewing the coverage by each program (in other words, before moving on) the students were asked what they learned from the clips, how informative they were, and whether they made manifest the complexity of race relations. Additionally students were asked to rate whether the clips were biased either for or against Obama. They were also asked to rate the funniness of the Stewart and Colbert clips. After the survey discussions were held with the students (similar to focus groups) where their comments on the clips were noted, and later recorded and evaluated.

Results from Survey Experiment

As seen in Table 2, overall, respondents felt that they learned the most from the ABC News video. The ANOVA revealed that there are no significant differences in the learning ratings of the ABC clip based on ideology. Interestingly, TDS and TCR learning ratings and the associated ANOVAs, demonstrated that there were significant differences in perceptions of learning between the ideological groupings. Moderates felt that they learned more from each show compared to either conservatives or liberals. Conservatives rated both TDS and TCR particularly low in terms of what they learned.

Table 2: Learning, Information, Race, Funniness

	Conservative (20)	Moderate (15)	Liberal (16)	Overall	F-test
Learned					
ABC	3.90	3.60	3.00	3.55	2.102
TDS	1.95	3.20	2.13	2.39	3.821*
TCR	1.65	2.93	2.56	2.33	4.085*
Information					
ABC	4.15	4.27	3.44	3.91	2.015
TDS	2.25	3.93	3.19	3.06	5.455**
TCR	1.95	3.60	2.63	2.65	4.582*
Complexity of Race					
ABC	2.65	3.47	2.81	2.89	1.174
TDS	2.60	4.07	3.50	3.31	3.354*
TCR	1.05	2.20	1.75	1.63	2.824

Funny	Conservative (20)	Moderate (15)	Liberal (16)	Overall	F-test
TDS	1.75	1.67	1.44	1.61	.939
TCR	2.20	1.73	1.81	1.88	2.035

NOTES: ** p. < .01; * p. <.05. For first three questions, scale = 0 (low) to 6 (high). For the funny question, the lower the mean, the funnier the clip was rated. Three respondents did not indicate an ideological preference, total n = 54.

Information

Respondents also felt that they received the most information from the ABC News clip (see Table 2) and the ANOVAs demonstrated no significant differences between ideological groupings. However, once again, there were significant differences among the ideologies when it came to rating the information gained from TDS and TCR. In particular, moderates and liberals, compared to conservatives, rated both shows higher in terms of information.

Complexity of Race

Overall, respondents believed TDS best dealt with the complexity of race relations (Table 2). Again, while there were no significant differences between mean scores for the ABC News clip, both liberals and moderates were significantly more impressed with how Stewart's show dealt with race relations. However, there were no differences among ideological groupings on racial complexity and TCR.

Funny

In Table 2, there was no ideological differences in how the experiment participants rated the funniness of Colbert and Stewart and this finding is consistent with LaMarre, et al. (2009).

Perceived Bias

In Table 3, 50 percent of the conservatives thought that the ABC clip was neutral while 45 percent of conservatives thought that it was biased against Obama. 80 percent of the moderates thought that the ABC News video was biased against Obama as did 75 percent of the liberals. Thus, while the participants thought that they learned more from the ABC clip, they clearly did not think it was a neutral piece of journalism. Interestingly, 50 percent of conservatives thought that TDS's coverage was biased against Obama, whereas only 40 percent of moderates and 25 percent of liberals thought that it was biased against Obama. Finally, 35 percent of conservatives thought that Colbert's segment was biased against Obama, compared to 20 percent of the moderates and 44 percent of the liberals. These findings are interesting and with Colbert, at least, they back up LaMarre, et al. (2009). They show that conservatives believe Colbert is a conservative since we would expect that conservative experiment participants would believe that Colbert was not biased against Obama. Liberal experiment participants seem more in on the satire expressed by Colbert.

Table 3: Bias For or Against Obama

	Conserv.	Moderates	Liberals	Overall
ABC News				
Biased in favor of Obama	1 (5%)	0 (0%)	0 (0%)	1 (2%)
Neutral	10 (50%)	3 (20%)	4 (25%)	19 (35%)
Biased against Obama	9 (45%)	12 (80%)	12 (75%)	34 (63%)
The Daily Show				
Biased in favor of Obama	1 (5%)	0 (0%)	3 (19%)	4 (6%)

	Conserv.	Moderates	Liberals	Overall
Neutral 9	(45%)	9 (60%)	9 (56%)	29 (54%)
Biased against Obama	10 (50%)	6 (40%)	4 (25%)	21 (40%)
The Colbert Report				
Biased in favor of Obama	4 (20%)	4 (27%)	1 (6%)	9 (17%)
Neutral	9 (45%)	8 (53%)	8 (50%)	26 (48%)
Biased against Obama	7 (35%)	3 (20%)	7 (44%)	19 (35%)

Discussion

We were surprised that the experiment's participants believed that they learned the most from, and received the most information from, the ABC clip. Indeed, Fox, Koloen, and Sahin (2007) found no differences in substantive coverage between the real news and the fake news (*The Daily Show*) and Colletta (2009) argues that as TV viewers we are sophisticated and understand the entertainment quality of contemporary journalism. Yet, it appears that overall our participants, at least, do not necessarily understand the constructions and postmodern collages of contemporary journalism. In addition, there appear to be ideological factors that predispose individuals' reactions to TCR and TDS. In particular, moderates learned the most from the TDS and TCR clips, followed by liberals. This backs up the point made by Baumgartner and Morris (2008) and Colletta (2009) that you have to be "in on the joke" to appreciate the purpose of these two shows. Conservatives did not feel that they learned from the TDS and TCR clips. Furthermore, while Baumgarter and Morris (2008) found that TCR produced changes in attitudes toward more conservative beliefs, our data indicates that our respondents, mainly college freshman, were generally (but not always) able to distinguish the more liberal intentions of both shows.

We are puzzled why moderates would be more satisfied by the fake news shows coverage than were liberals. One possibility is that both TDS and TCR clips included tough stances toward Obama. Jon Stewart plays much of the same snippets of Jeremiah Wright did ABC and Stewart acts shocked at what he is hearing. Such activities probably resonated negatively with liberals. Conservatives, on the hand, were likely unhappy with Stewart's summary of Obama's speech ("he talked to us like an adult"). Interestingly, and consistent with Baumgartner and Morris (2008), many participants in the Idaho debriefing were also unaware that Colbert was a liberal playing a conservative and some felt betrayed when they found out. Thus, Colbert's aggressive stance at the beginning of his clip turned off liberals and his later mocking of John McCain for his association with the religious right turned off conservatives. Moderates, by definition, like to see both sides of the story so they were more impressed with both Stewart and Colbert than were liberals or conservatives. Yet, it is surprising that moderates reported finding more information in, and learning more from, ABC's coverage because that clip had literally no "other side" to it. Perhaps it is difficult to test postmodern constructed realities when there is no logic to any of it.

It is also intriguing that respondents overall believed *The Daily Show* better captured the complexity of race relations. Once again, both liberals and moderates were more impressed with how TDS dealt with race relations. Such a finding goes beyond Fox, Koloen, and Sahin (2008) suggesting that the fake news can, on occasion at least, be more substantive than the real news. Thus, while respondents overall thought they gained more information and learned more about Wright from the real news (ABC), respondents overall thought that the TDS dealt better with the complexity of race relations. Therefore, minimally, our working hypothesis is partially confirmed. While the real news, according to our participants, brought out more information about Jeremiah Wright, the fake news (at least TDS) dealt better with race relations.

This study helps confirm the idea that the fake news may be more real than the real news, using the definition established herein. And, though correlation does not equal causation, there are many examples of how Stewart and Colbert's coverage seemed to alter mainstream coverage by breaking through the false shell, by reframing the policy debate, and by putting new issues on the table and taking other ones off the agenda. From their exposure of death panel silliness, to their coverage of the Henry Louis Gates, Jr., incident, from catching Fox News' use of old film to exaggerate the size of a crowd, to pointing out Glenn Beck's ties to a company that sells gold, their coverage appears to result in issue coverage dissipating or being altered by the "real" news.

Studies have shown (Westen 2008, 368) that when people learn about priming, for example, learning about the mortality salience effect (which predisposes people to a more conservative mind-set), its impact is counteracted. Therefore, puncturing the use of sacred rhetoric (Marietta 2008), pointing out incongruities and hypocrisy in narratives, and breaking one side's use of the press's complicity in monological arguments (Clemons and McBeth 2009, 237); plus helping to produce a better informed public that is also less inclined to blindly trust the mainstream media (Fox, Koloen, and Sahin 2007), surely constitutes impacting political opinions and furthering an authentic democratic discourse, potentially improving public policy. That is significant.

Acknowledgments

The authors would like to thank Rachel Brown for her help with the experiment and both research and editorial assistance.

References

ABC News. 2008. "Obama's Pastor: God Damn America, U.S. to Blame for 9-11." http://abcnews.go.com/Blotter/DemocraticDebate/story?id=4443788&page=1. (Accessed on July 9, 2010).

Baumgartner, Jody C. and Jonathan S. Morris. 2008. "One 'Nation,' under Stephen? The Effects of *The Colbert Report* on American Youth." *Journal of Broadcast & Electronic Media* 52(4): 622–643.

Cantor, Paul A. 2001. *Gilligan Unbounded: Pop Culture in the Age of Globalization.* Lanham, MD: Rowman & Littlefield Publishers, Inc.

Clemons, Randy S. and Mark K. McBeth. 2009. *Public Policy Praxis: A Case Approach for Understanding Policy and Analysis.* 2nd Edition. New York: Pearson Longman.

Colleta, Lisa. 2009. "Political Satire and Postmodern Irony in the Age of Stephen Colbert and Jon Stewart." *The Journal of Popular Culture* 42(5):856–874.

Edelman, Murray. 1964. *The Symbolic Uses of Politics.* Champaign, IL: University of Illinois Press.

Foy, Joseph J., ed. 2010. *Homer Simpson Goes to Washington: American Politics Through Popular Culture.* Lexington: University of Kentucky Press.

Fox, Julia R., Glory Koloen, and Volkan Sahin. 2007. "No Joke: A Comparison of Substance in *The Daily Show with Jon Stewart* and Broadcast Network Television Coverage of the 2004 Presidential Election Campaign." *Journal of Broadcasting & Electronic Media* 51(2): 213–227.

Gigerenezer, Gerd. 2007. *Gut Feelings: The Intelligence of the Unconscious.* New York: Viking.

Gladwell, Malcolm. 2005. *Blink: The Power of Thinking Without Thinking.* New York: Back Bay Backs/Little Brown and Company.

Holbert, R. Lance and Nick Geidner. 2009. The 2008 Election: Highlighting the Need to Explore Additional Communication Subfields to Advance Political Communication Studies. *Communication Studies*, vol. 60.4: 344–358.

Holbert, R. Lance, Jennifer L. Lambe, Anthony D. Dudo, Kristin A. Carlton. 2007. "Primacy Effects of *The Daily Show* and National TV News Viewing: Young Viewers, Political Gratifications, and Internal Political Self-Efficacy." *Journal of Broadcasting and Electronic Media*, Vol. 51.1: 344–358.

Knowlton, Brian and Jody Cantor. 2008. "Obama's Camp Caught up in Minister's Controversia Remarks." *New York Times*, March 17. http://www.nytimes.com/2008/03/17/world/americas/17iht-campaign.5.11196520.html (accessed January 15, 2010).

Lakoff, George. 2004. *Don't Think of an Elephant: Know Your Values and Frame the Debate—the Essential Guide for Progressives.* Vermont: Chelsea Green Publishing.

LaMarre, Heather L., Kristen D. Landreville, and Michael A. Bean. 2009. "The Irony of Satire Political Ideology and the Motivation to See What You Want to See in *The Colbert Report.*" *The International Journal of Press/Politics*, Vol. 14: 212–231.

Loftus, Elizabeth F. 1997. "Creating False Memories." *Scientific American.* 277.3: 70–75.

Marietta, Morgan. 2008. "From My Cold Dead Hands: Democratic Consequences of Sacred Rhetoric." *The Journal of Politics.* 70.3: 767–779.

Miller, Hugh T. 2002. *Postmodern Public Policy.* Albany: State University of New York Press.

_____, and Charles J. Fox. 2006. *Postmodern Public Administration.* New York: M. E. Sharpe.

New York Times. 2008. "The Third Presidential Debate." http://elections.nytimes.com/2008/president/debates/transcripts/third-presidential-debate.html (Accessed on July 9, 2010).

Pew & the Press. 2007. *Public Knowledge of Current Affairs Little Changed by News and Information Revolutions What Americans Know: 1989–2007.* http://people-press.org/report/319/public-knowledge-of-current-affairs-little-changed-by-news-and-information-revolutions (Accessed on February 1, 2010).

Reuters. 2008. "Election Star Joe the Plumber Lacks License." http://www.reuters.com/article/idUSTRE49F57Q20081017 (Accessed January 20, 2010).

Shane, Scott. 2008. "Obama and 60's bomber: A Look into Crossed Paths." *The New York*

Times. October 3. http://www.nytimes.com/2008/10/04/us/politics/04ayers.html (Accessed January 20, 2010).

Stone, Deborah. 2002. *Policy Paradox: The Art of Political Decision Making*, rev. ed. New York: W. W. Norton

Strom, Stephanie. 2008. "On Obama, ACORN, and Voter Registration." *New York Times.* October 10. http://www.nytimes.com/2008/10/11/us/politics/11acorn.html (Accessed January 21, 2010.

The Colbert Report. 2008. "Yes We Can." March 18. http://www.colbertnation.com/the-colbert-report-videos/164122/march-18-2008/yes-we-can (Accessed July 9, 2010)

_____. 2008. "The Word: The Gospel of John." March 19. http://www.colbertnation.com/the-colbert-report-videos/164382/march-19-2008/the-word — the-gospel-of-john (Accessed July 9, 2010).

_____. 2008. "Campaign Personal Attacks." http://www.colbertnation.com/the-colbert-report-videos/187621/october-09-2008/campaign-personal-attacks — david-gergen, October 9 (Accessed on July 9, 2010).

_____. Nd. "The Word: Fantasyland." October 21. http://www.colbertnation.com/the-colbert-report-videos/188889/october-21-2008/the-word —-fantasyland (Accessed July 9, 2010).

_____. 2008. "McCain Loves the Middle Class." October 22. http://www.colbertnation.com/the-colbert-report-videos/188930/october-22-2008/mccain-loves-the-middle-class (Accessed July 9, 2010).

The Daily Show. 2008. "Barack's Wright Response." March 18. http://www.thedailyshow.com/watch/tue-march-18-2008/barack-s-wright-response (accessed July 19, 2010).

_____. 2008. "Joe the Plumber's House." October 16. http://www.thedailyshow.com/watch/thu-october-16-2008/joe-the-plumber-s-house (accessed July 9, 2010).

_____. 2008. "Word War." October 16. http://www.thedailyshow.com/watch/thu-october-16-2008/word-war-iii (accessed July 9, 2010).

_____. 2008. "Community Organizers." October 30. http://www.thedailyshow.com/watch/thu-october-30-2008/community-organizers (accessed July 8, 2010).

Westen, Drew. 2008. *The Political Brain: The Role of Emotion in Deciding the Fate of the Nation.* New York: Public Affairs.

Jon Stewart a Heretic?
Surely You Jest

Political Participation and Discussion Among
Viewers of Late-Night Comedy Programming

DANNAGAL GOLDTHWAITE YOUNG *and*
SARAH E. ESRALEW

For the past decade, political communication scholars have extended their research outside of the bounds of traditional news programming in the application of mass communication theories. Recent research has acknowledged the importance of entertainment programs in processes of political socialization and opinion formation; (Holbert, Pillion, Tschida, Armfield, Kinder, Cherry, and Daulton 2003; Holbrook and Hill 2005; Moy, Xenos, and Hess 2006; Xenos and Becker 2009; Young 2006; 2004). Late-night comedy programs such as those hosted by Jay Leno and David Letterman have been analyzed to assess their potential role in informing or influencing their audiences. With research reports from Pew suggesting that young people report receiving political information from these shows, and overtime trends suggesting an increase in exposure to these programs among young people (Pew 2004), the topic has become a favorite among scholars and journalists alike.

The Daily Show with Jon Stewart on Comedy Central, which parodies a traditional news program and offers satirical critiques of public officials and the press, presents a different format from network late-night comedy shows. *The Daily Show* offers several distinct and politically relevant forms of content in each 22 minute episode. First, the news segments presented as "headlines" at the beginning of the show and "on location" by news "correspondents" throughout the program offer the audience pointed political satire that is critical of politicians, policies, parties, and other political players. Second, each episode presents an informal interview between host Jon Stewart and a politically savvy guest, including public officials, former public officials, political strategists, journalists, historians, and scholars (see Baym, 2007). Finally, the show itself is presented as a news parody, complete with reporters in the field, interviews with faux "experts," as well as graphics, charts, and other trappings of a modern cable news program.

Current scholarly opinion on *The Daily Show* is split between those who see it as beneficial and those who see it as problematic for democracy. On the one hand, some (see Baym, 2005; Jones, 2005; Young, 2007) see *The Daily Show* as a positive alternative form of journalism, one that challenges the norms of objectivity, holds politicians accountable, and deconstructs the symbiotic relationship between journalists and politicians. On the other hand, because of the program's critical view of politicians and governing institutions (including the press), other scholars (see Baumgartner and Morris, 2006; Hart and Hartelius, 2007) have argued that *The Daily Show* may foster alienation and disengagement from the political process. Our primary goal in this project is to advance the conversation between these two opposing factions by exploring various political behaviors and how they correlate with viewing of *The Daily Show*.

Late-Night Comedy? Or *The Daily Show* with Jon Stewart

"The stance of late-night humor is fundamentally cynical; each politician is defined only by his or her most glaring weaknesses, and the system produces only venal corrupt candidates unfit for the office" write Jamieson and Waldman (2002, p. 68). Content analyses of late-night comedy programs including *The Tonight Show* with Jay Leno, *The Late Show* with David Letterman, and *The Daily Show* with Jon Stewart, conclude that indeed the jokes made on these programs focus on personalities more often than policies, and paint an overwhelmingly negative picture of— for example — sex-hungry (President Clinton), unintelligent (President Bush), and pandering (John Kerry) political figures (Niven, Lichter and Amundson, 2003; Young, 2004). Given the repetitive nature of these themes in late-night political jokes across programs (Niven, Lichter and Amundson, 2003), scholars have sought to understand how exposure to these shows might affect viewers' perceptions of politicians as well as trust in government and political engagement (Baumgartner and Morris, 2006; Cao and Brewer, 2008; Moy, Xenos, and Hess, 2005).

Research in this area has resulted in mixed findings. In their study of the effects of the *Daily Show* on young Americans, Baumgartner and Morris

(2006) found that exposure to the *Daily Show* was associated with decreased ratings of political candidates and increased cynicism towards government and the media. However, the same study showed that *Daily Show* viewers experienced increased confidence in their ability to understand politics. Moy, Xenos, and Hess (2005) found that exposure to late-night comedy programming was associated with increased vote intention and political discussion, but only among political sophisticates. Meanwhile, Cao and Brewer (2006) found a positive association between exposure to *political comedy shows* (*Saturday Night Live* and *The Daily Show*) and one's likelihood of having attended a campaign event or having joined an organization, though no significant relationships were found when looking at exposure to late-night comedy programs like *The Tonight show* or *The Late Show.*

Cao and Brewer (2006) are not alone in their finding regarding the unique audience of *The Daily Show* compared to other forms of late-night programming. Research on the various late-night comedy programs has found significant and important differences in the content and audiences of different late-night programs. Using data from the National Annenberg Election Survey and from Pew, Young and Tisinger (2006) demonstrate that viewers of *The Daily Show* are more politically knowledgeable, attentive, and tuned into other forms of news than are viewers of other late-night comedy shows. In a time-series study exploring how exposure to *The Tonight Show*, *The Late Show*, and the *Daily Show* subsequently stimulated attention to other forms of news during the 2004 primaries, Feldman and Young (2008) illustrate that viewers of late-night programming experienced far steeper rates of temporary increases in news attention than nonviewers of late-night comedy. Meanwhile, viewers of *The Daily Show* experienced similarly steep rates of increased news attention, but *without* the precipitous decline following the primaries. Recent work by Xenos and Becker (2009) indicated through experimental analyses that viewers of *The Daily Show* showed enhanced rates of information-seeking after viewing *TDS*, a finding consistent with the normatively healthy outcomes associated with the gateway hypothesis.

These studies of the unique role of *The Daily Show* in the political environment add empirical evidence to support the call of scholars who urge that we treat *The Daily Show* as something distinct from more generic late-night comedy programming. Among them is Baym (2005), who suggests that we consider *The Daily Show* as more illustrative of an alternative form of journalism than would be suggested by the playful "fake news" moniker it wears. This observation is supported empirically by Fox, Koloen, and Sahin (2007), whose content analyses documented that story length on the *Daily Show* surpassed that of traditional broadcast news segments and that the average Daily Show segment was on par with traditional news in terms of the amount of *substantive* information presented. Jones (2005) goes a step further, arguing that the Daily Show provides an important alterative to elite political discourse: an accessible, powerful and critical voice that may empower citizens in a way that traditional news cannot.

While the punch-line oriented political jokes offered in the late-night fare of Leno and Letterman tend to reduce candidates to their least flattering caricatures, *The Daily Show*'s humorous segments are more likely to cover substantive political policies and institutions (Fox et al., 2007). The key here is that Stewart's program is illustrative, not just of political humor, but of true political *satire* (Holbert, 2005). Substantive satirical programming is rich with policy information and discussions of media and electoral processes. Political *satire* plays a critical role in a democratic society in that it "...encourages critical debate, sheds light upon perceived wrongs within society and government, points out hypocrisy, and makes political criticism accessible to the average citizen" (Caufield, 2007, p. 4). As such, this kind of content, unlike a short joke about John McCain being old or John Kerry being dull, taps into a deeper and broader kind of knowledge base to be appreciated in the manner in which it was intended.

The Daily Show: Towards a Healthy Democracy?

Hart and Hartelius (2007) criticize Jon Stewart for "engaging in unbridled political cynicism" and for "...not stimulating a polis to have new and productive thoughts" (p. 264). "Like his ancient predecessors," the authors argue, "he merely produces inertia." (p. 264). Yet, the political satire presented in *The Daily Show* is in keeping with the norms of satire practiced in ancient Greece and Rome, at the heart of which is "...an intent to bring about improvement" (Elliot, 2004). In many ways, *The Daily Show* taps into the same positive construct at the heart of Gray's (2004) treatise on the cartoon, *The Simpsons*. Gray contends that *The Simpsons* inspires, not cynicism, but rather Sloterdijk's concept of "kynicism," an "alternative cynicism that is capable of being continuous, communal, discussion-forming, reconstructive, and even optimistic." *The Daily Show* covers current events and offers viewers a shared public experience. By exposing the blunders of government and the press through its satirical segments, *The Daily Show*'s implicit argument is that something better is possible. To provoke stimulating and healthy political behaviors, perhaps offering specific solutions is unnecessary. Writes Gray (2005), "...where cynicism is morose, resigned, and apathetic, kynicism invokes the power or laughing and parodic/satiric ridicule, and is anything but apathetic." Perhaps the mere suggestions that alternatives to the status quo do exist is enough to combat apathy and stimulate viewer engagement.

At odds with the notion that *The Daily Show* might discourage "new and productive thoughts" (Hart and Hartelius, 2007, p. 264) are Jon Stewart's interviews, offering civil and substantive discourse between the host and various political figures, journalists, and scholars which may foster viewer discussion and engagement (Baym, 2007). While *The Daily Show's* satirical critiques may ignite viewer discussion and encourage the audience to consider alternatives, the interviews illustrate what Baym (2007) refers to as a "rational-critical dialogue," that is, deliberative democratic discourse in action; people — often holding opposite points of view — engaging one another in a respectful, honest — and often humorous — discussion of issues. Through these mechanisms, the program may foster viewer political discussion, both through the presentation of engaging political perspectives based on the news of the day, and through the modeling of a variety of political dialogue that seeks not to polarize or to persuade, but to explore political ideas.

Those who see *The Daily Show* as potentially harmful often center their critique on the question of the *Daily Show's* impact on political alienation or cynicism (Baumgartner and Morris, 2006; Hart and Hartelius, 2006). However, due to problems of measurement and conceptualization (incumbent versus systemic) of the "cynicism" or trust in government measure (see Levi and Stoker, 2000; Hetherington, 2001), this project will focus on the *Daily Show's* impact on other normatively positive political behaviors and characteristics. If *The Daily Show* is more substantive and policy-based than traditional late-night fare and as substantive as traditional news (Fox et al., 2007), and if, through substantive political satire and interviews, the show "...encourages critical debate, sheds light upon perceived wrongs within society and government, points out hypocrisy, and makes political criticism accessible to the average citizen" (Caufield, 2007, p. 4), then we should witness positive associations between viewing *the Daily Show* and constructs illustrative of healthy democratic practices, namely political participation and political discussion:

Political Participation
H1. Exposure to *The Daily Show* will be associated with increased rates of participation in politics.
Political Discussion
H2. Exposure to *The Daily Show* will be associated with increased rates of political discussion with friends, family, coworkers, and online.

Political Knowledge as an Effects Moderator

In his conversation about the beneficial impact of the *Simpsons*, Gray (2005) suggests that we must acknowledge parody's limitations, including the inability of some viewers to catch-on to the satirical component in the first place. As mentioned earlier, satire requires a certain level of political knowledge for the message to be processed in the spirit in which it was intended by the producer. Consistent with this assumption, several studies on the effects of the late-night comedy indicate that its effects depend on the viewer's level of political sophistication. Studying the persuasion and priming effects of late-night programming in general, Young (2004, 2006) found more pronounced effects on those viewers who were less politically knowledgeable. Similarly, looking at the impact of soft news programming on subsequent attention paid to foreign affairs, Baum (2003) found the most beneficial effects of late-night comedy on the least sophisticated viewers. In contrast, Moy, Xenos, and Hess (2005) found increases in vote intention and political discussion to occur among those late-night comedy viewers *highest* in political knowledge.

Generally speaking, political knowledge has been thought to hinder the persuasive effects of individual political messages on the message receiver (McGuire, 1968, 1972; Zaller, 1992). However, when political messages are deemed relevant or come from a trusted source (Miller and Krosnick, 2000), political sophisticates have been found to experience greater message effects than less sophisticated viewers. It could be the case that when looking at outcomes like persuasion, priming, or stimulation of attention to politics, the less knowledgeable viewer of late-night comedy shows has a) more room to move in the dependent variable and b) fewer alternative or competing sources (both internal and external) to buffer these effects. However, when dealing with political outcomes that are more behavioral — like political participation, political discussion, or voting, perhaps viewers less equipped with political knowledge are also "farther away" from these outward demonstrations of political engagement. In keeping with the basic assumptions of McGuire's information processing paradigm, behavior change ought to come *last,* after message presentation, attention, comprehension, yielding and retention (1968). Hence, for political sophisticates whose associative political mental models are elaborate, accessible, and organized, such programming should stimulate an already salient interest in politics, hence inducing them to demonstrate outward signs of their engagement, including more participation in and discussion about politics. Therefore, we imagine that these proposed behavioral effects of exposure to *The Daily Show* should be greater and more positive among political sophisticates.

> H3. Increased political participation and political discussion as a function of exposure to *The Daily Show*, will be greatest among the most politically knowledgeable viewers of the show.

Method

To test Hypotheses 1–3, data from the 2004 National Annenberg Election Survey was used. During the 2004 election campaign, the Annenberg Public Policy Center conducted a year-long rolling cross-sectional survey of Americans. The National Annenberg Election Survey is the largest academic survey of the American electorate ever conducted. The survey went in the field on Tuesday, October 7, 2003 and was in the field through the 2004 Presidential election. Households were randomly selected using a random-digit dialing technique. Each night a sample of those households was contacted and telephone interviews were conducted with American adults living in those homes. The overall response rate (using the American Association for Public Opinion Research's RR1) was 22 percent.

Measures

Dependent Variables

POLITICAL PARTICIPATION. From early January through early March, 2004, the survey included a series of items to capture forms of political participation in the primaries. These included: "During this presidential campaign, (have you talked/did you talk) to any people and try to show them why they should vote for or against one of the presidential candidates?" (Yes coded 1, No coded 0, don't know and refused coded missing); "During this presidential campaign, (have you gone/did you go) to any political meetings, rallies, speeches, dinners, or things like that in support of a particular presidential candidate?" (Yes coded 1, No coded 0, don't know and refused coded missing); "During this presidential campaign, (have you done/did you do) any other work for one of the presidential candidates?" (Yes coded 1, No coded 0, don't know and refused coded missing); "During this presidential campaign, (have you given/did you give) money to any of the presidential candidates?" (Yes coded 1, No coded 0, don't know and refused coded missing); "During this presidential campaign, (have you worn/did you wear) a presidential campaign button, put a campaign sticker on your car, or placed a sign in your window or in front of your house?" (Yes coded 1, No coded 0, don't know and refused coded missing). Political participation was calculated as the sum of these five items. The Alpha for this scale is .62 (M = .75, SD = 1.06). Because these items were only included during the primaries, when looking at this item as a dependent variable, the sample is limited to only those participants interviewed during the early months of the campaign.

POLITICAL DISCUSSION. Respondents were asked about three different forms of political discussion: "How many days in the past week did you discuss politics with your family or friends?" (M = 2.95, SD = 2.49), "How many days in the past week did you discuss politics with people at work" (M = 1.52, SD = 2.10), "and "How many days in the past week did you discuss politics online with people over email, in chat rooms, or using listservs or instant messaging services?" (M = .42, SD = 1.28).

Independent Variables

To tease out the independent effects of exposure to *The Daily Show,* all models run to test H1–2 were run twice, once with *Daily Show* specific exposure, and once with exposure to late-night programming in general. By including this more general measure in our models, we can better understand if any effect of exposure to *The Daily Show* could be attributed to late-night comedy programming in general, or if it is restricted to — or more pronounced for — viewers of *The Daily Show* versus the other programs.

GENERAL LATE-NIGHT COMEDY EXPOSURE. To understand how exposure to *The Daily Show* functions in these models compared to more traditional talk show style late-night comedy programming, we included a variable for "general late-night comedy exposure." How many days in the past week did you watch late-night comedy programs like *The Late Show* with David Letterman, the *Tonight Show* with Jay Leno or *The Daily Show* with Jon Stewart. (Coded 0–7, Don't know and Refused coded missing). (M = .87, SD = 1.66).

DAILY SHOW SPECIFIC EXPOSURE. In addition to the "days in the past week" exposure to late-night comedy measure, the NAES also includes an item which captures which late-night program the respondent watches "most often." To create a measure of exposure to *The Daily Show* with Jon Stewart, a product term was created, multiplying the dummy variable for *The Daily Show* watched most often times the number of days in the past week the subject reported watching late-night comedy. This product term is referred to as "Daily Show specific exposure" (M = .14, SD = .75). Admittedly, because this construct excludes those respondents who watch *TDS* less often than other late-night programs, it does not capture all respondents' exposure to *TDS*. However, for the purposes of this project, the product term was deemed more informative — and hence, preferable — to alternative measures, including (a) exposure to late-night comedy in general or (b) a dummy variable indicating that the respondent watches *The Daily Show* more than other late-night shows.

Control Variables

OVERALL CANDIDATE EVALUATION: For each of the following people in politics (Bush and Kerry), please tell me if your opinion is favorable or unfavorable using a scale from 0 to 10. Zero means very unfavorable, and 10 means very favorable. Five means you do not feel favorable or unfavorable toward that person. (Kerry M = 5.06, SD = 3.01) (Bush M = 5.37, SD = 3.63)

GENDER. Female = 1, Male = 0 (M = .55, SD = .50)

AGE. What is your age? (Don't know, Refused coded missing) (M = 47.99, SD = 16.59)

EDUCATION. What is the last grade or class you completed in school? Grade 8 or lower (7), some high school (10.5), high school diploma or equivalent (12), technical or vocational school after high school (14), some college (14), associate's or two-year degree (14), four year college degree (16), graduate or professional school- no degree (17), graduate or professional degree (18). (Don't know and refused coded missing). (M = 14.24, SD = 2.47)

PARTY IDENTIFICATION. Generally speaking, do you usually think of yourself as a Republican, a Democrat, an Independent or something else? (Democrat M = .34, SD = .47; Republican M = .32, SD = .47)

POLITICAL IDEOLOGY. Generally speaking, would you describe your political views as very conservative (1), conservative (2), moderate (3), liberal (4), or very liberal (5)? (M = 2.81, SD = .99)

TRADITIONAL POLITICAL MEDIA EXPOSURE. All media exposure variables are asked in the format: "Now I would like to ask about where you got your news during the past week. Please tell me how many days in the past week you did each of the following. How many days in the past week did you..." All responses coded 0–7, Don't know and Refused coded missing.

- Watch the national network news on TV — by national network news, I mean Peter Jennings on ABC, Dan Rather on CBS, Tom Brokaw on NBC, and Jim Lehrer News Hour on PBS. (M = 2.67, SD = 2.64)
- Watch a 24 hour cable news channel, such as CNN, Fox News Channel or MSNBC. (M = 3.01, SD = 2.84)
- Watch local TV news — for example, "Eyewitness News" or "Action News" (M = 4.06, SD = 2.75)
- Read a daily newspaper (M = 3.78, SD = 2.90)
- Listen to NPR, also known as National Public Radio (M = 1.19 SD = 2.23)
- (Apart from NPR) Listen to radio shows that invite listeners to call in to discuss current events: Political Talk Radio (M = 1.28, SD = 2.18)

FOLLOW POLITICS. Some people seem to follow what is going on in government and public affairs most of the time, whether there is an election or not. Others are not that interested, or are interested in other things. Would you say you follow what is going on in government and public affairs most of the time (3), some of the time (2), only now and then (1), or hardly at all (0)? (Don't know and Refused coded missing). (M = 2.10, SD = .91)

CIVICS KNOWLEDGE. Measured as the total number correct of four items. Correct answers (shown in parentheses) were coded as "1" and incorrect, don't know, or refused were coded "0." (M = 2.55, SD = 1.23, Alpha = .60, N = 30,469).

- Do you happen to know what job or political office is now held by Dick Cheney? (Vice President)
- Who has the final responsibility to determine if a law is constitutional or not? Is it the president, the Congress, or the Supreme Court? (Supreme Court)
- How much of a majority is required for the U.S. Senate and House to override a presidential veto? (2/3)
- Do you happen to know which party has the most members in the United States House of Representatives? (Republican)

Analytical Procedure and Results

Main Effects

To test H1 regarding the effects of exposure to *The Daily Show* on political participation, we ran OLS regression models to predict political participation in the primaries using *Daily Show* viewing, late-night comedy viewing, other media use and sociodemographic controls. As illustrated in Table 1, being a strong partisan (Democrat or Republican) was the strongest correlate of participation in the primaries in 2004. Controlling for party identification and Bush favorability as well as other socio-demographic and media viewing variables, viewing late-night comedy programming was a significant positive correlate of political participation (B = .02, SE = .01, p < .05), a relationship that was even stronger among people who watched *The Daily Show* (B = .08, SE = .02, p < .001). Hence, H1 is supported. Because of the large sample sizes in these models (N > 4000), many of the variables are statistically significant: education, following politics, political knowledge, as well as various forms of media use. However, the fact that exposure to *The Daily Show* is a significant and *positive,* not negative, predictor of political participation should give pause to those critics who see the show as a harmful influence that breeds inertia.

Table 1. Political Participation: OLS Regressions predicting 5 item political participation scale with late-night comedy viewing and *Daily Show*-specific exposure.

	General Late-night comedy viewing	Daily Show specific exposure
	B (SE)	B (SE)
Intercept	-.42** (.14)	-.43** (.14)
Female	.08* (.03)	.08* (.03)
Age	.00 (.00)	.00 (.00)
Education	.02*** (.01)	.02*** (.01)
Republican	.38*** (.04)	.38*** (.04)
Democrat	.32*** (.04)	.33*** (.04)
Political ideology (1 = very conservative, 5 = very liberal)	.03# (.02)	.03 (.02)
Following politics	.22*** (.02)	.22*** (.02)
Civics knowledge (# correct out of 4)	.05** (.02)	.05** (.02)
Bush favorability (0–10)	-.03*** (.01)	-.03*** (.01)
Kerry favorability (0–10)	-.01 (.01)	-.01 (.01)
Days in the past week watched/read/listened to:		
National network news	.01 (.01)	.01 (.01)
Cable news	.02*** (.01)	.02*** (.01)
Local news	-.02** (.01)	-.02** (.01)
Newspaper	.02** (.01)	.02** (.01)

	General Late-night comedy viewing	Daily Show specific exposure
Political Talk Radio (other than NPR)	.05***	.05***
	(.01)	(.01)
NPR	.04***	.04***
	(.01)	(.01)
Late-night comedy viewing	.02*	—
	(.01)	—
Daily Show specific exposure	—	.08***
	—	(.02)
N	4509	4491
R^2	.14	.14

NOTE. ***$p < .001$; **$p < .01$; *$p < .05$; #$p < .1$

Next, we tested H2 regarding the relationship between exposure to *The Daily Show* and political discussion in various contexts. To test H2, six models were run, two predicting each of the three forms of political discussion (with friends and family, at work, and online) — once with late-night comedy viewing as the independent variable of interest, and once with the proxy for *Daily Show* specific exposure as the independent variable of interest. Results are shown in Table 2. As illustrated in the table, general late-night comedy viewing was a significant positive predictor of political discussion with friends and family ($B = .04$, $SE = .01$, $p < .001$), and online ($B = .04$, $SE = .01$, $p < .001$) (though not with people at work), and viewing *The Daily Show* was a significant positive predictor of predictor ($p < .001$) of all three forms of political discussion.

Table 2. OLS Regressions predicting various forms of political discussion with late-night comedy viewing and Daily Show specific exposure.

Discuss Politics with:	Friends and Family		People at Work		People Online	
	Late-night	Daily Show	Late-night	Daily Show	Late-night	Daily Show
	B (SE)	B (SE)	B (SE)	B (SE)	B (SE)	B (SE)
Intercept	-.25*	-.25*	1.61***	1.61***	-.27***	-.26**
	(.12)	(.12)	(.11)	(.11)	(.09)	(.09)
Female	.33***	.33***	-.48***	-.48***	.08***	.07***
	(.03)	(.03)	(.03)	(.03)	(.02)	(.02)

Discuss Politics with:	Friends and Family		People at Work		People Online	
	Late-night	*Daily Show*	*Late-night*	*Daily Show*	*Late-night*	*Daily Show*
	B (SE)	B (SE)	B (SE)	B (SE)	B (SE)	B (SE)
Age	-.01*** (.00)	-.01*** (.00)	-.04*** (.00)	-.04*** (.00)	.00 (.00)	.00 (.00)
Education	.04*** (.01)	.04*** (.01)	.03*** (.01)	.03*** (.01)	.01** (.01)	.01** (.01)
Republican	.17*** (..04)	.17*** (.04)	.02 (.04)	.02 (.04)	.08** (.03)	.08** (.03)
Democrat	.10** (.04)	.10** (.04)	.11** (.03)	.11** (.03)	.01 (.03)	.01 (.03)
Political ideology	.03* (.02)	.03# (.02)	.01 (.02)	.01 (.02)	.04*** (.01)	.04*** (.01)
Following politics	.76*** (.02)	.79*** (.02)	.39*** (.01)	.38*** (.02)	.16*** (.01)	.16*** (.01)
Civics knowledge (0–4)	.22*** (.01)	.22*** (.01)	.03* (.01)	.03* (.01)	.02# (.01)	.02 (.01)
Bush favorability (0–10)	-.07*** (.01)	-.06*** (.01)	-.02*** (.01)	-.02*** (.01)	-.03*** (.00)	-.03*** (.00)
Kerry favorability (0–10)	-.04*** (.01)	-.04*** (.01)	-.01* (.01)	-.01* (.01)	-.02*** (.00)	-.02*** (.00)
National network news	.04*** (.01)	.04*** (.01)	.01# (.02)	.01# (.02)	.01 (.00)	.01# (.00)
Cable news	.15*** (.01)	.15*** (.01)	.06*** (.01)	.06*** (.01)	.02*** (.00)	.02*** (.00)
Local news	.00 (.01)	.01 (.01)	.02** (.01)	.02** (.01)	-.02*** (.00)	-.01** (.00)
Newspaper	.04*** (.01)	.05*** (.01)	.05*** (.01)	.05*** (.01)	.01* (.00)	.01** (.00)
Political Talk Radio (other than NPR)	.10*** (.01)	.10*** (.01)	.10*** (.01)	.10*** (.01)	.02*** (.00)	.03*** (.00)
NPR	.11*** (.01)	.11*** (.01)	.06*** (.01)	.06*** (.01)	.03*** (.00)	.02*** (.00)
Late-night comedy viewing	.04*** (.01)	— —	.01 (.01)	— —	.04*** (.01)	— —

Discuss Politics with:	Friends and Family		People at Work		People Online	
	Late-night	Daily Show	Late-night	Daily Show	Late-night	Daily Show
	B (SE)	B (SE)	B (SE)	B (SE)	B (SE)	B (SE)
Daily Show exposure	—	.15***	—	.06**	—	.10***
	—	(.02)	—	(.02)	—	(.01)
N	24193	24088	24219	24114	19246	19173
R^2	.27	.27	.16	.16	.04	.04

NOTE. ***$p<.001$, **$p<.01$, *$p<.05$, #$p<.1$

Interactions with Political Knowledge

To assess the extent to which late-night comedy's relationships with these normative behaviors varied as a function of the political sophistication of the viewer, the models above were re-run, with the addition of an interaction between civics knowledge and exposure to late-night comedy or with the proxy for *Daily Sh*ow specific exposure. These analyses yielded eight regression models, six predicting various forms of political discussion, and two predicting political participation. None of the interactions with political knowledge produced statistically significant findings. Hence, these data do not support the contention that political knowledge moderates the relationship between exposure to late-night comedy programming and political participation or political discussion.

Discussion

Through a series of cross-sectional analyses using data from the 2004 National Annenberg Election Survey, we have illustrated positive and significant correlations between viewing *The Daily Show* with Jon Stewart on the one hand, and positive political behaviors on the other. Instead of arguing about the normative implications of "political cynicism" or a lack of trust in government, we avoid this measurement debacle altogether by looking directly at political behaviors that are indicative of a healthy and active democracy: participation in the campaign and discussing politics with various cohorts. By assessing the relationship between *Daily Show* viewing and these specific forms of quantifiable political behaviors it becomes evident that viewers of *The Daily Show* are *not* disengaged from the political process. If anything, people watching late-night comedy programming are *more* engaged and participatory than people who don't watch these comedy shows — and this is particularly true among those who report watching *The Daily Show* most often.

When it comes to discussing politics with friends, family, coworkers, and people online, people watching *The Daily Show* and other late-night comedy shows are ahead of the curve. The same is true for political participation during the primaries. Our data suggest that *The Daily Show* and late-night comedy in general are part of a diet of healthy political characteristics and behaviors, all of which correlate positively with political participation, discussion, and debate viewing. Among the other, even stronger characteristics of participatory and politically talkative citizens are following politics, education, strong party identification, and exposure to various traditional forms of political media, including National Public Radio, political talk radio, cable news, and newspapers.

As we consider what these findings mean more broadly, it is important to remember that these results do not present evidence of *effects* of exposure to late-night comedy. Instead, they offer a "snapshot" of a citizenry for whom exposure and behavior are positively correlated. Hence, viewers of *The Daily Show* were also those who participated in the campaign, and were engaged in political discussion. It is possible — perhaps even *likely*— that what we have captured is the profile of a kind of political junkie — one for whom watching *The Daily Show* is a part of a politically active lifestyle and media diet. Hence, these correlations may reflect a category of people who share these functional political traits and behaviors. In fact, the strong predictive power of the "following politics" variable in all of these models lends credence to this claim, as it appears to be one of the key factors driving these positive outcomes.

These findings advance our understanding of late-night comedy audiences in the context of political life. Scholars to date have disagreed about whether political satire alienates or engages the public. Our project suggests that viewers of political satire participate in and talk about politics — both behaviors that support the notion of "engagement" over that of "alienation." And while Cao and Brewer's (2008) work advanced this conversation with data regarding political *participation* rates among *Daily Show* viewers, the project presented here is first consideration of the relationship between late-night comedy viewing and political discussion. Interestingly, in our analyses exploring the moderating role of political knowledge in these processes, no significant findings emerged. In other words, these positive correlations between viewing *TDS* and discussing and participating in political life are not stronger or weaker for political sophisticates than those low in political knowledge. The healthy trends emerge among all political knowledge groups.

Of course these findings are just one piece of evidence in an ongoing analysis of the role of political satire in a Democracy. These results cannot tell us if people were more or less politically engaged going into the viewing experience, but merely that viewing *TDS* is associated with other positive political behaviors. While the cross-sectional nature of these data compromises our ability to draw causal claims, this non-experimental approach does add a much needed element of ecological validity and generalizability to our conversation about political satire. Researchers are urged to consider other methods, such as panel studies or experiments to address the lingering questions of causality. Such approaches will help us isolate the causal dimensions of the relationships identified in the current project and the mechanism through which political knowledge might moderate these effects.

References

Baum, M. A. 2003. *Soft News Goes to War*. Princeton, NJ: Princeton University Press.

Baumgartner, J. and Morris, J. S. 2006. "The *Daily Show* Effect: Candidate Evaluations, Efficacy, and the American Youth." *American Politics Research*. 34: 341–367.

Baym, G. 2005. "The Daily Show: Discursive Integration and the Reinvention of Political Journalism." *Political Communication*. 22: 259–276.

_____. 2007. "Crafting New Communicative Models in the Televisual Sphere: Political Interviews on *The Daily Sh*ow." *Political Communication*. 10: 93–115.

Cao, X. and Brewer, P. R. 2008. "Political Comedy Shows and Public Participation in Politics." *International Journal of Public Opinion Research*. 20: 90–99.

Caufield, R. 2008. "The Influence of "Infoenterpropagainment": Exploring the Power of Political Satire as a Distinct Form of Political Humor." In *Laughing Matters: Humor and American Politics in the Media Age*, eds. Baumgartner, J. C. and J. S. Morris, 3–20. New York: Routledge.

Delli Carpini, M. X. and Williams, B. A. 1994. "'Fictional' and 'Non-fictional' Television celebrates Earth Day: Or, politics is comedy plus pretense." *Cultural Studies*. 8: 74–98.

Delli Carpini, M. X., and Keeter, S. 1996. *What Americans Know About Politics and Why It Matters*. New Haven, CT: Yale University Press.

Donohue, G. A.; Tichenor, P. J.; and Olien, C. N. 1975. "Mass Media and the Knowledge Gap: A Hypothesis Reconsidered." *Communication Research*. 2: 3–23.

Elliott, R. C. 2004. "The Nature of Satire." In *Encyclopaedia Britannica*, "Satire," 2004.

Fox, J. R., Koloen, G. and Sahin, V. 2007. "No Joke: A Comparison of Substance in *The Daily Show with Jon Stewart* and Broadcast Network Television Coverage of the 2004 Presidential Election Campaign." *Journal of Broadcasting & Electronic Media*. 51: 213–227.

Gray, J. 2005. *Watching with the Simpsons*. Routledge: London.

Hart, R. P. and Hartelius, J. 2007. "The Political Sins of Jon Stewart. *Critical Studies in Media Communication*." 24: 263–272.

Hetherington, M. 2001. "Declining Trust and a Shrinking Policy Agenda: Why the Media Scholars Should Care." In *Communication in US Elections: New Agendas*, eds. Ron Hart and Donald R. Shaw, 105–21. Lanham, MD: Rowman and Littlefield.

Holbert, R. L., Pillion, O., et al. 2003. "*The WestWing* as Endorsement of the American Presidency: Expanding the Domain of Priming in Political Communication." *Journal of Communication*. 53: 427–443.

Holbrook, T. M. 2002. "Presidential Campaigns and the Knowledge Gap." *Political Communication*. 19: 437–454.

Jamieson, K. H. and Waldman, P. 2003. *The Press Effect: Politicians, Journalists, and the Stories that Shape the Political World*. London: Oxford University Press

Jones, J.P. 2005. "Entertaining Politics: New Political Television and Civic Culture." Lanham, Md.: Rowman & Littlefield Publishers.

Levi, M. and Stoker, L. 2000. "Political Trust and Trustworthiness." *Annual Review of Political Science.* 3: 475–507.

McGuire, W, J. 1968. "Personality and Attitude Change: An Information-Processing Theory." In *Psychological foundations of attitudes*, eds. A. G. Greenwald, T. C., Brock, and T. M. Ostrom, 171—196. San Diego, CA: Academic Press.

Miller, J. M. and Krosnick, J. A. 2000. "News Media Impact on the Ingredients of Presidential Evaluations: Politically Knowledgeable Citizens Are Guided by a Trusted Source." *American Journal of Political Science.* 44: 295–309.

Moy, P., Xenos, M. A., and Hess, V. K. 2006. "Priming Effects of Late-night Comedy, *International Journal of Public Opinion Research.*" 18: 198–210.

_____. 2005. "Communication and Citizenship: Mapping the Political Effects of Infotainment." *Mass Communication & Society.* 8: 111–131.

National Annenberg Election Survey. 2004. "*Daily Show* Viewers Knowledgeable About Presidential Campaign." September 21. Available at: http://www.annenbergpublicpolicycenter. org/naes/2004_03_late-night-knowledge-2_9–21_pr.pdf.

Niven, D. Lichter, S. R., and Amundson, D. 2003. "The Political Content of Late-night Comedy." *Press/Politics* 8: 118–133.

Pew Research Center for the People and the Press. 2004. "Cable and Internet Loom Large in Fragmented PoliticalNewsUniverse." January 11. Available at: http://people-press.org/reports/display .php3?ReportID=200.

_____. 2002. *Public's News Habits Little Changed Since September 11.* Available at: http://people-press.org/reports/display.php3?ReportID=156

_____. 2000. *Audiences Fragmented and Skeptical: The Tough Job of Communicating with Voters.* Available at: http://www.people-press.org/jan00rpt.htm

Prior, Markus. 2007. *Post-Broadcast Democracy: How Media Choice Increases Inequality in Political Involvement and Polarizes Elections.* Cambridge University Press.

Tichenor, P. J.; Donohue, G. A.; and Olien, C. N. 1970. "Mass Media Flow and Differential Growth in Knowledge." *Public Opinion Quarterly.* 34: 159–170.

Xenos, M. A. and Becker, A. B. 2009. "Moments of Zen: Effects of *the Daily Show* on Information Seeking and Political Learning." *Political Communication.* 26: 317–332.

Young, D. G. 2006. "Late-night Comedy and the Salience of the Candidates' Caricatured Traits in the 2000 Election." *Mass Communication and Society* 9: 339–366.

_____. 2004. "Late-night Comedy in Election 2000: Its Influence on Candidate Trait Ratings and the Moderating Effects of Political Knowledge." *Journal of Broadcasting and Electronic Media.* 48: 1–22.

_____, and Tisinger, R. 2006. "Dispelling Late-night Myths: News Consumption Among Late-night Comedy Viewers and the Predictors of Exposure to Various Late-night Shows." *The Harvard International Journal of Press/Politics.* 11: 113–134.

Young, D. G., Tisinger, R. M., et al. 2006. "The Power of Numbers: Examining Subpopulations with the NAES." In *Capturing Campaign Dynamics. The National Annenberg Election Survey: Design, Method, and Data,* 2nd ed., ed. Dan Romer, Kate Kenski, Christopher Adasiewicz, and Kathleen Hall Jamieson. Oxford: Oxford University Press.

Young, D. G. 2007. "*The Daily Show* as New Journalism." In *Laughing Matters: Humor and American Politics in the Media Age,* eds. J. S. Morris and J. C. Baumgartner, 241–259. New York: Routledge.

Zaller, J. 1992. *The Nature and Origins of Mass Opinion.* New York: Cambridge University Press.

Irony and the News

Speaking Through Cool to American Youth

RICHARD VAN HEERTRUM

Introduction

David Harvey (1989), among many, have argued that irony is the dominant affective state of youth today. Irony, in the space between figurative and literal meaning, defines a separation from deeper emotional or political commitment, a space for cool detachment. The popularity of *The Daily Show* and *The Colbert Report* (DR/CR) arguably relate directly to this postmodern predilection, as they use irony as a vehicle for critique that protects them from the appearance of deeper political engagement, even as they clearly engage more deeply with politics than many of their more serious contemporaries. In this essay, I argue that the two shows have garnered such popularity and critical acclaim based on an underlying dynamic that relates directly to the political stance of many youth today — a critique of the current order of things connected to cynicism about the possibility of real change.

While the election of Barak Obama certainly highlighted an underlying hope, the relatively rapid descent of his popularity and precipitous move to the center may provide further evidence of this cynicism as protection from authentic commitment. Rather than arguing, as some have, that DS/CR foster cynicism in their audiences (Baumgartner and Morris, 2006), I instead believe that their popularity relates to an underlying irony and cynicism that resonate with those youth drawn to the show. This seems particularly true given studies that find both that DS/CR audiences are as or more informed than more mainstream sources and more educated; for example, *Daily Show* viewers are 78 percent more likely to have four or more years of college education in comparison to the average American, while Bill O'Reilly's is only 24 percent more likely (Long, 2004) and Baumgartner and Morris found that almost 50 percent of college kids were watching one or both shows in 2004. I relate this analysis to broader debates on the cool, anti-intellectualism and neoliberalism, arguing the shows provide powerful evidence of the importance of irony to understanding contemporary youth culture and a powerful space for political information and critique that essentially speaks "the language" of American youth today.

Youth and the Culture of Cool

Today the tentacles of media culture continue to spread outward across the social and political landscape, altering the very dynamics of how we live and perceive the world around us. A 2009 study from the Kaiser Family Foundation exemplified its broad reach, finding that "generation M" (those aged 8 to 18) consume the equivalent of over 7½ hours of media and technology each day, effectively occupying a third of their waking life (Rideout, Foehr, and Roberts, 2010). According to PBS's *Frontline* and the American Academy of Pediatrics, kids are inundated with over 3,000 advertisements a day and watch 1,023 hours of television a year, outstripping school by over 100 hours (Goodman, 2001). And Pew finds they rely heavily on television and the Internet to get political news, increasingly mock news programs like *Saturday Night Live, The David Letterman Show* and, of course, *The Daily Show* and *Colbert Report* (Online news audience larger, more diverse: News audience increasingly politicized, 2004). When we add videogames, movies and music, it is clear that media exposure far exceeds time spent with family and friends, in school or any other activity, becoming the de facto in locus parenti.

This only amplifies the concerns of social theorists, who have long argued for the essential role of the culture industry in contemporary society, particularly as it relates to the creation of opinion, meaning and official knowledge. Today media's influence continues to grow, framing and refracting the lenses through which we view the world. Media provides youth in particular with representations of identity and preferable normative behavior, defining not only the form of social life but an increasing proportion of its content as well. Increasingly, youth appear to identify themselves within market constructed stereotypes and modes of behavior that influence their fashion, hairstyle, artistic tastes, social interaction and perceptions of gender, race, class and sexuality. At the heart of the consumer culture for youth is the selling of "cool" — generally codified in challenging authority, apoliticism, anti-intellectualism and rejection of everything perceived as "uncool" or "outdated."

One could further argue that media culture complements an increasingly administered quotidian life, driving youth from the public sphere, active democratic citizenship and free thought by selling identities that replicate commodified models and ideals and through the shrinking of public spaces where they can develop social and cooperative skills (Giroux, 2003). On the other hand, media has also opened up new spaces of possibility for social interaction, political mobilization and dialogue and alternative knowledge systems and information sources. The Internet is reinventing modes of social and political engagement, alternative media and political documentaries are offering alternative perspectives and strong critique and new spaces are opening for dialogue and debate. But where do *The Daily Show* and *Colbert Report* fit in this formula? Before analyzing that question in depth, I want to explore what I label the "culture of the cool" and its relationship to DS/CR.

The cool in Hollywood and on television are generally apolitical, tending toward individualized, self-interested behavior — as for example in reality television (Andrejevic, 2004; Couldry, 2006; Giroux, 2004), crime and mafia flicks or comedies and drama targeted at youth — and ironically distance themselves from the political. The cool, the heroic and the desirable in films and on television often engender the central tenets of neoliberalism[1]— stressing solipsism and greed, individuals over community and the state and an ahistorical fatalism that rejects the possibility of radical change. The cool are often apolitical and anti-intellectual, defined by their ability to step outside cultural norms and mainstream culture, while sometimes reinforcing them in the end. They are individualistic and rebellious, reject authority (bureaucracy and the state) and tend to focus on surface over substance. And they are commodified and sold back to teens through manufacturers of apparel, health and beauty, cosmetics and fragrances, shoe companies, sports association, electronics companies, advertising agencies and, of course, movie studios and television.

Yet who are these constructed cool figures? Clearly there are diverse manifestations, across gender, race, ethnicity and sexual orientation, but they often have similar attributes. First is a strident individualism and rejection of authority. The cool is generally detached and ironic, and though rejection of social norms could be seen as transgressive, the irony promoted here is often related to the distance between what is said and what is meant. The cool steps outside the normative and in the process challenges those norms, foregrounding the individual and the freedom to rebel. The rejection of authority calls that authority into question and critiques it from without, potentially offering alternatives to conventional wisdom and hegemonic discourses. This irony has arguably become one of the major ways that youth interact today, distancing themselves from hope, substance and authentic interaction and instead existing in a state of perpetual distrust and undiscerning mockery. At a deeper level, it appears to relate to a deep-seated but unrealized desire for authenticity; even if authenticity itself might be a social construct. In any case, it is hard not to connect this affective stance to the exemplars of the commercial world and their cool distance from politics, social norms and respect for anything. While many youth idols like Brittany Spears, the Jonas brothers and Miley Cyrus embrace commercialism fully, the cool are generally defined by attempts to step outside the crass world of commercialism while embracing it indirectly. Urban Outfitters is a good example of this trend taking the cool from the streets and offering it in an easy-to-find, reasonably-priced commodified form. A French Connection UK (FCUK) billboard in Hollywood shows the general tenor of this marketing approach, "Apparently there are more important things than fashion. Yeah right."

The youth market is plush with ironic messages from "Princess" T-shirts to more sexually suggestive themes to Diesel's new "Be Stupid" advertisement campaign to young fashion magazines focused predominantly on fashion, beauty and surface appeal to the endless array of entertainment news outlets that focus on the absurd foibles of the rich and famous. In a postmodern world of pastiche and bricolage, the Goo Goo Dolls line "when everything feels like a movie, you bleed just to know you're alive," seems an apropos representation of the crisis of representation itself. Irony then becomes a defensive affective stance used to distance oneself from the instability of the contemporary subject position (Langstraat, 2002). Yet this irony precludes a way out of the impasse, ensuring that lack of respect for authority, social institutions and democracy itself become normalized and naturalized, subsumed under the tidal wave of consumer culture and its pleasure on the cheap. This is the essence of the youth cynicism that dominates today, fortified by exemplars that focus on fame, fortune and beauty as the apogee of existence and intelligence, deep rumination, civic engagement and substance as idealistic, unrealistic and uncool attributed we should run from. There is no reality to grasp at, so why not embrace the spectacle society and its titillating simulated world?

One instantiation of the cool figure is one that never engage in politics at any level (e.g,, *Friends, Seinfeld, Entourage, Arrested Development, Californication, 30 Rock,* etc.), thus demonstrating the verboten status of the political among the cool, charismatic and lovable. We can think of the films of Wes Anderson (*Bottle Rockets, Rushmore, The Royal Tenenbaums, A Life Aquatic*), a series of bands like *Blink 182* that base their act on irony, stores like Urban Outfitters and cynical teen films like *The Chumscrubber* (2005), *Brick* (2005) and *Alpha Dog* (2006). And we see the same trend among youth-targeted television and movies that seldom focus on anything but the cool, famous or popular and very rarely on broader political questions (e.g. *Hannah Montana, (500) Days of Summer* (2009), *Mean Girls* (2004), *Clueless* (1995) or the *Scream* series), relying predominantly on irony as the way that teens talk to and interact with each other. Even the relatively radical *Dawson's Creek, 90210* or *Mel-*

rose Place (at the time), which crossed traditional thresholds of sexual politics, rarely moved on to larger social issues.

Beyond irony, the cool has often become synonymous with the lovable dolt or naïve ingénue who exists in the oblivious world of contentment and happiness, usually underwritten by an almost fanatical selfishness. From Will Ferrell, Owen Wilson and Jimmy Fallon to Homer Simpson, Forrest Gump, the South Park kids and Peter Griffin to Phoebe Buffay, Amy Smart and Jessica Simpson, we have become increasingly enamored with the raffish dolt, the obtuse buffoon and the naïve lackey. Through these characters and personalities, we valorize those who accept society as it is and float through life without worry while criticizing those who actually ruminate on anything of substance. They are apolitical, anti-intellectual and uncritically embracing of the status quo they mock, serving as a contrast to the newly defined "elite," namely those nerds, ivory tower professors and other cultural liberals that drink latte, do well in school and actually like theatre, novels and art house movies (Frank, 2004). This seems particularly true on *South Park, The Simpsons* and *The Family Guy,* where idle ignorance is consistently placed above intelligence, activism and really social engagement of any kind outside the satisfaction of individual want. It seems to relate to a broader social meme to valorize youth and innocence above all else, often involving the infantilization of American males in sitcoms and popular film (Faludi, 1999). The *Family Guy* is a telling example, a show based on referentially parodying popular culture — essentially a full realization of pastiche and bricolage without a real plot. Like *The Simpsons* on methamphetamines, irony is the language of the show, but without any of its predecessor's social commentary or valorization of family and community (and *The Cleveland Show* expands their empire outward).

A quintessential example of this anti-intellectual, naive trope is Adam Sandler, who in one film after another valorizes ignorance, street smarts over intelligence and violence as the appropriate response to almost any affront. The loose remake *Mr. Deeds* (2002), for example, centers on a sweet-natured, small-town everyman who resorts to violence to right any wrong. In one scene, we are shown the evil artists and intellectual elites of New York (an opera singer, New Yorker writer and patron of the arts) who openly mock him in a foolish, elitist way. The naïve figure is given a favorable representation and promoted as innately superior to those who have more education, more sophistication and do not see the world through his credulous, doughy eyes. Similar characters emerge in *Happy Gilmore* (1996), *The Waterboy* (1998), *The Wedding Singer* (1998), *Big Daddy* (1999), *Click* (2006) and *I Now Pronounce You Chuck and Larry* (2007). This is also true of most films emerging from *Saturday Night Live* alum over the past several years including those of Will

Ferrell (*Old School, Anchorman, Semi-Pro, Talladega Nights* and *Elf*), Rob Schneider (*The Hot Chick, The Animal, Deuce Bigelow: Male Gigolo*), Mike Meyers (*Austin Powers* and *The Love Guru*) and even Tina Fey (*Baby Mama*) in addition to other big name comedy stars like Owen Wilson, Seth Rogan, Vince Vaughn, Bradley Cooper and Mathew McConaughey. It appears Peter Pan syndrome has become the dominant male pathology of comedy today — offering teenage boys an older version of themselves to embrace and replicate.

A recent study by USC offered evidence of the power of identification with the cool, finding that TV personalities and the famous in general tend to be more narcissistic than the average American, but may be pulling the population closer to their point-of-view. As researcher Campbell argues, "By definition, it's supposed to be reality, and you have a sample of people who are more self-absorbed, more entitled, more vain than the normal population, that is going to pull the population in the direction of narcissism. If the self-absorption you see on *Laguna Beach* or *The Real World* is viewed as normal, the culture will be pushed in that direction" (Abcarian, 2006). Other studies confirm this perspective, finding entering college students more narcissistic than their predecessors, setting up a clear path between changing social values and their affects on the next generation. And two recent books, *The Cheating Culture* (Callahan, 2004) and *Making Good* (Fischman, Solomon, Greenspan, and Gardner, 2004), found a dramatic increase in cheating, both in schools and among certain professions, seemingly replicating these figures and increasingly sports stars like bicyclist Floyd Landis, baseball players Barry Bonds, Jose Canseco and Kenny Rogers and runners Justin Gatlin and Marion Jones, who portray themselves as victims of a culture of cheating that permeates much of the sports world today. One could argue simply that there is very little to believe in anymore, so why not reject it all.

The point is that the distrust in human nature and social institutions neoliberalism promotes are reinforced on a daily basis on television and in movies, videogames and music. The citizen as consumer is a theme that is consistently spread across these mediums, rearticulating choice in market terms as in voting for the next *American Idol*, with Nintendo commercials bragging of their distance from politics and Urban Outfitters selling t-shirts in 2004 that read "Voting is for Old People" to amplify the point. The PBS Frontline documentary *Merchants of Cool (2003)* offers a compelling presentation of the ways these various manifestations of the cool are brought together and intimately tied with the consumer culture and media industries. Using interviews with Robert McChesney, Mark Crispin Miller, Douglas Rushkoff and a host of teen marketing and media experts, the film documents the ways in which "cool" has become a commodity sought, found and then packaged back to teens on a grand scale. The big five media companies (Disney, Viacom, News Corp., Universal/Vivendi and AOL/Time Warner)—who collectively control 90 percent of the music industry, all the major film studios, most of the cable and network television stations and programming and a huge portion of the book, magazine and print market — revolve largely around using cool as a marketing tool that introduces and reinforces the central tenets of consumer culture without any real reference to what kids actually want, need or dream of; or what may make them happy.

The cool in this case is emptied of its content, becoming but its surface manifestation in fashion, hairstyle, clothing, music, films, modes of comportment and interaction and the like. It essentially reinforces Nick Hornby's prescient comment from *High Fidelity* that what matters now is what you like, not what you are like. A series of marketer researchers and "cool seekers" essentially scour the streets looking for those kids on the edge of the latest trends (the top 20 percent known as "trend setters" or "early adopters"), then interview them or follow them around finding out what they like, how they talk, who they are listening to and any other details that could be adapted to media content and commodified products. Other teens are then inundated with the various commodity forms, to the tune of 3,000 discrete ads each day and over 10,000,000 by the time they reach 18 and television, movies, music and goods that replicate the surface content. These commercials seem to work, as teens spent an astounding $179 billion in 2007 alone (Mui 2007). Yet the irony is that in commodifying and popularizing the cool, they essentially kill it and after a short amount of time must find the next cool thing. As Mulvey (1993) argued, popular culture bridges the gap between commodity as spectacle and the figure of the woman as spectacle, bringing together the fetishism of Marx and Freud. The cool offers a manifestation of this confluence, where sexuality and commodity fetishism are brought together in ways that most teens cannot help but find appealing.

Marketers have found out that kids in recent years became cynical to advertisers who engage in these activities and have become largely immune to traditional modes of advertising, just as one could argue they are immune to the traditional mainstream press. So new forms that are more subversive and cross-sectional have become the norm, with MTV, the fashion industry, the music industry and corporations working in tandem to find "cool" ways to sell the cool. Sprite is a perfect example, marketing itself in the 1990s through irony, by mocking the very process of selling itself, then when that lost its caché, using cleverly constructed "events" to buy their way into hip hop culture and align themselves with it, becoming in the process the fastest growing soft drink in the world. Like MTV, Sprite and all the corporations in this vein are essentially selling a lifestyle — which is access to the cool through proximity to the world of fame, money and consumer culture. Yet who are the figures they are selling?

The point is the nature of the perpetual cycle is cynical at its core. The kids want to be cool and thus reject the mainstream appeal and consumer culture that attempts to commodify them, or at least see it for what it is, yet they end up embracing the very thing they are trying to reject as every form of rebellion is quickly commodified and folded into the consumer culture spectacle society. Hebdige (1979) explored youth subcultures and resistance and the ways it was increasingly co-opted, commodified and incorporated into consumer culture over 30 years ago, but the trend has accelerated in the period since. Along with other Birmingham theorists, he focused on youth culture as a potential space for resistance and opposition as well, creating distinct forms of identity and group formation that challenged dominant institutions and modes of thought and behavior. But he also saw the ways popular culture tended to co-opt rebellion as a sellable commodity.

Just as Lacan argued that we lived in a world of unstable subject positions that created a form of neurosis, the contemporary spectacle society only amplifies these concerns. And when teens do replicate those cool figures, this only accentuates the detachment from real social engagement, as the cool recognizes the inauthentic nature of all those around them and thus mocks them from a safe distance that reaffirms the fact that they are in on the grand joke and lie that is postmodern society. This affective stance fits perfectly with the nature of being a teenager to begin with. Many clearly embrace the system without this neurotic relationship, but they are nonetheless buying into cool on the cheap as well. There is great variety among youth today from the most base and anti-intellectual instantiation of the cool to much more nuanced, critical irony on the edges and in various countercultural movements. Yet in most cases, there appears to be an underlying and unmet desire for authenticity that goes largely unrealized. Many teens want to be on the cutting edge and yet that cutting edge is too slippery and is forever falling back into the mainstream. They end up stuck in a world where everything does in fact seem like the movies and reality itself, together with their subjective identity, called into question. So to be cool or simply to exist in this social structure almost requires irony and cynicism as a defense against the constant barrage of artificiality in the guise of authenticity from marketers, television characters, film personalities and politicians.

Cynicism, Media and Youth

Jean-François Lyotard (1974) once argued that cynicism was endemic to modernity, "capitalism offers nothing to believe in; cynicism is its morality."

He believed that the same tendencies that led society toward fascism were also implicitly cynical in nature. The modern man believed in nothing, not even his guilt or responsibility, and his repression thus came not as a punishment but as a result of the universal law of equitable exchange engendered in capitalism. This tendency has only amplified in the postmodern epoch, as incredulity toward metanarratives, further skepticism of language and politics and failed utopian projects became the norm. The very distrust of these failed utopian projects bred distrust of any alternative to liberal democracy and capitalism (even as people distrusted both), thus avowing an explicit cynicism to all but the most abstract forms of social change.[2] This relates to the youth culture discussed above, as it is arguably cynical at its core.

Sloterdijk (1987) took a similar stance, arguing that cynicism was the dominant operating model in contemporary Western society — at both the institutional and personal level — though he places the phenomena more in relation to the false promises of ideology critique and utopian hopes that culminated in the post–60s malaise. He sees cynicism as "enlightened false consciousness," where people recognized the failure of reason and rationality Enlightenment had promised as a panacea to social ills and became largely asocial, borderline melancholics and thus immune to ideology critique and its unearthing of the truth; a position shared by Zizek in *The Sublime Object of Ideology* (1997). Contemporary society was both well off and miserable, existing in the *unhappy consciousness* of understanding the central insights of Enlightenment thinking, but aware of the inability to enact them. Science and technology had failed to improve the human condition in the larger sense and in fact strengthened a sense of unfreedom buoyed by collective distrust and alienation.

Sloterdijk saw cynicism as an ontological condition, founded on the failures of the past and perceived notions about future possibility. Langstraat (2002), on the other hand, sees cynicism as the dominant affective modality of our time, the psychological response to shifting emotional identification led by mass-media consciousness and a loss of authenticity. She defines this state as *miasmic cynicism* where overdetermined narratives, loss of a stable subject position and grand narratives and the undermining of corporeal reality to disorienting simulacra predominate. Both thus focus on postmodernity and what Jameson (1991) has defined as a "waning of affect" or "depthlessness" of emotive experience. David Harvey (1989) further articulates this position as one where instantaneity and disposability create "time space compression" and a feeling of disorientation and alienation from society and oneself (predominantly through the media). Essentially, capitalism and consumer culture rearticulate our wants, needs and desires then only deliver partial, disposable satisfaction that leads to the perpetuation of the system. As Marcuse (1966) argued, repressive desublimation ensues, where we accept the system and the crumbs of satisfaction and desire fulfillment it offers. This is particularly true of youth, who have grown up in a world of media influence that even those of us in Generation X cannot really understand. They are often legally drugged from an early age, move on to illegal drugs and alcohol abuse as they grow (or their parents medicine cabinet), take antidepressants at alarming rates, have eating disorders and generally appear to be both materially well-off and melancholic.

Even the notion of progress changes in a cynical world, framed largely in economic and technological terms that ignore whether that progress actually improves the human condition. And in the political realm, a similar aesthetic prevails with much of the punditocracy spouting intransient ideological positions or providing horse race/he said she said coverage, too morose and boring for most youth today. News media thus helps rearticulate social responsibility and obligation as consuming as much as possible and working to succeed in one's chosen profession.

Just as the FCC came to define the public interest as whatever entertains them, media has come to establish a "how to" public sphere, where politics becomes simply signing on to an ideological position without much forethought or discussion. As media influence grew, Habermas (1962) followed C. Wright Mills (1951) in arguing that electronic media was radically transforming the public sphere from one that facilitates rational debate and the free exchange of disparate opinions to a source for shaping, constructing and limiting public discourse and stultifying plurality, debate and free thought. Mills earlier argued that entertainment media was becoming a potent instrument for social control starting in the 50s, often because it was accepted without the apprehension of propaganda instruments and thus consumed with little critical analysis or forethought. Postman (1985) goes further in arguing that media and television altered the nature of the political toward entertainment, sound bites and away from reasoned debate.

Galtung and Vincent (2003) and Chomsky (2002) offer more recent manifestations of this argument, claiming that media tends to frame political issues in dualistic terms that constrict the options available to public debate and cut off the channels for compromise or real change. McChesney and Kellner further this analysis by arguing that television and media culture have undermined democracy and politics itself, by placing entertainment and spectacle above substance. McChesney (2004) enumerates the ways in which media consolidation has limited the voices and perspectives available to the public and placed business interests above more traditional democratic roles for the press, leading to inadequate, biased journalism and hyper-commercialism. He then argues that "by the late twentieth century, media policy making was the private playground of a handful of powerful corporate lobbies and trade associations" (McChesney, 2004, p. 8). And Kellner (2005) has extended the work of Guy Debord and the Situationalists, exploring the spectacle society and ways that entertainment and commodification have undermined the role of the fourth estate. He believes the spectacle nature of popular media distracts the public from the substance of politics today, tying current media policy and practice to conservative government policy including the spread of neoliberal ideology, the two Iraq Wars, the post–9/11 war on terror and the attack on civil liberties and democratic principles of governance and popular representation.

Yet youth culture today does not appear to fit as readily into these deterministic, economistic explanations. They appear more savvy as media consumer, recognizing the lies and rhetorical strategies used by politicians and the media. Instead I believe cynicism and ironic distance are more powerful explanations for their behavior. And it is here that DS/CR become important in speaking the language of youth — based on irony, or distance from the expected reaction to the spectacle society and the absurdity of contemporary politics and essentially cynicism about things ever changing. Not all youth are this savvy, but if one looks at the amount of cheating going on, the levels of distrust in media and politicians and the general tendency to disconnect from politics, or to embrace alternatives to the two mainstream parties (or Obama's rather nebulous discourse of "hope"), it is fair to say that youth today are not the naïve dupes that critical theorists saw in the 50s. And among the truly savvy youth, the *Daily Show* and *Colbert Report* are the ideal vehicle.

Deconstructing the Daily Show and Colbert

Woody Allen once said "comedy is tragedy plus time," a line related to Charlie Chaplin's insight that "life is tragedy when seen in close-up, but a comedy in long-shot." The point is that comedy is really defined by distance from tragedy, either of time or location. Irony is one way to provide that space by separating literal from figurative meaning. It is the ideal language for a cynical age, as it allows critique without commitment, truth without emotional attachment. One could argue that this is the appeal of *The Daily Show* and *Colbert Report.* Sure they make us laugh, but our laughter is of a satirical sort brought on by the recognition that what they mock is often of a very serious nature, whether it be lying politicians, war, corporate malfeasance, or a media that has largely abrogated its responsibility as the fourth estate — checking the powerful by holding them accountable for their words and actions. It is not an accident, I think, that Jon Stewart ended up fourth on a list of journalists that were most admired in 2007, tied in the ranking with anchormen Brian Williams, Tom Brokaw, Dan Rather and cable host Anderson Cooper (Center, 2008).

In a 2006 interview in *Rolling Stone,* Ben Karlin, Stewart's production partner who oversees both shows argued, "the biggest mistake people make is thinking that Jon and Stephen sit down before every show and say, 'OK, how are we going to change the world? Or any bullshit like that. They both really just want to get a laugh." Stewart, in fact, argues in the same interview "[we are] emotional but apolitical," "we are not warriors in anyone's army" and "I still don't consider myself political. People confuse political interest with interest in current events." And yet in the same article the two offer some of the most incisive critique you will hear from contemporary media personalities.

Colbert, for example, offers the following commentary on Bill O'Reilly, the obvious inspiration for his mock personality, "You know, actually, I have a genuine admiration for O'Reilly's ability to do his show. I'd love to be able to put a chain of words together the way he does [*snaps his fingers*] without much thought as to what it might mean, compared to what you said about the same subject the night before." This could describe much conservative discourse today. Stewart follows this up deconstructing the Republican Party, "The cornerstone of politics these days is grievance. It's really hard to keep that going when you're in power.... And what are they most angry about? People who play the victim card." And in deconstructing Bush, Stewart offers the salient argument that Bush is "uncurious about the world" while Colbert goes further to challenge the left's rather uncritical perspective on the ex-President, "Bush is not dumb. He speaks to us like we're dumb."

And this is what Colbert does week after week, with the audience in on the joke. He makes up facts to suit his perspective, creates a personality so enamored with himself that he is constantly selling manifestations of that personality to the public (read O'Reilly, Hannity and Limbaugh) and bamboozles guests into sometimes accepting absurd claims: "And the person folds, 'cause they don't realize I have no problem making things up, because I have no credibility to lose." Mocking conservatives he has come up with the word "Truthiness" and likes to say things like "I'm not a fan of facts. Facts can change all the time, but my opinion will never change." And yet this is not completely true, as a series of studies have shown that their coverage of, for example, the 2004 election were as substantive as "real" news (Hollander, 2005; Long, 2004; Young, 2004) and that their fans are often more informed than those consuming other, more reputable news sources (Center, 2007)

As the *Rolling Stone* article argues, they are the "Cronkite and Murrow for an ironic millennium." While real network news loses audiences, and even Fox has seen its numbers diminish in recent years, Stewart's show became the hot destination for politicians, authors, celebrities and anyone who "wants to sell books or seem hip." Even Pakistani President Pervez Musharraf was on the show, as were almost all the main candidates for president, making it an almost de rigueur stop for anyone attempting to appeal to the Nation's youth. Maybe the greatest irony is that those who are often the victims of the shows ironic critique feel required to appear before Stewart and act as if they themselves are in on the joke.

Beyond deconstructing politics, Stewart and Colbert are particularly adept at critiquing the mainstream media, from the safe distance of their stance as comedians and apolitical representatives of the people. And yet when asked by the *New York Times* how his show did such a good job digging up politicians contradicting himself he drolly replied, "a clerk and a video machine." The coolness and ironic distance of the shows and their hosts belies the substance of their critique, their ability to dig deep and not only show the manipulative nature of politicians and their "great faith in institutional absurdity" but the ways in which the mainstream media fails to do its job.

To be fair, Stewart relies on a very talented staff of writers and researchers. At the center is Adam Chodikoff, the show's chief researcher and video wiz who has an encyclopedic memory and the ability to find so many of the clips the show uses in showing the contradictions and lies of the Bush administration or other politicians: "Chodikoff 'sees the whole picture, says Rob Kutner, one of the show's writers. He's 'in the news matrix. He spots patterns, trends, the forces of history. He remembers a politician saying the opposite thing three years ago and gets us to that video" (Farhi, 2008). The interesting question is how a show with a small staff more interested in getting a laugh than holding politicians accountable can be so much better at their job then huge multimedia conglomerates with large research and journalist staffs. Could it be that the mainstream media has become part of mainstream politics in a way that disincentives them from providing this critique? Chodikoff says he relies predominantly on "recall and hustle and a few good TiVos."

Essentially the two shows are taking on a task mainstream media has largely abandoned — holding politicians and the media accountable for what they say and do (and don't say and don't do). *Daily Show* writer Elliott Kalan highlights their role, arguing the major problems with the mainstream media involve overreaction and early reaction — based too much on "a scoop" or "breaking news," rather than in depth content (Tenore, 2009). Segment Producer Patrick King goes further arguing "Too often, journalists' political coverage — and that of media critics — ends up being sanitized and nothing but a perfunctory he said/she said exchange" (Tenore, 2009). The show essentially steps in where the mainstream and other cable media often leave off, equally adept at critiquing media and politicians who, like those in the Bush administration, have led the degradation of political discourse in America. During the Bush years, they became one of the strongest voices challenging the absurdity of the War on Terror, the doublespeak around the Iraq War, the rhetorical flourish of the Bush tax cuts, misrepresentation of corporate malfeasance and, really, the corruption at the heart of the political and economic worlds.

More recently, the show caught Sean Hannity using video from Glenn Beck's protest footage instead of his own, smaller event, skewered CNN for saying "let's leave it there" during critical parts of an interview, lambasted Jim Cramer for repeating corporate spin instead of investigating the truth on CNBC, the mainstream media in general for its nonstop coverage of the faked "Balloon Boy" incident and continues to deconstruct the hypocrisy of the right in challenging and obstructing anything and everything Obama does. One of its most powerful components, now all but absent from the mainstream media, is a larger critique of political corruption and the relationship between money and policy. Stewart, for example, skewered John McCain and others for not supporting Net Neutrality in January arguing, "It's kinda like creating a carpool lane on the Internet, except instead of high-occupancy vehicles, only rich assholes will be able to drive in it." He mentions in the piece that McCain receives more Telco cash than any other member of Congress. This is the kind of critique that is rarely (or really never) seen on network news, and very rarely on anything but MSNBC, who themselves have media pundits that use irony like Rachel Maddow and Keith Olbermann. Using clips, he holds politicians, experts and the media itself accountable for their actions — mocking as he critiques thus using the language of youth to make them more informed about the key issues in politics from one day to the next. This is particularly important if one believes that youth are largely immunized from artifice, even as they engage in it themselves, and recognize that a large, though shrinking percentage of the show's audience is college students. In the Net Neutrality piece, Stewart included a clip from Joe Wilson of Florida arguing that the Internet marketplace has helped liberate Iran, Iraq and Afghanistan, then mocked the absurdity of the claim by pretending to believe it. He did this with a look that has become his signature, a dumbfounded credulity in the face of absurdity that has a glimmer of ironic knowing that tells the audience we are in on the joke.

One could then argue that Stewart and Colbert may in fact benefit from their comedic sheen, as it protects them from the limitations of being seen as "liberal" commentators (à la Maddow or Olbermann on MSNBC). That is why when Stewart went on the now defunct *Crossfire* a few years ago and critiqued the hosts for damaging America with their incendiary version of political discourse, it garnered massive media attention. The critique from the comedian who happens to have a news show provided some cover from any underlying ideological commitment — clearly viewed as negative not only by savvy young viewers, but those who believe media can and should be "objective." The general nature of their political engagement is mocking indifference and diffidence, rarely crossing over to embrace either party or any political or social movement. By equal opportunity mockery, that includes both sides of the political spectrum and much in between, they ensure that we recognize the artificiality and manipulation at the heart of all politics. Yet is this cynical in nature, or does it provide a valuable voice to counter the degradation of political discourse and media coverage today? In the final section, I briefly consider this argument.

Politically Relevant or Inspiring Cynicism?

So are the *Daily Show with Jon Stewart* and *Colbert Report* as apolitical as they sometimes pretend to be? Do they inspire cynicism in their audience? I think the answer to both questions is clearly no. Stewart in particular provides an important voice to the sophisticated young viewers turned off by the earnestness and purported "objectivity" of mainstream news. Both provide a powerful critique of the mainstream media and the rhetorical strategies the two parties employ toward influencing and manipulating the political will of the people, even as they orient themselves more to the critique of the right, this seems appropriate given their control of the political discourse over the past 30 years.

The shows are, of course, not alone in using satire and irony as mechanisms of political critique. Within the media Olbermann, Maddow, Michael Moore, Bill Maher and a host of other minor players all use satire as one tool in their repertoire. And political satiric films like *In the Loop* (2009), *Looking for Comedy in the Muslim World* (2006), *C.S.A.: The Confederate States of America* (2004), *The Onion Movie* (2008) and most Moore films all use irony to appeal to larger audiences then, say, the documentaries of Robert Greenwald and his leftist contemporaries. That was the intended purpose of satire from the beginning, with a long lineage tracing back to Diogenes, Erasmus, Shakespeare, Jonathon Swift and the like. This is where Stewart and Colbert diverge from parody, more intent on humor than critique. *Saturday Night Live* is also cited by some as an increasingly important source of political coverage for teen audiences, but they are more intent on making fun than actually deconstructing political issues or holding the media accountable for their coverage.

One could argue that, in the spectacle society, the laughter that Bakhtin once saw as transgressive becomes more in line with Adorno, the laughter of quiescence, of servitude and ironic conformity (Bakhtin, 1982). It becomes the laughter of enlightened skepticism that Sloterdijk (1987) sees in the west, with the masses in on the Wizard sitting behind the iron curtain, but unwilling or unable to do anything to pull the sheet back and demand a different ruler. Yet irony can also be a powerful force for social change and given contemporary affective predilections, it is fair to argue that irony is an important element in overcoming miasmic cynicism, as long as it is combined with critique and hope (Langstraat, 2002).

Cynicism could then be seen as a great unrealized potential; the radical who has retreated from the world of engagement but is really a cloaked romantic waiting for that one honest man that can spark the revolution, or a revaluation of values that embraces the true spirit of utopia (freedom, sensual pleasure, more robust notion of happiness, embrace of difference, equality), even as they doubt his presence. One could argue that the spirit with which many youth embraced Obama's campaign and election signals the tenuous line between cynicism and hope and it is here where shows like DS/CR can play a role.

In fact Sloterdijk saw irony and a particular form of cynicism as embodying radical potential. He argues irony, rejection and mockery are potentially revolutionary forces that can undermine the various failed attempts at improving the human condition. To this end, he calls for a stance of irony toward the world, a radical laughter and satirical spirit that can rupture the society from the outside in. He then argues that the "critical addiction to making things better" should be abandoned, replaced by a focus on affective identification as a radical strategy for change. He wants to reactivate what he calls kynicism, the satirical tradition that focuses on finding ready answers rather than brooding over unsolvable, deeper questions. He believes attempts at maintaining Enlightenment rationality lead to inauthentic ways of being and acting that simply reinforce that which they hope to overcome.

Instead he wants, like Marcuse, to create a world where reason and emotions come together to create an empathetic communion with experience. He wants a world of sophistry, spontaneity and chaos, even as the entire project of society has been to limit these impulses. Jon Steward and Stephen Colbert seem to exist at least at the edges of this project, mocking politicians and the media from a safe distance without ever offering any alternative. In showing the absurdity of much of the political discourse today, they provide a space to enact broader critique for the mainstream, largely educated audiences that watch their show.

Langstraat (2002) on the other hand argues for the space between Enlightenment and cynicism, arguing that cynicism defines the contradictions between inauthenticity and the desire for authenticity and suspicion of Enlightenment and reason and the desire to finally realize them. At some level, I wonder if that lack of authenticity is at the heart of youth culture today. The constantly changing fashion and music trends, counter-cultural movements, internet culture and the like all seem intent on escaping the grasp of a consumer culture youth embrace and shun simultaneously. And the DS/CR fit well with this sensibility, critiquing all the inauthentic discourse from politicians and the media while using laughter to position themselves above it all; often by embracing a naivety they clearly critique.

I follow these thinkers in believing that there is a place for the cynic in contemporary politics, particularly as a source of immanent critique or perpetual deconstruction, a space to challenge and shock and to open the possibility for critical reflection and action. This is exactly what Stewart and Colbert do, holding everyone up to the microscope of truth and consistency. But I have serious reservations of its place as a radical stance in and of itself. The cynic described above tends to feed the sort of cynicism that has arguably plagued American society for too long (Bewes, 1997; Caldwell, 2006; Cappella, 1997; Chaloupka, 1999). They do check the cynicism of the elites and the failure of so many efforts at social transformation. And yet they simultaneously lack the components I believe are key to positive social transformation: hope and an affirmative politics that complements critique. Cynicism rejects the system tout court and offers no avenue to transcend that reality. It demands all of the individual and nothing of the community and is thus solitary, solipsistic and asocial. Satire, irony and perpetual critique are necessary, but I do not believe they are enough.

Interestingly, a noteworthy finding from Forbes last year showed that both the *Daily Show* and *Colbert Report* have aging audiences, with more over 50 tuning in and 14 percent and 15 percent declines in youth viewership, respectively. Could the two shows be the latest victim of the constant search for the cool? Most cool has a shelf life much shorter than the 11 years Stewart has been hosting *The Daily Show*, and one can see both a push toward more serious critique and a waning of the novelty of his approach and joie de vivre. If this is the case, one hopes others step in to continue the critique of the media and degraded political discourse — confronting the powerful with their own lies and deception. Until then, *The Daily Show* and *Colbert Report* remain at the forefront of a battle they refuse to openly engage.

Notes

1. Like many, I see neoliberalism as the dominant global paradigm today, founded as a project of market liberation, government retrenchment and dismantling of the social safety net.

Its defining principle is that the market has the power to efficiently and effectively mediate the production and allocation of economic and social goods from consumer products to governance to medical care, energy, retirement funding and education. Toward this end, it calls for privatization, market liberation (domestically and abroad), diminished government oversight, lower marginal personal and corporate taxation and, really, establishment of market ethics and rationality across economic, political and social institutions. (Giroux 2004; Macedo, Dendrinos, and Gounari 2003; Stiglitz 2002)

2. Here for example we find Levinas' incantation for a universal responsibility to the other (in a sort of Kantian idealist turn), without a firm explanation for this ethical responsibility or how to actualize it in concrete social relations (Levinas 1969). We find Foucault's argument for micro politics and Deleuze and Guattari's deterritorialized, rhizomatic and solitary structures of rebellion (Deleuze and Guattari 1987). And we find more recent manifestations of these arguments in Hardt and Negri, who bring together a multitude who can somehow assemble at some point to negate the emergent Empire (Hardt and Negri 2004).

References

Abcarian, R. 2006. "Narcissists in the Spotlight." Retrieved April 17, 2007 from www.dailytid ings.com/print_article.php?pagename=/2006/0916/stories/0916_bp_narcissism.php

Andrejevic, M. 2004. *Reality TV: The Work of Being Watched.* Lanham, MD: Rowman & Littlefield.

Bakhtin, M. M. 1982. *The Dialogical Imagination* (C. Emerson and M. Holquist, Trans.). Austin: University of Texas Press.

Baumgartner, J., and Morris, J. 2006. "The Daily Show Effect: Candidate Evaluations, Efficacy and American Youth." *American Politics Research.* 34.3: 341–367.

Bewes, T. 1997. *Cynicism and Postmodernity.* New York: Verso.

Caldwell, W. W. 2006. *Cynicism and the Evolution of the American Dream* (1st ed. ed.). Washington, D.C.: Potomac Books, Inc.

Callahan, D. 2004. *The Cheating Culture: Why More Americans Are Doing Wrong to Get Ahead.* Orlando, FL: Harcourt.

Cappella, J. N. 1997. *Spiral of Cynicism: The Press and the Public Good.* New York: Oxford University Press.

Center, P. R. 2007. *Public Knowledge of Current Affairs Little Changed by News and Information Revolutions*: Pew Research Center.

_____. 2008. *The Daily Show: Journalism, Satire of Just Laughs:* PewResearchCenter Publications.

Chaloupka, W. 1999. *Everybody Knows: Cynicism in America.* Minnesota: University of Minnesota Press.

Chomsky, N., and Herman, E. 2002. *Manufacturing Consent: The Political Economy of the Mass Media.* New York: Pantheon Books.

Couldry, N. 2006. "Reality TV, or the Secret Theatre of Neoliberalism." *Hermes* (37).

Deleuze, G., and Guattari, F. 1987. *A Thousand Plateaus: Capitalism and Schizophrenia.* Minneapolis, MN: University of Minnesota Press.

Faludi, S. 1999. *Stiffed: The Betrayal of the American Male.* New York: William Morrow & Company.

Farhi, P. 2008. "It's Funny How Funny Just the Facts Can Be: 'Daily Show' Staffer Mines News for Laughs," April 30. *The Washington Post.*

Fischman, W., Solomon, B., Greenspan, D., and Gardner, H. 2004. *Making Good: How Young People Cope with Moral Dilemmas at Work.* Cambridge: Harvard University Press.

Frank, T. 2004. *What's the Matter with Kansas?* New York: Metropolitan Books.

Galtung, J., and Vincent, R. 2003. *U.S. Glasnost: Political Themes in U.S. Media Discourse.* New Jersey: Hampton Press.

Giroux, H. 2003. *Public Spaces, Private Lives: Democracy Beyond 9/11*. Lanham, MY: Rowman & Littlefield.

_____. 2004. *The Terror of Neoliberalism: Authoritarianism and the Eclipse of Democracy*. London: Paradigm Publishers.

Goodman, B. (Writer). 2001. "Merchants of Cool [Television]," *Frontline*. United States: Public Broadcast Company.

Habermas, J. 1962. *The Structural Transformation of the Public Sphere: An Inquiry into a Category of Bourgeois Society*. Cambridge, MA: MIT Press.

Hardt, M., and Negri, A. 2004. *Multitude: War and Democracy in the Age of Empire*. New York: The Penguin Press.

Harvey, D. 1989. *The Condition of Postmodernity: An Enquiry into the Origins of Cultural Change*. Cambridge: Blackwell.

Hebdige, D. 1979. *Subculture: The Meaning of Style*. New York: Routledge.

Hollander, B. A. 2005. "Late-night Learning: Do Entertainment Programs Increase Political Campaign Knowledge for Young Viewers?" *Journal of Broadcasting & Electronic Media*. 49: 402–415.

Jameson, F. 1991. *Postmodernism or, the Cultural Logic of late Capitalism*. Durham, NC: Duke University Press.

Kellner, D. 2003. *Media Spectacle*. New York: Routledge.

_____. 2005. *Media Spectacle and the Crisis of Democracy: Terrorism, War, and Election Battles*. New York: Paradigm Publishers.

Langstraat, L. 2002. "The Point Is There Is No Point: Miasmic Cynicism and Cultural Studies Composition." *JAC: A Journal of Composition Theory*. 22.2: 293–325.

Levinas, E. 1969. *Totality and Infinity: An Essay on Exteriority* (A. Lingis, Trans.). Indiana: Duquesne University Press.

Long, B. 2004. "'Daily Show' Viewers Ace Political Quiz." Retrieved 2/10/2010.

Lyotard, J. F. 1974. "Capitalisme Energumene." *Critique, 306*.

Macedo, D., Dendrinos, B., and Gounari, P. 2003. *The Hegemony of English*. Boulder, CO.: Paradigm Publishers.

Marcuse, H. 1966. *Eros and Civilization: A Philosophical Inquiry into Freud*. Boston: Beacon Press.

McChesney, R. 2004. *The Problem of the Media: U.S. Communication Politics in the 21st Century*. New York: Monthly Review Press.

Mills, C. W. 1951. *White Collar*. Boston: Beacon Press.

Mui, Y. 2007. "As the Kids Go Buy; 61 Teens Descend on Tysons, and We're There to Watch," June 4. *Washington Post*, p. D1.

Mulvey, L. 1993. "Some Thoughts on Theories of Fetishism in the Context of Contemporary Culture." *October, 65* (Summer), 3–20.

Online News Audience Larger, More Diverse: News Audience Increasingly Politicized. 2004. Washington, DC.

Postman, N. 1985. *Amusing Ourselves to Death: Public Discourse in the Age of Show Business*. New York: Penguin Books.

Rideout, V., Foehr, U., and Roberts, D. 2010. *Generation M: Media in the Lives of 8- to 18-Year Olds*.

Sloterdijk, P. 1987. *Critique of Cynical Reason*. Minneapolis: University of Minnesota Press.

Stiglitz, J. 2002. *Globalization and Its Discontents*. New York: W.W. Norton & Company.

Tenore, M. J. 2009. "'Daily Show' Producers, Writers Say They're Serious About Media Criticism." *Poynter Online*.

Young, D. 2004. *Daily Show Viewers Knowledgeable About Presidential Campaign, National Annenberg Election Survey Shows*. Philadelphia, PA: Annenberg Public Policy Center.

Zizek, S. 1997. *The Sublime Object of Ideology*. New York: Verso Books.

Wise Fools

Jon Stewart and Stephen Colbert as Modern-Day Jesters in the American Court

JULIA R. FOX

While court jesters no longer exist, Jon Stewart and Stephen Colbert function in much the same way as court jesters in European and Asian monarchies once did. Like court jesters of old, Stewart and Colbert — politically marginalized with their "fake news" formats — criticize the ruling administration in a manner that is humorous and therefore non-threatening while also insightful and brutally honest. And just as the other court members could not violate social norms and similarly criticize their monarchs without harming their own social standing (and possibly even their physical well being), "real" journalists, bound by norms of objectivity, cannot risk their credibility and perhaps even their professional standing by similarly criticizing the White House. Freed from such conventions, Stewart and Colbert can be both scathing in their criticism of politicians and, at the same time, whimsical, if not downright sophomoric, in their critiques. Yet, just as jesters were often quite close to their monarchs, so, too, Stewart and Colbert have had the very same politicians they've lambasted appear as guests on their shows. In so doing, they link their audience with America's most powerful politicians as jesters served to link monarchs with their subjects. Silly and sophomoric though they may seem, Stewart and Colbert serve a critically important political function much the same as court jesters did in centuries past. In this essay, I will review the history and political role as well as the psychological and social functions of the court jester and place Stewart and Colbert firmly in that role in contemporary American politics.

To understand how Stewart and Colbert fit in today's political system requires not only contemporary social and political context but historical grounding as well, and for this it is important to consider the role of court jesters, particularly the wise fools amongst their ranks. While jesters are most often thought of as part of European courts of the Middle Ages, they were widespread figures throughout Asia and Africa as well, and over a much longer period of time (Otto 2001; Willeford 1969). The first known jester was Danga, either a pygmy or dwarf jester who resided in the court of Pharaoh Pepi (Otto 2001; Willeford 1969). The earliest recorded references to court fools date back to the 12th century (Welsford 1935/1968), and the first court fool in England to be officially recorded as having the title of jester was James Lockwood, later known simply as Lockye, in Nottingham in 1548 (Southworth 1998). Otto (2001) documents jesters spanning more than 2500 years of history, from 2325 B.C. to as recently as 1896, in such diverse places as England, Scotland, France, Germany, Italy, Spain, Holland, Ireland, Sweden, Austria, Hungary, Russia, Bavaria, Bohemia, China, Persia, Turkey, India, Egypt, Uganda, Constantinople, Baghdad, and Polynesia. Despite this diverse range of historical eras and locales, Otto (2001, xvi, xvii) argues the court jester was "a universal character, more or less interchangeable regardless of the time or the culture in which he happens to cavort — the same techniques, the same functions, the same license" and further argues that there has been "a deep and widespread social need" for jesters throughout history.

The court jester belongs to a larger and even more diverse group of fools (Billington 1984; Willeford 1969). Fool figures have been prominent throughout history. The diversity of real-world fools includes not only court jesters of European and Asian monarchies but also Zuni and Navajo ritual clown dancers; revelers from the Medieval Feast of Fools, itself a vestige of the ancient Roman saturnalia; and even, more recently, the Marx Brothers, Charlie Chaplin, and Buster Keaton (Willeford 1969). Fools have appeared in a variety of media over the years including the fool literature of the Middle Ages and the Renaissance, Skakespearean dramas, circus and vaudeville skits, slapstick films, paintings, cartoons, and playing cards (Willeford 1969). Despite the superficial differences among the various fool types, there remain a number of common elements. Most notably, all draw our attention to the folly of a situation, whether it be a scene in a play or film, a skit in a circus or vaudeville act, or the real-world drama that unfolds daily on the political stage. Because "folly is one of the supreme facts about human nature, perhaps even about the world," (Willeford 1969, xv), these fools in their various forms have remained relevant throughout the course of human history.

Stewart and Colbert are merely the latest incarnations of a character that is not bound by time but is part of the very fabric of the human experience, embodying a fundamentally human response to our social and political environments. Stewart himself acknowledged as much on his show, when he noted,

"Comedians do social commentary through comedy. That's how it's worked for thousands of years.... I'm just doing what idiots like me have done for thousands of years" (Stewart, April 20, 2010). As he has existed throughout history so, too, will the fool presumably continue to adopt new forms in the future. That he should now appear in mock newscasts on television should come as no surprise, as television is the dominant medium of our time and the particulars of a fool's performance are shaped by the shared values, culture, and experiences of his contemporary audience (Willeford 1969). And even these most recent incarnations of the fool in Stewart's and Colbert's on-air personalities have historical precedent in using a news format. By the late 1600s, traveling fools, often referred to as Merry Andrews or Jack Puddings, were the most popular entertainment at country fairs (Billington 1984). "Satire was the entertainment offered and, in a country where news outside the cities was scarce, it would not be surprising if satirical newsvendors and their tumblers were received kindly," (Billington 1984, 59). So it appears even their fake news formats have deep roots going back well beyond earlier instantiations on broadcast television (e.g. *Saturday Night Live*'s Weekend Update segment), back in fact more than three hundred years to the farcical newsvendors of the 17th century English country fairs.

In addition to having a similar format, the fake news presentations of then and now aimed their satirical barbs at similar targets, as the traveling fools' satire often targeted those with political power and authority (Billington 1984). For example, one fool accompanying a mountebank — a traveling, often quack, doctor — declared the doctor had cured "twelve Foreign Ministers of State of those twin plagues, Bribery and infidelity; six kings of a Tyrannical fever; the whole conclave of Cardinals of Pride, Laziness, and Hypocrisy; and the present Pope of the Antichristian Evil" (Billington 1984, 62). And just as Stewart and Colbert are immensely popular with today's viewing audience so, too, the traveling fools were more successful than other, more serious strolling actors of their time (Billington 1984). Further, they are also similarly politically motivated; the 17th century traveling fools tapped into Elizabethan disillusionment with the government and the church (Billington 1984), just as today Stewart's and Colbert's material taps into contemporary disillusionment with politicians and others in positions of authority (e.g. those in charge of the country's financial institutions).

In reviewing the history of court jesters and fools, it is important to distinguish between a fool who is lacking sense and one who feigns folly for entertainment's sake. This distinction goes back to Elizabethan England, with the former being known as naturals and the latter as artificial fools (Willeford 1969). Some of the natural fools may have been coerced into service (Billington 1984), sometimes under a legal process known as "begging for a fool" in which a jury could find a man to be purus idiota and he would become the property of the crown (Billington 1984; Willeford 1969). Other presumed natural fools turned out to be not as witless as originally thought. Will Somers of Henry VIII's court and, later in the 16th century, Richard Tarlton, both from Shropshire, were discovered in their country abodes but willingly joined the court as a way to better themselves and their fellow townsmen, for the fool was not only well compensated for his antics but also often had the ear of the king and could get him to grant people special favors (Billington 1984; Willeford 1969).

At the opposite end of the spectrum, artificial fools were not only *not* lacking in reason, they were often among the most educated men in the country (Billington 1984). For instance, George Buchanan, boyhood tutor and later counselor to James VI of Scotland, a writer and poet who also tutored and translated for Mary Queen of Scots, was best known as James' jester (Billington 1984; Otto 2001); John Haywood was a jester-scholar in Henry VIII's court; John Scogin, in Edward IV's court, studied at Oxford; and John Skelton, also Oxford and Cambridge educated, tutored young Henry VIII before becoming a jester (Otto 2001). Skelton was known not only for his sharp satire, as might be expected of one so well educated, but also for his buffoonery (Otto 2001). In Germany, Solomon Jacob Morgenstern, dressed in motley clothes, even held a scholarly debate on folly in which all professors were summoned by royal command to take part (Welsford 1935/1968). Elizabethan fool William Kemp authored two books—*A knack to know a Knave* and *Kemps Nine Daies Wonder;* the latter detailed his nine-day journey dancing from London to Norwich, a public relations tour done in 1599 to repair his reputation after being dismissed from a dramatic company (Billington 1984). By then, jesters like Kemp and Richard Tarlton were also appearing on the public stage as well as entertaining in the royal court (Billington 1984). Tarlton's solo improvisational performances at the end of the plays became the main draw at the theater (Billington 1984). In fact, Tarlton is considered "the first court fool to achieve national celebrity for his genius as a comedian" (Southworth 1998, 114). Other popular London theaters in the early 1600s also began employing professional fools who used satire to skewer those in high society and positions of authority (Billington 1984).

Clearly, Stewart and Colbert belong to the artificial fools, where they are in elite company with some of the most famous court jesters. Those pretending to be fools "stand somewhere between the reality, possibly horrible, of idiocy or madness, and its character as a show, something to be entertained by and, if taken seriously, loved rather than despised" (Willeford 1969, 10). For some, Stewart and Colbert are merely entertaining. Yet, for others, they are taken seriously, and loved, in Stewart's case as a legitimate source of news; indeed, a sizable portion of young voters 18–30 rely on *The Daily Show* as their primary source of presidential campaign information (Pew Research Center 2004). This legitimacy is not without merit — Stewart has a long-established precedent of conducting mostly-serious interviews with politicians appearing on his show, and in one case Democratic presidential hopeful John Edwards actually used *The Daily Show* as a platform to announce his candidacy for president of the United States.

In fact, much has been made recently of how Stewart and Colbert are the new faces of television news — a 2006 *Rolling Stone* magazine cover article referred to them as America's anchors, with writer Maureen Dowd (2006) arguing, "While real network news withers, Stewart's show has become the hot destination for anyone who wants to sell books or seem hip, from presidential candidates to military dictators.... They're the Cronkite and Murrow of an ironic millennium" (Dowd 2006, 54).

Yet, while Colbert and Stewart may be as influential, if not more so, than their traditional news counterparts, they, like the jesters of the royal courts, have no official status in the political system (Southworth 1998; Welsford 1935/1968; Willeford 1969), including the fourth estate, as they were quick to point out to Maureen Dowd in her interview with them for *Rolling Stone* magazine:

> DOWD: When you came to the *Times*, Jon, you said the lesson of the Oscars and the White House Correspondents dinner was that you guys should not be talking to "the Establishment."
>
> STEWART: It's not that we shouldn't be talking. It's that we shouldn't care.
>
> COLBERT: We can't care.
>
> STEWART: What people in Washington don't understand is that we're not running for re-election. We don't have to parse every word for fear that it appears in our opponent's commercial and suddenly renders us impotent.
>
> COLBERT: We claim no respectability. There's no status I would not surrender for a joke. So we don't have to defend anything [Dowd 2006, 58].

Similarly, earlier in the interview Colbert noted, "I have no credibility to lose" (Dowd 2006, 56).

This unique social position of the fool is at once outside of society, as Stewart and Colbert alluded to in their response to Dowd, and also bound by social norms and mores, a "paradoxical position of virtual outlawry combined with utter dependence on the support of the social group to which he belongs" (Welsford 1935/1968, 55). Colbert and Stewart are clearly outlaws from the traditional fourth estate of mainstream news media, yet they depend upon that system for their very existence, as all of their humor stems from either the folly of the political world or the journalists who cover it. In addition to this dependence on "the Establishment," as Maureen Dowd called it, Willeford (1969) notes that fools often have strong connections to the very social and cultural boundaries they are thought to transgress. Many, such as Saxon King Edmund Ironside's jester, Rahere, and Henry I's 12th-century court jester, had great favor and independence (Billington 1984). Similarly, Stewart and Colbert have strong connections within our cultural and social boundaries with the political elite, who appear on their shows and with whom they rub elbows at events such as the White House Correspondents Dinner. Yet, Stewart and Colbert clearly transgress these boundaries in their ridicule and sophomoric acts as they dwell amongst the common folk of their live studio audiences, just as many jesters stayed connected with the common folk in their countries (2001).

Putting them further outside of European Christian society, some court jesters — often the highly educated ones — were Jewish. The Russian Czar Peter the Great's jester, La Costa, was a Portuguese Jew who was extremely knowledgeable and spoke several languages (Otto 2001). There was also a Hasidic Jewish fool named Motke, and the most famous Spanish jester, Zuniga, was a Jewish convert who called himself the Duke of Jerusalem (Otto 2001). Although Stewart, who often references his Jewish heritage on his program, has not given himself any such titles, he does go by the stage name of Jon Stewart, a derivative of his given name Jonathan Stuart Leibowitz. As his production partner, Ben Karlin, noted in the *Rolling Stone* article, "Jon is driven by the forces of guilt and shame and fear of being on the outside that gives Jews their comic angst" (Dowd 2006, 56).

Just as the jester's harlequin costume suggests both order in its geometric pattern and chaos in its crazy-quilt design, for the fool there is a delicate balancing act of being in between the boundaries of the ordered social world and chaos (Welsford 1935/1968; Willeford 1969). Neither Colbert nor Stewart are physically deformed, as fools often were (Welsford 1935/1968; Willeford 1969), nor are they motley in appearance; yet, in their folly they, too, draw our attention to the often fine line between social order and chaos. When Maureen Dowd remarked there were so many levels to Colbert's show it sometimes made her head hurt, Colbert replied, "Then we've succeeded. We want people to be in pain and confused" (Dowd 2006, 56). In her interview with Stewart and Colbert, Dowd's first question hinted at this delicate balancing act the two perform nightly between order and chaos, when she asked:

A fake news show, "The Daily Show," spawned a fake commentator, Colbert, who makes his own fake reality defending the fake reality of a real president, and has government officials on who know the joke but are still willing to be mocked by someone fake. Your shows are like mirrors within mirrors, using a cycle of fakery to get to the truth. You've tapped into a sense in society that nothing, from reality shows to Bushworld, is real anymore. Do you guys ever get confused by your hall of mirrors?

Here, Dowd's analogy of mirrors is particularly interesting, as the fool is often depicted holding a mirror; the fool's image in the king's reflection serves as a reminder of the king's flaws and foibles (Southworth 1998; Willeford 1969). Further, the images in the mirrors the fools hold are often reversed, suggesting the farcical view of the world that jesters uniquely provide (Willeford 1969).

These reversed images of our world reflected through the fool's mirror suggest the fool's unique ability to transcend the border between chaos and order, paradoxically seeming to belong to neither one nor the other yet at the same time embodying the confusion between them as if they were one and the same. Similarly, in responding to Dowd's question as to whether their humor ever goes too far, Stewart's response suggests that nothing he could say or do could ever be more chaotic than the reality of which he jests:

> I don't understand how anyone can consider jokes about this stuff worse than the reality of it. We're not out to provoke. We're not out to shock. There is no joy in stepping over a line. I don't think there's any way to possibly offend in a comedic sense when reality has such a desperate foundation to it [Dowd 2006, 56].

To truly understand this paradox the fool poses regarding order and chaos is to understand the nature of folly itself, which Erasmus suggested in the 16th century was a basic part of human nature (Willeford 1969). Madness as a permanent condition is certainly undesirable, but momentary flights of folly can be viewed as actual moments of clarity that afford "a transformation of consciousness that would allow us to see things more truly" (Willeford 1969, 25). While most of us are not fools, we recognize this transformative characteristic in fool figures, and in so doing also achieve the same transformation of consciousness ourselves. To understand this symbolism of the fool requires "empathic imagination" as well as "intellectual judgment" (Willeford 1969, xviii). Thus, the audiences of Stewart and Colbert must have the requisite knowledge of civics and current events to truly appreciate the underlying folly of the political situations that they skewer. If indeed, as Dowd suggests, Stewart and Colbert are the Cronkite and Murrow of an ironic millennium, then they are also the Cronkite and Murrow of an ironic generation, an audience that must still be embedded in the political system in order to appreciate their humor and at least understand if no longer adhere to the role of traditional journalists in order to fully appreciate the parody of Stewart and Colbert.

Along with their requisite sophisticated irony, as with jester John Skelton, known for his sharp wit but also his buffoonery, there is a simplistic, often outlandish side to Stewart's and Colbert's fooling as well, often in the form of silly jokes and sight gags. Stewart at times employs physical comedy that includes exaggerated facial expressions, and he has been known to engage in slapstick antics such as taking a sip of water and spitting it out upon hearing an outrageous soundbite from a politician. In one instance, Stewart carried this gag to an extreme, spitting out first water, then cereal, and then rainbow-colored candies as he heard the name Dick Sweat, then gave "kudos" to Mr. Sweat for "putting up with this kind of juvenile bullshit" (Stewart, February 15, 2010).

But the fool's simple exterior belies his complex yet critically important role in the political system, as "the surface of folly sometimes breaks open to reveal surprising depths, and these are as much a part of what the fool finally is as are his shallowness and triviality" (Willeford 1969, xxi). In their costumed revelry, fools can be both "meaningless and meaningful, worthless and valuable" (Willeford 1969, xx). Stewart and Colbert, while "costumed" in the traditional suit of a television news anchor, often employ meaningless sophomoric antics, such as spitting our food and drink on set, that have no real worth compared to traditional news coverage of events. Yet, Stewart, at least, was found in a content analysis by this author and her colleagues to be just as substantive as the network newscasts in his coverage of the 2004 presidential campaign (Fox, Koloen, and Sahin 2007).

Furthermore, Stewart often goes beyond what real newscasters, who are bound by professional norms and routines to remain neutral in their coverage (Borden and Tew 2007; Fox and Park 2006), can or will do. In responding to criticism leveled on Fox News' *The O'Reilly Factor* the previous evening, by Bernie Goldberg, that Stewart had crossed the line from comedy to social commentary, Stewart replied, "You can't criticize me for not being fair and balanced — that's your slogan, which, by the way, you never follow" (Stewart, April 20, 2010). Stewart's ability to go further than traditional journalists in exposing the folly of political events and actors makes his commentary *more* meaningful and valuable than his traditional news counterparts. Even in a rare instance when Stewart noted the mainstream media correctly reported President Obama's reversal of position from candidate Obama's statement on the campaign trail that health care reform compromise sessions would be broadcast on C-SPAN, his remarks were truly a back-handed compliment, "You make it so hard for me when you do your job" (Stewart, January 7, 2010).

More typically, it is Stewart's show that contrasts politicians' statements with contradictory remarks they previously made. Presumably, broadcast and cable news networks have larger budgets and more personnel specifically trained to be journalists, and thus should have the resources and the where-withal to be both aware of the politician's reversal of position and able to dig through previous footage to find and air the conflicting sound bite. Yet, it is Stewart and his smaller staff of humor writers who consistently call our atten-tion to the hypocrisy of our political leaders by contrasting soundbites that expose their flip-flops on political positions, pointing both to the folly and the truth of the situation. When asked at a *New York Times* lunch how he is able to continually do this, he responded, "A clerk and a video machine" (Dowd 2006, 54), clearly implying that the traditional news media could cer-tainly do the same on a more regular basis. In his relentless critiques of sup-posedly serious journalists, Stewart exposes not only the folly of politicians but also members of the fourth estate, themselves important actors on the political stage who should be acting as watchdogs on behalf of the citizenry.

As noted, Stewart is mainly serious while interviewing political guests on his show, although he does intersperse a few jokes here and there. For example, when he interviewed Congressman Anthony Weiner about a pro-posed medicare buy-in, Stewart noted that Senator John McCain had said he was against it because Weiner was for it. "My question for you," Stewart asked Weiner, "is — is he a dick?" (Stewart, February 15, 2010).

Colbert, on the other hand, remains inane throughout his political inter-views. Yet, through the surface of his folly there is depth as well. For example, as part of an ongoing series in which he interviews members of Congress in their offices, Colbert interviewed Mike Quigley, the congressman from the "fightin'" 5th district of Illinois, noting that Dan Rostenkowski, who went to prison, and Rod Blagojevitch, who was impeached as governor of Illinois, both held that seat and asking the congressman if he'd decided which prison he wants to go to (Colbert, February 12, 2010). While the joke itself may be inconsequential, it is a reminder of the political corruption for which the state of Illinois, and its 5th congressional district in particular, are infamous, allow-ing us, as we view Colbert's performance, a moment of folly in which to reflect on the politics of that state. In his in-studio interviews, Colbert ego-tistically runs in a victorious fashion from his anchor desk to join his guest, already on stage and seated waiting for Colbert, who waves to his audience and soaks in their applause as he runs past — as if Colbert and, by extension, the folly which he will expose in his interview, and not the guest are the real focus of attention. Even President Obama's press secretary, Robert Gibbs, has joked that the president might appear on *The Daily Show*, but not Colbert, as he has yet to see a politician best Colbert in an interview (Colbert, March 1, 2010). Similarly, and perhaps appropriately given the French pronunciation of Colbert's name, the last officially recognized court fool in France, l'Angely, was known to strike fear in the hearts even of scholars who dined at court, who refrained from engaging in conversation with him lest they be made to look like fools in front of the king (Welsford 1935/1968).

Just as anyone at court was fair game for court jesters, no political player is safe from skewering by Stewart or Colbert. During the Bush administration, Republicans more often than not bore the brunt of Stewart's sarcasm. But with the Democrats in charge he pokes fun at their leaders, too. For example, MSNBC's *Morning Joe* news program showed a clip from *The Daily Show* of Stewart criticizing House Speaker Nancy Pelosi (Licht, March 3, 2010). Before going to break, MSNBC showed the clip of Stewart criticizing Pelosi for saying previously that there would be high moral and ethical standards in the house, then saying in a more recent soundbite that Congressman Charles Rangel did not hurt the country when he violated the House ethics rules. The clip then showed Stewart at the anchor desk asking a picture of Pelosi, "Does botox also paralyze your moral compass?" When *Morning Joe* returned from commercial break, Scarborough noted that Stewart was going after Democrats now that they're in charge.

Like other entertainers at court, many court jesters were also musicians, actors, and/or singers. But, they were unique among the entertainers in the court not just for their humor but also in the privileges afforded them, particularly the license to speak freely (Otto 2001). "It is the right to present indirect and even forthright mockery of universal human foibles and more precisely aimed critical advice, sharp edges softened with colorful and witty wrapping," (Otto 2001, 100). Although jesters were sometimes beaten, banished, or even beheaded for their criticisms, most often their wit (or lack thereof, in the case of natural fools) allowed them to say what no one else in the court dared (Otto 2001). Both Chinese as well as European jesters had the privilege of speaking without offense, provided they spoke in jokes or songs (Otto 2001). Seventeenth century poet and jester Friedrich Taubmann, for example, used humor to rebuke Duke Friedrich Wilhelm of Weimer into acting more humanely and to expose corruption, and in China, jester Baldy Chunyu used a riddle to let the king know that he was forsaking his duties for drinking and womanizing. Similarly, court jester Tom Killigrew drew Charles II's attention to his negligence of duties in pursuing pleasures of the flesh by walking in on Charles during a night of carousing; according to Otto's (2001, 121) account of the incident, Charles remarked, "'Now we shall hear of our faults.' But Killigrew denied him the satisfaction, 'No, faith! I don't care to trouble myself with that which all the town talks of.'"

It was their foolishness that gave these jesters license to speak freely — and truthfully — to the king when others in court dared not. The word jest, with its roots in the French geste (exploits), now refers to brief witticisms but previously referred to a mocking tale and before that specifically a mock heroic tale which considers the relationship between the fool and the hero/king, with the fool being a foil to the latter (Willeford 1969). Toward the end of the Middle Ages and the beginning of the Renaissance, fools were often depicted as arguing with a king (Gifford 1979). In reality, the jester's and the king's exchanges were mostly in good fun, as in the verse-capping in which Henry VIII and Will Somers would often engage. Otto (2001, 16) details one example where Henry began, "'The bud is spread, the Rose is red, the leafe is green,' which Somers paries with 'A wench 'tis sed, was found in your bed, besides/the Queene."

Most of Stewart's and Colbert's criticisms and good-natured ribbings of presidents are leveled from their anchors desks, and not actually in the presence of the commander in chief. However, at the White House Correspondents dinner, Colbert lambasted fellow attendee President Bush in person in front of the Washington press corps, not unlike a jester jokingly ridiculing the king in the presence of the rest of the court. In the *Rolling Stone* interview, Maureen Dowd asked Colbert if he thought the president understood the irony:

> COLBERT: We had a very nice conversation beforehand about that subject, actually, I said how nice it is that I, who am satirical and whose comedy can be critical of the administration, get to do this.
>
> DOWD: Did he talk to you after?
>
> COLBERT: He said, "Well done."
>
> STEWART: As in, how he would like to cook Stephen's hide on the barbeque [Dowd 2006, 58].

This exchange touches upon the complex relationship between court jesters and kings of the Middle Ages and Renaissance that is mirrored today in the relationships between Colbert, Stewart, and the United States presidents. Because the king condoned the jester's antics, they were seen as an extension of the king's will and, therefore, his power, and thus even the fool's jokes at the king's expense were tolerated (Willeford 1969). For example, at a bull fight in 1638, the jester to King Philip IV sat at the foot of the throne wearing the crown and holding the king's scepter (Otto 2001). On one level, this might have suggested that the king was a fool. But, on another level, it reinforces the sovereignty of the king in permitting his jester to do this. "Allowing his kingly dignity to be mocked in a sense reinforced that dignity" (Otto 2001, 51). That such joking at the expense of the king was "allowed and even encouraged implies that the social institutions and the persons in power are strong enough to tolerate it; thus it serves the interests of authority and of social cohesion" (Willeford 1969, 155). Because the king allowed the jester to mock him, the mockery did not undermine but actually reinforced the king's authority, just as Stewart's and Colbert's mockery reinforces the power of our democracy to allow and even welcome such criticism. Any threats were further diminished due to the playful nature of the jester's jokes and antics (Willeford 1969), just as Stewart's and Colbert's humor diminishes the threat their criticisms might otherwise pose to undermine our political system..

However, as Willeford (1969) also noted, this playful joking also expressed the power of the fool in being able to make fun of the king. In one extreme instance, the power of the fool and the king were literally reversed when George Buchanan, in a ploy to get James VI of Scotland to carefully read documents before signing them, was able to get the king to carelessly sign a document transferring regal authority to Buchanan for 15 days. Stewart's and Colbert's ultimate power may not be in calling into question our political and media elites for their various blunders, but in reconfirming the strength of the core values on which our political system is based. In their ability to do so, both Stewart, author of a book titled *AMERICA (THE BOOK): A Citizen's Guide to Democracy Inaction*, and Colbert, author of *I Am America and So Can You*, forge a deeper connection beyond any particular administration in power to the U.S. political system itself. While their at times chaotic performances expose many flaws in our political system, their fake news shows are presented within the constraints of our ordered society — serving both to point out the folly and failings within our system while also maintaining the order of that very system in exercising the freedom that allows such criticism without sanction.

The Latin derivation of fool from follis is a wind bag, suggesting that fools words are "only air, empty of meaning" (Willeford 1969, 10). This suggests a lack of any real power or influence to what they say, but it also gives license to fools to speak harsh truths that serious speakers often cannot or will not speak. While traditional journalists are bound by professional norms and practices to carefully measure their words and consider the power and amplification that the traditional news anchor desk gives them, foolish news anchors like Stewart and Colbert are free to say whatever they please. Thus the words of fools — harsh truths tempered with humor — can have significance, sometimes even more so than more serious or measured responses. Yet, as Willeford (1969) warns, the paradox of the wise fool should not by oversimplified in an abstraction that loses an understanding of the fool himself, and, more importantly, what he means to us. The fool's psychological function is the embodiment of folly itself as a uniquely and universally human way of adapting to the social world (Willeford 1969). Our responses to fools tap into our own understanding of the world, with subsequent social implications as well. We are not simply "getting" Stewart's and Colbert's jokes as both meaningless and meaningful but are also getting in touch with our own knowledge and experiences of folly in the political world.

Although the court jester as he was once known no longer exists, the need for him may be greater now than ever. As Otto (2001, 258) noted, "Close to those at the apex of power, he could temper extremes of mood and rein in excessive power." In the deeply divisive political climate of 21st century America, we need our modern-day court jesters. Otherwise, "Who is to laugh at us and remind us of mortal inadequacy? Who is to present our humanists and dictators with cap and bells?" (Welsford 1935/1968, 194). Who, indeed?

References

Billington, S. 1984. *A Social History of the Fool*. NY: St. Martin's Press.

Borden, S. L., and Tew, C. 2007. "The Role of Journalist and the Performance of Journalism: Ethical Lessons from 'Fake' News (Seriously)." *Journal of Mass Media Ethics*. 22.4: 300–314.

Colbert, S. (Executive Producer). 2010, February 12. *The Colbert Report* [Television broadcast]. New York: Comedy Central.

_____. (Executive Producer). 2010, March 1. *The Colbert Report* [Television broadcast]. New York: Comedy Central.

Dowd, M. 2006. "America's Anchors." *Rolling Stone*. November 16. Issue # 1013, 52–58, 139.

Fox, J. R., Koloen, G., and Sahin, V. 2007. "No Joke: A Comparison of Substance in *The Daily Show with Jon Stewart* and Broadcast Network Television Coverage of the 2004 Presidential Election Campaign." *Journal of Broadcasting & Electronic Media*. 51.2: 213–227.

Fox, J. R., and Park B. 2006. "The 'I' of Embedded Reporting: An Analysis of CNN Coverage of the Shock and Awe Campaign." *Journal of Broadcasting & Electronic Media*. 50.1: 36–51.

Gifford, D. J. 1979. "Iconographical Notes Towards a Definition of the Medieval Fool." In *The Fool and the Trickster*, ed. P. Williams. Cambridge: D. S. Brewer Ltd.

Licht, C. (Executive Producer). 2010, March 3. *Morning Joe* [Television broadcast]. New York: MSNBC.

Otto, B. 2001. *Fools Are Everywhere: The Court Jester Around the World*. Chicago: The University of Chicago Press.

Pew Research Center for the People & the Press. 2004, January 11. *Cable and Internet Loom Large in Fragmented Political Universe: Perceptions of Partisan Bias Seen as Growing*. Washington, DC.

Southworth, J. 1998. *Fools and Jesters at the English Court*. Thrupp: Sutton Publishing Ltd.

Stewart, J. (Executive Producer). 2010, January 7. *The Daily Show* [Television broadcast]. New York: Comedy Central.

_____. (Executive Producer). 2010, February 15. *The Daily Show* [Television broadcast]. New York: Comedy Central.

_____. (Executive Producer). 2010, April 20. *The Daily Show* [Television broadcast]. New York: Comedy Central.

Weslford, E. 1968. *The Fool: His Social and Literary History*. Great Britain: Latimer Trend & Co Ltd Whitstable. (First printed 1935 London: Faber and Faber Limited).

Willeford, W. 1969. *The Fool and His Scepter: A Study in Clowns and Jesters and Their Audience*. Evanston, IL: Northwestern University Press.

I Am the Mainstream Media
(and So Can You!)

ROBERT T. TALLY, JR.

On its February 10, 2010 broadcast, *The Daily Show* with Jon Stewart opened with a satirical monologue in which Stewart explored the possible slogans that a "fake news" program on the Comedy Central television network might use in covering the day's leading story, a massive snowstorm blanketing the eastern seaboard. Employing what should be recognized as nonsense words appropriate to such a venue (and, by contrast, words that should be entirely inappropriate for "real news" programs), Stewart begins to introduce the terms, *Snowmageddon*, *Snowpocalypse*, and eventually *Snowtorious B.I.G.*, only to be cut off each time by clips of other mainstream network news shows — on CNN, NBC, and MSNBC — using those very words. A mock-chagrined Stewart bemoans the fact that mainstream news channels (the "big boys"), with their greater financial and meteorological resources, have usurped what should have been the birthright of comedy writers on *The Daily Show*.

The humor in this bit, and similar bits on almost every other episode of the program, derives from the powerful critique of the mainstream media: What is funny about the piece is not *The Daily Show*'s own writing or in comedian Jon Stewart's performance (although these certainly enhance the experience), but rather that the so-called "real news" programs are so ridiculous. To use phrases like *Snowmageddon* or *Snowpocalypse* in a serious news broadcast, with real news to cover, should be viewed as unprofessional, if not shameful. But, far from it, such silliness is now the actual stuff of mainstream television news. Stewart's fake news is funny *because* of its trenchant exposure of the silliness of real news. As Jeffrey Jones has put it, "As a parody of television news shows, it skewers the absurdity and contradictions that pass for 'news'" (2005, 54). The key point is not that satirical, fake news is taken as

149

seriously as real news (although hard evidence, as well as hue and cry, suggest it is [see Fox et al. 2007; Cave 2004]), but that all "news" has become transformed into entertainment-television that no longer bears much, if any, relation to the "real." The social significance of fake news programs like *The Daily Show* and *The Colbert Report* is disclosed in their assiduous critique, not of the news itself— that is, the underlying reality or story (in the example above, the February snowstorm)— but of the purported agents of journalistic information-dissemination: the news programs themselves. From the fake news' critique of the real news, one recognizes the hyperreality of the news more generally.

The Hyperreality of Fake News

One can see this clearly in the very form of both Comedy Central programs, produced in mockery of real news, yet they are absolutely faithful replicas of news shows like those on CNN and FOX News. The satirical copy is nevertheless absolutely authentic. In *Travels in Hyperreality*, Umberto Eco writes that America is "a country obsessed with realism, where, if a reconstruction is to be credible, it must be absolutely iconic, a perfect likeness, a 'real' copy of the reality being represented" (Eco 1986, 4). This functions equally well for satirical or for more reverent simulations, illustrating Eco's (and Jean Baudrillard's) notion of *hyperreality*, in which the simulacrum supplants the real by acquiring a kind of experiential authenticity. In the hyperreal, the "authentic fake" takes on a reality far more salient than the reality itself, all the more so for being fake. In a ruse of history, perhaps, the idea that fake news, *by being fake*, is actually more real than real news (at least, as it appears on television) is not only possible, but now seems likely.

The Daily Show and *The Colbert Report* seem humorously apt examples of the hyperreality of fake news, but part of their aptness lies in the effectiveness of their critical program. Satire in the form of news is not new, but Comedy Central's duo have become a much more socially significant force, not just poking fun at figures *in* the news, but launching a full-scale attack on the media and the messages simultaneously. Earlier examples of "fake news" include Monte Python's frequent use of the format, along with *Saturday Night Live*'s "Weekend Update," and Canada's *This Hour Has 22 Minutes*, just to name a few. However, in most cases, these programs have presented themselves in the formal clothing of a news show in order to engage in topical humor about items or figures in the news (e.g., politicians, celebrities, events). But this critique of the newsmakers did not usually include a critique of the news-reporters, except in rare cases or perhaps by implication. *The Daily Show* and *The Colbert Report*, by contrast, explicitly make the critique of the mainstream media their principal aim; in Colbert's case, this satire of the mainstream media reaches its apotheosis.

A good demonstration of the difference between satire using the fake news format and the more thoroughgoing social critique of the media in these two fake news programs might be seen in the remarkable transformation of *The Daily Show* after its change of hosts. Whereas Craig Kilbourn's *Daily Show* was a lighthearted spoof, mainly of local television news shows, which added political humor and sidebar "on location" reports of various characters and oddities, Jon Stewart's is a national and international force, shaping the debates while participating in and poking fun at them, and above all displaying a critical disdain for the very "real" television journalists covering the stories for the cable and broadcast news networks. With Stewart, *The Daily Show* has become a better comedy by also becoming a more *real* fake news show — in the sense that it has significant effects on the so-called "real world." *The Colbert Report* goes even further, as it allows Stephen Colbert to adopt the persona of a right-wing pundit, thereby dropping any pretense to objective television journalism, which in turn makes possible an even more savage critique of politics and the media. In Colbert's monologues, even the spoken critique carries with it a further critique: a metacritique or hypercritique, whose on-screen spirit is made manifest in the marginal gloss accompanying Colbert's "The Word" segment. The nonsense of Colbert's book-title, *I Am America (and So Can You!)* embodies the greater sense of immanent social critique, precisely because Colbert can attack the very thing he purports to be, which is a hyperreal personage: the fake newsman who is more real than the supposedly mainstream journalists.

The hyperreality of these fake news programs is not based on the much vaunted or much maligned, and largely dubious, proposition that some people "get their news" from Stewart or Colbert. Rather, what is hyperreal about the shows is that they dramatically enact the underlying critique of the media, by showing that the mainstream news is altogether artificial, constructed according to formulae and processes easily decoded by comedy writers and attentive viewers. *The Daily Show* and *The Colbert Report* shape the social field even as they lampoon it. Above all, these programs impress upon the viewers the profound sense that the mainstream media's real news is not much more real than its satirical or parodic copies. Hence, the distinction between the real and the fake begins to recede, and the television-information nexus reveals itself to be little more than a critical apprehension of various sorts of simulations — some in the form of breathless coverage of a "balloon boy hoax" on CNN, others in the form of mock-breathless accounts of "the threat of global darkening" on *The Daily Show*. This is not so much *the desert of the real*, in Baudrillard's infamous phrase (1994, 1), as *the plenum of the fake*.

In suggesting that television news, whether understood as fake or real, is actually hyperreal, I do not mean to say that it comports directly with the semiological meaning of the term. However, I do argue that certain aspects of the notion of hyperreality are revealing in the context of the social significance of fake news. In his notorious essay, "The Precession of Simulacra," Baudrillard delineates the process by which the representation of reality withers away in what Guy Debord had called the "society of the spectacle." Baudrillard's examination of the *image* (that is, the purported representation of reality) offers a view of the image produced by and in the news as well. Baudrillard lists and interprets "the successive phases of the image" as follows:

> it is the reflection of a profound reality;
> it masks and denatures a profound reality;
> it masks the absence of a profound reality;
> it has no relation to any reality whatsoever: it is its own pure simulacrum.
>
> In the first case, the image is a *good* appearance — representation is of a sacramental order. In the second, it is an evil appearance — it is of the order of maleficence. In the third, it plays at being an appearance — it is of the order of sorcery. In the fourth, it is no longer of the order of appearances, but of simulation [Baudrillard 1994, 6].

In the context of fake news and the social significance thereof, one could add that one of the key things that *The Daily Show* with Jon Stewart and *The Colbert Report* do, on an almost nightly basis, is guide their viewers through just this process, substituting the mainstream media's news imagery for Baudrillard's image.

Examples are simply too numerous, but one can easily see the ways that both shows contrast, say, Fox News' or CNN's presentation of an event with the "reality" of what happened. At this first level, the joke is just how incompetent the mainstream news is, as it inevitably seems to "get the story wrong," or, in Baudrillard's terms, it does a poor job of "reflecting" the underlying reality. At the next level, the fake news shows may look into the active masking or concealing of reality by purportedly objective news organization — to cite a recent example, Jon Stewart exposed Fox News' use of footage from a different event to make it seem as though more people attended another rally in Washington — thus allowing fake news to serve the traditional function of ideology-critique, revealing the truth underneath the deliberate or negligent falsehoods of the mainstream media. In the third case, the fake news shows may reveal that the mainstream media's coverage is of something nonexistent entirely, or perhaps it is coverage of a news item of such little consequence that any coverage is a clear misuse of resources — as with the many "threats" with no substance behind them, or the non-news of celebrity gossip and the like. Finally, there is the inevitable notion of news as a self-perpetuating image-generation machine, in which the very news to be reported is only that of other news reports. This becomes the most vicious of vicious cycles, where the news reports only that others are reporting upon it, back and forth, signifiers without signified, signs without referents. In the end, and this is the most devastating critique leveled by the fake news of *The Daily Show* and *The Colbert Report*, all news is disclosed to be a hyperreality of its own, largely if not completely cut off from any actual and meaningful reality.

Obviously, this is not to say that there is no real news to cover, or that no one actually does any real journalism. The demystifying operations of fake news, *contra* a more properly Baudrillardian analysis, require that there be something real to hold up in opposition to the CNNs and Foxes and MSNBCs out there. Stewart and Colbert must bear in mind some real world, if only a proxy for reality, that the mainstream media is somehow misrepresenting, whether through incompetence, lack or conflict of interest, or corruption. Hence, the phenomenon may not be entirely *hyperreal* in the more technical sense in which the term used by Baudrillard or Eco, but the notion that fake news may serve the journalistic profession more faithfully (and therefore be more "real") than real news leads one to rethink the terms a bit. In Baudrillard's metaphor — drawn from Jorge Luis Borges's famous cartographers whose map was coextensive with the territory it purported to represent — the "territory" of the real news is subsumed by the "map" of its Stewart and Colbert spoofs. Of course, in the society of the spectacle, juiced up even more by the accelerated spectacles available through cable television and the internet, the *real* events that the *real* news program is supposedly covering may be further lost to us the viewers, as we find ourselves deeper and deeper in Plato's cave.

Indeed, the fakery of fake news makes it all the more interesting in its hyperreality. As Eco has pointed out, "Disneyland is more hyperrealistic than the wax museum, precisely because the latter still tries to make us believe that what we are seeing reproduces reality absolutely, whereas Disneyland makes it clear that within its magic enclosure it is fantasy that is absolutely reproduced" (Eco 1986, 43). In this formulation, it would be real news that presents the false representations but insists on their representative accuracy, and the fake news of *The Daily Show* and *The Colbert Report* that provides the authentic fakery of the hyperreal.

Yet I also want to suggest that in their hyperrealism, *The Daily Show* and *The Colbert Report* perform that critical function that most real news cannot, or at least is less likely to be able to do than in an earlier epoch. Many apologists for the mainstream news organizations like to imagine that journalists serve a watchdog function, using their investigative powers to uncover wrongdoing and using their information-dissemination media to broadcast the results. In this, as one jeremiad after another has noted in recent years, the decline of the press is directly linked to a decline in democracy, as the sacred role of the fourth estate is to maintain vigilance over those in power and to speak to and for those outside of it (see, for example, Jones 2009). This is indeed part of the thrust of Jon Stewart's own notorious appearance on *Crossfire*, when he accused the show (and all others like it) of ignoring real problems while they instead generated much heat and little light in meaningless partisan squabbling. Fake news pokes through the pretense of journalistic solemnity, and calls attention to the seemingly hypocritical or self-serving activities of the mainstream media. In a sense, the fake news is able to perform more critical social critique than investigative journalism could in an era of 24-hour news cycles and constant commercial interruption. Perhaps the kitschy, parodic play of the signifiers can (and in this case does) serve as viable social critique; indeed, it can do so better than merely oppositional forms of the actual mainstream media precisely *because* it operates in the form of satirical fake news.

Although *The Daily Show* and *The Colbert Report* are first and foremost television shows, with audiences to entertain and sponsors to satisfy, they have also exerted no small influence on the political discourse in the United States and abroad. (Of course, the same could be said for those other television news programs, which also have audiences to entertain and sponsors to satisfy.) What sets the two Comedy Central shows apart, from other news programs and from other comedy programs, is their profoundly critical spirit. As both Jon Stewart and Stephen Colbert have proved, in many cases this form of critical satire does not necessarily allow itself to be funny, and certainly does not try to appeal to the broadest audiences, as would most shows designed for entertainment. The movement from political satire, as ancient as comedy itself, to this immanent critique of the mainstream media itself has real-world effects. The social significance of these two fake news programs can be illustrated by looking at how *The Daily Show* transformed itself from mere comedy to biting social critique, and at how the persona of Stephen Colbert has disrupted the sign-system of political and media discourse.

From Topical Humor to Fake News: On the Structural Transformation of *The Daily Show*

Using a fake news format to lampoon public figures or to entertain is nothing new. Satire, especially political satire, is well suited to the format of fake news, since the underlying substance of the jokes (i.e., politics, politicians, political issues) are known to the audience largely through the medium of news programming. *Saturday Night Live*'s "Weekend Update," as much a staple of the long-running comedy sketch show as the opening monologue or the musical guest, has had great success in re-presenting the week's key news stories with humorous effects or as set-ups to jokes. To a certain extent, the very form of "Weekend Update" also allows it to poke fun at the television news broadcasts. Sometimes this is explicit, as in Jane Curtin and Dan Aykroyd's "Point/Counterpoint" (itself an actual segment of CBS's *60 Minutes* at the time) sketches, and at others it may be implied, as with the inane banter between anchors Amy Poehler and Seth Meyers. Yet, in the main, the objects of the show's derision were the people *in* the news, not those broadcasting the news.

A telling example of the formal and substantive difference lies in the remarkable transformation of *The Daily Show* from its inception in 1996, with Craig Kilborn as its host, to what it has become in the Jon Stewart era. Formally, at least, *The Daily Show* with Craig Kilborn was above all a spoof of *local* news, and its forays into national and international affairs were presented in such a way as to highlight the glib superficiality of a smarmy local-news anchor, rather than with the *gravitas* (a word journalists so love) of a national news anchorman, of a Walter Cronkite, Dan Rather, or Tom Brokaw. The program originally underscored its resemblance to local news shows by introducing, along with its anchorman, its use of a news van and of such technology as the TDS 5000 color copier (in parody of local news programs' hype over "eye in the sky" helicopters and Doppler radar). Although many of Kilborn's jokes dealt with national news stories — this was the era of Monica Lewinsky, after all — the overall feel of the show was less *newsy*, and the news format was really just a framing device for the joke-telling. The field reports filed by such intrepid journalists as Stephen Colbert himself certainly had little or nothing to do with the "news" presented by Kilborn (see Plume 2003, 6). *The Daily Show* was actually developed to replace the more topical, and more intelligent, program *Politically Incorrect*, which used a talk show (rather than news) format as the platform for its political satire. In the beginning, *The Daily Show* was set up to allow a bit of topical, political humor on what was manifestly a comedy, not news, program.

The very look of the anchor tells part of the story. Craig Kilborn, a former college basketball player, is the tall, blond, handsome all-American boy from the heartland (Minnesota). He had previously worked as an ESPN *SportsCenter* anchor, and maintained the on-screen persona of an athletic, mischievous frat-boy (a character he easily reprised in the film *Old School*, in which he plays the athletic, mischievous, aging frat-boy type). Kilborn's look accentuates the jokes, as the clean-cut, fresh-faced smart-aleck smirks at the news of the day. At about 5'7", with dark hair, projecting himself as a self-conscious (one might even say, self-promotional) Jewish nebbish from New

Jersey, Jon Stewart cuts the figure of an anti–Kilborn, the corporeal embodiment of a franchise's "change-of-direction." Although he is also handsome
and clean-cut, Stewart's humor frequently comes from the disjunction between
the clever but impotent little guy and the larger powers that be (a franchise
that Woody Allen has made his stock and trade). Kilborn's boyish Goliath
breezily strode alongside and among the powerful, whereas Stewart's on-screen
persona vacillates between cowed underling and outraged outsider, a mouse
that might sometimes roar.

More noteworthy in the transformation of *The Daily Show* were the
changes to the guest list after Stewart seized the reins, although one might
note a bit of a chicken-and-egg conundrum in this, since it is obvious that
the increased newsiness of *The Daily Show with Jon Stewart* is both the cause
and the result of the greater participation by politicians and others working
more directly in the political arena. Nevertheless, during the two years of
Craig Kilborn's term as anchorman, not a single politician, government official, or even politically oriented writer or journalist appeared as a guest on the
show. Kilborne's guests included actors (Jason Priestly), comedians (Janeane
Garofalo), and musicians (Travis Tritt); only one journalist appeared as a
guest, Deborah Norville, and Norville's own "news" show (*Inside Edition*),
which also focused primarily on the entertainment industry, was not much
more newsy than *The Daily Show* itself. In 1999, the year Jon Stewart took
over, the guest list remained limited to entertainers, with the possible exception of former Senator Bob Dole, who entertained thoroughly during his two-
part interview on December 7–8, 1999. By the next year, however, *The Daily
Show* devoted an entire episode to a New Hampshire primary (featuring Senator Dole), as well as two full weeks to the Republican and Democratic Party
conventions, and hosted such politically oriented guests as Bob Dole (again),
journalists Wolf Blitzer, Sam Donaldson, Peter Jennings, David Frost, and
Greta Van Susteren, Senators Arlen Specter, Joe Lieberman (then-Vice Presidential nominee), and consumer advocate and presidential candidate Ralph
Nader. Considering Comedy Central's commercial reluctance to allow political
positions to be aired for fear of alienating viewers, this was already a leap forward into a much more "real-news-like" fake news show. Of course, space
would not permit the listing of "real news" guests on *The Daily Show* in recent
years; suffice it to say that in 2009, such guests actually outnumbered those
in the strictly-speaking "entertainment industry." (This very fact should offer
occasion to question that distinction further, and the result of that questioning
might not reveal anything particularly salutary about the contemporary practices of politics or of entertainment.)

The look of the anchor and the type of guests were not the only changes.
Much of the substance of the writing changed as well. Referring to his own

time as a *Daily Show* correspondent in the Kilborn era, Stephen Colbert noted: "Those were more character-driven pieces. First of all, there were no desk pieces. Correspondents didn't do stuff like editorializing at the desk. The field pieces we did were character-driven pieces — like, you know, guys who believe in Bigfoot. Whereas now, everything is issue- and news-driven pieces, and a lot of editorializing at the desk. And a lot of use of the green screen to put us in false locations." Asked whether the change was a budgetary decision, Colbert emphasized: "No, no, no. It's editorial tone that Jon has changed. We're more of a news show — we were more of a magazine show then" (Plume 2003, 6). Colbert pointed out that Kilborn was not involved with field reports at all; Kilborn did the studio bits, and correspondents like Colbert would film the field reports, almost as if they were two separate shows. As Colbert put it, referring to the transition from the Kilborn to the Stewart eras:

> It really wasn't night-and-day, because you had the same writers, the same executive producer [...] You had the same correspondents — at first. And so, it was a gradual evolution. Jon didn't come in and say, "It's closing time, folks." He came in and said, "And let's see if we can't push this in this direction. Let's see if we can't maybe make the field pieces reflect something that's happening in the headlines of the day, so there's more of a natural transition, the show doesn't change tonally, completely." Which it would often do, from headlines into field pieces. It would be, like, something fairly clever about the Clinton administration — and then straight into a guy who was a Bigfoot hunter. It was quite jarring. That was the first thing I noticed, was that our field pieces were coming out of the news, and not in sort of opposition to them [Plume 2003, 7].

With the integration of the anchorman's (or comedian's) in-studio commentary and the field reports, *The Daily Show* became more like the real news, and much more capable of performing the social-critical function of fake news.

Jon Stewart's renovation and transformation of *The Daily Show* reveal the extent to which television needed, and audiences craved, what I have been calling (somewhat tongue-in-cheekily) "immanent critique," the satirical critique *of* the media *by* the media, here in the form of fake news. Stewart was less interested in jokes about Bill Clinton *per se*, and more interested in the ways that Clinton-jokes were dominating mainstream media while other crucial social issues were being overlooked. As Jones (2005, 54) notes, Stewart expresses "dismay over the artifice of public life — whether it is news reporting, political rhetoric, or entertainment talk" and "ridicules politicians and journalists for being fakes." *The Daily Show with Jon Stewart*, a fake news show, is almost perfectly suited to expose the fakery of real news.

Authentic Fakery: Stephen Colbert and *The Colbert Report*

The Colbert Report began as a spinoff of *The Daily Show*, with Stephen Colbert adopting a full-time persona of a conservative commentator along the lines of Rush Limbaugh, Sean Hannity, or especially Bill O'Reilly. Colbert had occasionally used this persona earlier on *The Daily Show* as a foil to liberal commentators or to Stewart himself; in their back-to-back time slots, with Stewart normally introducing *The Colbert Report* at the end of his show, the two are able to reprise their rivalry to humorous effect. That he chooses to give his persona the name "Stephen Colbert" only adds to the glorious ambiguities of fake and real news, and Colbert frequently supplements his own real biographical details (like being a Roman Catholic from Charleston, South Carolina) with fake ones (like being a local anchor in the 1980s for a small-town, North Carolina TV station). Colbert's show permits him to present the worldview of a character whose politics are both conservative and risible, thus allowing his show to be more overtly political than *The Daily Show*, since *The Colbert Report* is not so much fake news as reversed punditry.

Perhaps the coup de grace of Stephen Colbert's career thus far was his triumphant and controversial appearance at the White House Correspondents Association dinner on April 29, 2006, later reprinted as the appendix to *I Am America (and So Can You!)*. An immediate YouTube sensation that originally aired on C-SPAN, Colbert's speech satirically assailed President Bush and his administration, as expected, but it also reserved much of its biting and ironic criticism for those very members of the mainstream media who cover the White House. In Colbert's view — a view not at all dissimilar to Jon Stewart's deliberately less funny, but still trenchant critique of the media in his infamous *Crossfire* appearance in 2004 — the mainstream media had not only failed in its duty as a public watchdog, allowing the government to get away with policies that might have outraged many news readers or viewers, but it had actively facilitated these outrages, going along with if not promoting an anti-democratic agenda, and allowing itself to become a mere megaphone for the powers that be. The mainstream Washington-based journalists, who so like to think of themselves as essential checks on political power, were not watch-dogs, but lapdogs.

Under the circumstances, it is perhaps unsurprising that the vociferous negative reaction to Colbert humorous speech emerged at such a loud volume and over such a widespread area in the so-called mainstream media. For all of the claims that Colbert's piece was a "lame," "insulting," or that "He was a bully" (Cohen 2006), the rush to defend President Bush's honor by some in the affronted media seems more a form of wounded self-defense. After all, there was nothing surprising or unseemly about Colbert's political remarks in and of themselves: Colbert, Stewart, *Saturday Night Live,* Jay Leno, and hundreds of comedians had been delivering similar critiques of the administration on a nightly basis, and non-comedians elsewhere had not reserved their venom either. Nor were his remarks inappropriate in their setting, contrary to the misleading spin of some critics outraged by Colbert. For example, despite the claim that the White House Correspondents Association dinner was supposed to be a staid, respectful affair, it had frequently if not always been an occasion to "roast" the President, and Colbert's very presence there — that is, a *comedian* (not a statesman) was the invited speaker — shows just how much satire was *meant to be* guiding tone of the event. The speaker for the 2010 dinner was Jay Leno, and recent headliners have included only comedians: Wanda Sykes, David Letterman, and Cedric the Entertainer. In fact, Colbert's remarks were *exactly* the type of remarks one might hear at exactly this event, but for the fact that he attacked the media itself, rather than chiding the political figures alone.

The most damning critique of Colbert's speech was directed at the White House correspondents and by extension the mainstream media journalism. Mock-praising reporters for underplaying if not ignoring such stories as the effects of irresponsible tax cuts, faulty intelligence over apparently nonexistent weapons of mass destruction in Iraq, and the potentially devastating effects of global warming, Colbert reminded the press of its place in the nation:

> We Americans didn't want to know, and you had the courtesy not to try to find out. Those were good times, as far as we knew.
>
> But listen, let's review the rules. Here's how it works: the President makes decisions. He's the Decider. The press secretary announces those decisions, and you people of the press type those decisions down. Make, announce, type. Just put 'em through a spellcheck and go home. Get to know your family again. Make love to your wife. Write that novel you got kicking around in your head. You know — the one about the intrepid Washington reporter with the courage to stand up to the administration. You know — fiction! [Colbert 2008, 224].

"Or Fantasy," adds the marginal gloss, à la *The Colbert Report*'s "The Word." And this is Colbert's point. During the Bush Administration, much of the mainstream media operated as the administration's stenographers, allowing dubious if not downright misleading information to circulate as real news. That such a critique is delivered by a leading member of the "fake news" establishment adds to its satirical power.

The real outrage came not from Colbert's venue, his bad taste, or his actual comments; rather, the nerve touched by Colbert was so acutely felt because his speech, delivered in his persona as a media-pundit (and not as a comedian), revealed to many in the mainstream media exactly what they had become: simulacra of simulacra. Far from the real journalists they took such pride in being — let us not forget that the WHCA is a rather elite organization among mainstream journalists — they were at best hyperreal, becoming almost indistinguishable from the fake journalists in the world of satire, and less capable than they of recognizing their own fakery.

The media critics Jonathan Gray, Jeffrey P. Jones, and Ethan Thompson have nicely summed up the effects of the Colbert event, naming five particular aspects of media culture in the twenty-first century that this event disclosed:

> First, it speaks of the immense popularity of satire TV: being funny and smart sells and has proven a powerful draw for audiences' attention. Second, the rapid spread of the clip highlights satire's viral quality and cult appeal, along with the technological apparatus that now allows such satire to travel far beyond the television set almost instantaneously. Consigned to basic or pay cable channels (as it often is in the United States), satire has nevertheless frequently commanded public attention and conversation more convincingly than shows with ten times the broadcast audience. Third, since multiple commentators criticized the speech for not being funny, the speech illustrates how the presence of "humor" in political humor can rely quite heavily on one's political worldview. It demonstrates that some satire may not even intend to be funny in a belly laugh kind of way.
> Fourth, Colbert's boldness as a comedian in a room full of politicians and journalists crystallized the sad irony that contemporary satire TV often says what the press is too timid to say, proving itself a more critical interrogator of politicians at times and a more effective mouthpiece of the people's displeasure with those in power, including the press itself. Good satire such as Colbert's has a remarkable power to encapsulate public sentiment. Finally, then, the incident tells us of how satire can energize civic culture, engaging citizen-audiences (as few of Colbert's press corps audience can), inspiring public political discussion, and drawing citizens enthusiastically into the realm of the political with deft and dazzling ease [Gray et al. 2009, 4].

Colbert's speech ushered in a new phase of political satire in the context of fake news, establishing a different relationship to the media and its audience than political satire and humor had previously.

Colbert's persona, drawn largely as a caricature of various right-wing pundits (especially Fox News' Bill O'Reilly), makes him an even more effective fake-newsman and social critic than Jon Stewart in a way. In *The Daily Show*, Stewart's persona is that of the relatively objective journalist, and he has proven himself to be a fiercely sardonic critic of Democrats Bill Clinton and Joe Biden as well as Republicans George W. Bush and Sarah Palin. As Stewart himself has put it, "The point of view of the show is we're passionately opposed to bullshit. Is that liberal or conservative?" (quoted in Jones, 2005, 55). But Colbert, by posing as a right-wing conservative, need not oppose bullshit; he can promote bullshit, make sure everyone knows that it is bullshit, and insist that such bullshit is a core foundation of conservative political philosophy. Indeed, by portraying the very thing he is parodying, Colbert can more actively undermine the authority of his targets. This was partly what was on display in the WHCA dinner.

The upshot of this fake news is that the already blurred lines between fake and real become even less distinguishable. Take, for example, this bit of trivia: Colbert's book *I am America (and So Can You!)* reached No. 1 on the *New York Times* nonfiction best-seller list on October 28, 2007 and stayed there until December 2, 2007. The title that preceded it was Clarence Thomas's "real" autobiographical memoir, *My Grandfather's Son*, and the one that succeeded Colbert's was right-wing pundit Glenn Beck's satirical *An Inconvenient Book*. As the risk of making an absolutely churlish point, I would say that this particular chain of book-publishing events in the autumn of 2007 parallels the sort of social and cultural transformations that have made fake news so significant. However one views his political or judicial views, Thomas is an important, "newsworthy" figure, an associate justice of the United States Supreme Court, only the second person of color to occupy such a position, and someone whose life story — particularly in its compelling narrative of a black child rising from the segregated South to one of the highest positions of power in the country — is inherently worth paying attention to. Colbert's "fake" autobiography, offering parodic faux-politics and self-aggrandizing cultural commentary, makes no actual claim to cultural relevance, aside from the comedian's desire to poke fun at the current state of affairs. Its presence on the bestseller list does not diminish the importance of Thomas's memoir, but offers another kind of discourse. But Beck pushes this process even further. Like Colbert's book, his is fundamentally satirical (the title itself, a playful jab at former Senator and Vice President Al Gore's book and film, *An Inconvenient Truth*), yet Beck's adoring fans apparently do not view his political opinions, even when presented in a clearly satirical manner, to be fake in any way. That is, Beck has taken a form of "fake news" to an extremity whereby it collapses back upon itself in the form of "real" news commentary. The absolute evacuation of *gravitas* has therefore led to the weightlessness of the media in general, and the gravitational pull of "fakery" becomes the only ground upon which the news-media can rest at all.

Here again we see the hyperreality of fake news, where *The Colbert Report* actually becomes far more grounded in reality that many television news programs can be. By staking out a position, Colbert actually maintains a position — the opposite of that held by his fictional persona — something the news cannot allow itself to do in good conscience, whatever the far right or far left believe about media bias. In establishing itself only as the transparent eye of a society of the spectacle, the news dissipates its own reality in favor of a hyperreal or nonreal that becomes indistinguishable from it. Of all news on television, fake or real, Colbert's then stands as the most real.

Again, this is not to say that the fake news replaces real news, or to repeat the nonsense about how Jon Stewart and Stephen Colbert should be viewed as real journalists. When asked about whether audiences "get their news" from *The Daily Show*, Colbert expressed doubt, then explained: "I wish people would watch the real news before they watch our show, because we have two games. Our game is we make fun of the newsmakers, but we also make fun of the news style. They're missing half our joke if they don't keep up with the day-to-day changes of mass media news" (Plume 2003, 7). Yet, so effective has been the fake news of Stewart and Colbert that some have conceded, or rather asserted, that they are actually *real* journalists after all. For example, in an article on Stewart's controversial *Crossfire* appearance (tellingly titled "If You Interview Kissinger, Are You Still a Comedian?"), Dan Kennedy is quoted as saying that, "by offering serious media criticism," Stewart must assume the responsibilities of a journalist; "you can't interview Bill Clinton [and others] and still say you're a comedian" (Cave 2004). In other words, whether they like it or not, the fake news comedians Stewart and Colbert are now real news journalists and commentators. This may be the most hyper-real (or perhaps surreal) aspect of the blurring of the lines between journalism and entertainment, revealing the social significance of these fake news shows: Fake news is more real than real news precisely because it discloses just how fake the real news can be. Here it is, your moment of Zen. And that's the word.

References

Baudrillard, Jean. 1994. "The Precession of Simulacra." *Simulacra and Simulation*, trans. Sheila Faria Glaser. 1–42. Ann Arbor: University of Michigan Press.

Cave, Damien. 2004. "If You Interview Kissinger, Are You Still a Comedian?" October 24. *New York Times*.

Cohen, Richard. 2006. "So Not Funny." May 6. *Washington Post*. Available at: http://www.washingtonpost.com/wp-dyn/content/article/2006/05/03/AR2006050302202.html (accessed 10 February 2010).

Colbert, Stephen, et al. 2007. *I am America (and So Can You!)*. New York: Grand Central.

Debord, Guy. 1994. *The Society of the Spectacle*, trans. Donald Nicholson-Smith. New York: Zone Books.

Eco, Umberto. 1986. *Travels in Hyperreality*, trans. William Weaver. New York: Harcourt Brace.

Fox, Julia R., Glory Koloen, and Volkan Sahin. 2007. "No Joke: A Comparison of Substance in *The Daily Show with Jon Stewart* and Broadcast Network Television Coverage of the 2004 Presidential Election Campaign." *Journal of Broadcasting & Electronic Media* 51.2: 213–227.

Gray, Jonathan, Jeffrey P. Jones, and Ethan Thompson, eds. 2009. *Satire TV: Politics and Comedy in the Post-Network Era*. New York: New York University Press.

Jones, Alex S. 2009. *Losing the News: The Future of the News that Feeds Democracy.* Oxford: Oxford University Press.

Jones, Jeffrey P. 2005. *Entertaining Politics: The New Political Television and Civic Culture.* Lanham, Maryland: Rowman & Littlefield.

Plume, Ken. 2003. "An Interview with Stephen Colbert." *IGN.* August 11. Available at: http://movies.ign.com/articles/433/433111p6.html (accessed 17 January 2010).

It's All About Meme

The Art of the Interview and
the Insatiable Ego of the Colbert Bump

K. A. WISNIEWSKI

When Comedy Central audiences take their nightly double-shot of Jon Stewart and Stephen Colbert, there's a strange brew of subtlety from the left, right, and middle of the political spectrum that allows the viewer to find his or her own closure of current events, a sense of viewer-controlled interpretation that permits doubt and belief, seriousness and humor, right and wrong. Why does this particular ordering encourage critical thought and independent perspective? Could it be that the agitprop of Stewart followed by the absurd satire of Colbert is leaving audiences with a sense of self–determined politics? Did we vote? We did. Do we feel empowered to think, to laugh? We do. And we don't need it explained by the so-called objective news sources. Aware of the artifice of comedy, audiences of *The Daily Show* with Jon Stewart and *The Colbert Report* also become aware of the schema and mission of other news broadcasts. However, while the Comedy Central programs serve a dose of thought-provoking entertainment to many of its viewers, for many others it has become first, and, in some cases, the only source of politics and news.

When Jon Stewart replaced the one-dimensional egotist and former ESPN *SportsCenter* anchor Craig Kilborn in January 1999, *The Daily Show* shifted gears from a humorous recap of the entertainment world to a much more politically-focused and news-driven satire, eventually being self-described as "fake news." While assuming a new format and mission under the wing of Stewart — who also serves as a writer and executive producer — the show amplified its political agenda, adopting a more liberal-minded perspective on national and world events while parodying other, more conservative media outlets. By imitating and mocking these outlets, by recontextualizing clips of news previewed by them, and by offering new and engaging interviews with public figures, *The Daily Show* forces its audience to consider what's going on, how they feel about these issues, and what exactly constitutes fake news. Stewart is a comedian by trade and his show is marketed and showcased as comedy; however, by exposing the often absurd nature of the media and its lack of real content (and in political discourse at large) and by presenting alternative, under-represented opinions to currently debated issues depicted within these venues, the show and its host reveal a platform that is often read by its audience as the opposite of what it claims to be.

The very nature of comedy is that of tension and release. Freud saw humor as a space where one can release the melancholy, awkwardness, and aggression he or she feels towards something through laughter, and, similarly, Bakhtin argued that it allowed social analysis, reflection, and criticism (Freud 1960; Bakhtin 1981). Watts (1981, 117) furthers these ideas by claiming that in their responses to comedy, participants receive the immediate pleasures by means of recognizing, understanding, and applying modes of truth. In the cases of both *The Daily Show* and *The Colbert Report*, this truth arrives through a punch line exposing the fallacies and emptiness in a large portion of political discourse and the news that covers it. Audience pleasure derives from awareness that the shows are mimetic acts. The joke requires audiences to having some working knowledge of the issues at hand and of the misinformation, biases, inadequacies portrayed on serious news broadcasts. By exposing the artificiality of both players in public culture and media outlets and offering more perspectives to a debated issue, Amber Day (2009, 85–90) argues that these "fake" news broadcasts are, in some ways, more real than the shows they imitate. Building on these ideas, this essay explores how both shows contribute to contemporary political discourse and public culture in general. Focusing on the mimetic, interview segments from both shows reveals layers of critique, but, ultimately, it is in the cocky character of Colbert that we get the clearest and most potent message. In his "truth, unfiltered by rational argument," audiences witness the absurd, and often unpredictable, nature of ideas in the public sphere — of how they evolve and how they can promote languor or create change. Through this character, his parody of political commentators, and his relationship with guests and audiences, viewers gain access to how the political machine works and can recognize and breakdown for themselves the rhetoric spun by politicians and pundits alike.

A mirror capable of both reflecting cultural norms and ideas and influencing our outlook on the world and ourselves, there are critics who argue television is a medium unable or inappropriate for conveying serious political inquiry and prompting critical analysis. Largely conceived by its viewers as a place for diversion and entertainment, these critics might contend that these comedy shows, like sitcoms and talk shows, dangerously elevate entertainers to the status of pundits, comics and actors into heroes. This is the criticism maintained by Neil Postman (1985, 106), who wrote that, "Americans are the best entertained and quite likely the least well-informed people in the Western World." Here, Postman contends that television is for entertainment. This is the viewer expectation of the medium; therefore, even the "real" news and other serious broadcasts are irrational and trivial and read, on some level by the average viewer, as such, making television an inappropriate and problematic venue for serious discourse. But this, too, was the point of Jon Stewart himself on his appearance 2004 appearance on CNN's *Crossfire*, where he criticized, "You're doing theater when you should be doing debate." Unlike Postman, Stewart might contend that television is the perfect venue to debate vital political and social topics and not only relay them onto a larger audience but also include them in the discussions.

Both Morreale (2009, 121) and Erion (2007, 13) examine the Stewart interview and praise Stewart and his show for its socio-political critique, referring to it as a combination of "deliberative and epideictic rhetoric [that] combats cynicism" and "critical and educative," respectively. However, while Morreale sees Stewart "teaching deliberation," Erion reads the show as a comedy that "requires its audience to grasp a Postmanesque criticism of television news." Both are accurate. To understand many of the *Daily Show* jokes, audiences must understand the set-up of the joke, that is, the context of what is happening around the world or at least what is being broadcasted on the news. But audiences also learn by watching the show's commentators analyze, deconstruct, and rebuff clips and testimonies. Moreover, audience members become active participants themselves when they take what they've heard and learned beyond the couch or computer and discuss them with friends or co-workers. Thus, the passive, isolated television experience is "taken to the streets," to office water coolers with colleagues and coffee shops with friends, and deliberated in public settings.

As *The Daily Show* gained popularity, it has evolved as a much more serious venue for the kinds of discourse Stewart criticized in his *Crossfire* interview. It is still grounded in the comedic, ranging from the sophisticated parody of network broadcasts to the common toilet humor that winks and smiles at passing gas, but, since Stewart's emergence as an icon in public culture, it clearly has an agenda. It is no longer completely free from the ethics and responsibilities attached to journalists and related media. This is perhaps best visible in Stewart's interviews with Arkansas Governor Mike Huckabee. On January 10, 2007, the politician visited the show to promote a book entitled *From Hope to Higher Ground*. From the start of the interview, it is clear that Huckabee is aware of both the audience and the format of the show.

The word "stops" in his book's subtitle *12 Stops to Restoring America's Greatness* is emphasized and called into question by Stewart who asks for the rationale behind the word, "Do you think Americans fear stairs?," to which the politician cleverly and quickly responds, "They do. The StairMaster has injured a lot of people." He later quips that the title also gave Stewart something to mention on the show. From the opening alone, we see a seasoned Stewart throwing a softball witticism before preparing for the much more serious discussion ahead. Huckabee's "practical" approach in the book seems to mirror Stewart's mission in the sense that both target the average citizen. Huckabee interprets this everyday American as a person who doesn't think in polemic, ideological terms but rather in "vertical terms" of being progress or regression. Upon agreeing with this interpretation Stewart intervenes but the fear is "can we believe you?" But before the studio audience has a chance to laugh, Stewart reaches out to his guest to signal that this remark is not a personal criticism and sincerely comments on the problems of political rhetoric. The interview maintains a serious tone for the remainder of the time with only one other humorous moment, interestingly, sparked by Huckabee who speaks of the battle of politics and the problems of empty rhetoric by explaining that, if he retained this sensibility, he wouldn't have been able to "pass gas" in the House chamber. Stewart, surprised by the remark, responds slowly to the remark and, in his typical fashion, sips the contents of his mug on the desk to allow laughs to die down and retort that he doesn't care for that kind of humor.

Huckabee reappeared on December 9, 2008, and found himself lodged in an even more serious, somewhat heated debate on the definition of marriage in relation to homosexuality. Here, it is clear that Stewart again stretched beyond the show's comedic groundwork and stayed focused to deliver a sober interview on an issue on which he very clearly was passionate. Stewart's line of questioning here, again, was very deliberate; he closely followed a series notes sketching out and probing Huckabee's presumed arguments against gay marriage, eventually directly revealing his own viewpoints: "I disagree. I think segregation used to be the law until the courts intervened.... Religion is far more of a choice than homosexuality." Alluding to the politician's record that the pro-life movement is one of the greatest shames in American history, Stewart cites the ban on gay marriage as perhaps the second greatest, asserting, "It's a travesty that people have forced someone who is gay to have to make their case, that they deserve the same basic rights as someone else." The episode concludes with interviewer and interviewee having an insightful conversation on the complexities around definitions of not only marriage but also of rights, privileges, and lifestyle choices and essentially agreeing to disagree. The interview might be one of Stewart's finest and most critical and engaging moments, and it demonstrates that television can transmit thoughtful and substantial discourse and hold viewers' attention.

The problem of the show, however, is also revealed in these scenes. In the aforementioned articles by Morreale and Eiron, both writers view a show with a deliberate plan that "requires" audiences to meet that plan halfway. Generally speaking, Stewart interviews are light in the sense that there is a much more humorous dynamic at play, a planned attack to make reveal some paradoxical truth in the guests' actions or beliefs. Stewart — sometimes witty, sometimes silly — plays the welcoming host and offers guests the opportunity to escape their public selves and to connect with the studio audience. Of course, the guests (hopefully) realize that this is, in fact, a comedy show and that occasionally there will be jokes at their own expenses; for the less savvy guest, these punch lines can be unintentionally self-inflicting. Jonathan Gray (2009, 156) analyzes how public figures can quickly become victims in the wordplay of such interviews when they appear "out of touch and removed from everyday life and popular culture." Gray cites the live studio audience as aiding this transformation. Their laughs and applause to Stewart's cutting remarks, or the interviewee's ineptness, turns the guest — the focus of the interview — into an "outsider" and provides "a space for a range of American citizen-politician interactions and communication in which public image is anything but stable" (Gray 2009, 159). But the argument could go the opposite way. Like the broadcasters and journalists he parodies, Stewart relies heavily on audience support — the jokes only work if the audience is on the same page as the host. As seen in the Huckabee interviews, by imitating "real" broadcasts so closely, Stewart can fall into the same trap that he criticizes. The assumption is that the audience *will* meet him halfway and that they know enough of the issues to follow the host to his punch line, that they agree with the punch line. And if they don't, unlike the subjects of parody, there is no worry, for the show, after all, is *just* entertainment. Geoffrey Baym (2009, 127) might agree to some extent when he suggests that the *Daily Show* can be understood "not as fake but as oppositional news," providing a "critical challenge that is all but absent in the so-called real news."

While Stewart maintains this interviewer-interviewee model closely, there is much more play in the work of Stephen Colbert. Specifically deconstructing the "actors" of Colbert's interviews — the interviewed guest; interviewer himself; the studio audience; and the audience watching on a screen at home — reveals how *The Colbert Report* can *act* as a vehicle that not only demonstrates how mechanisms of imitation and contagion provide an explanation of how both a sense of self and national character and culture develop but also, through its ambiguous and over-the-top nature, allows a variety of interpretations, thus, potentially fostering critical thinking across a diverse audience whose worldviews span across the political spectrum. As previously high-lighted, as a comedian, Stewart's agenda is much more direct and obvious to his viewers; he often fulfills his role as dissenter, objector, and has become a sort of watchdog of American politics. Meanwhile, Colbert, a self-proclaimed actor, is much more difficult to read — masking agendas, performing charac-ters, harshly criticizing one aspect of American politics one moment only to rally the audience into a "U-S-A" chant the next. This ability to not only get the audience laughing but to also stir them into a frenzy or get them to par-ticipate in public action — whether its voting in elections, donating money to charities like DonorsChoose and the Yellow Ribbon Fund, or create and sub-mit entries to Colbert's "Green Screen Challenge"— shows the power of the show, the meme in action.

Coined by Richard Dawkins (1976, 192), a meme is merely a unit that of "cultural transmission" or imitation (see also, Blackmore 2000, 4–8). Essen-tially, studying memes is a way to explain how ideas and phenomena are spread, and, according to Susan Blackmore, doing so might lead to insights as to how culture develops over time. The title of this essay borrows the term "meme" to highlight a few points concerning Colbert. First, Colbert reveals the "contagion" of politics and news broadcasts and their ability to spread fear, anger, and mistrust. Second, in doing so, Colbert's parody has a power to unmake holistic metaphors; what is instead suggested is a power — or weak-ness — of these metaphors, of communicability. Lastly, while parody, Colbert still operates in a political and public forum and comedic formula. Colbert's jokes may destabilize and resist the state's established order, but it also relies on the structuralist rigor of the signifying system. For Bataille, contagion becomes communication, and all the world is a parody (Noys 2000, 21–22; Hegarty 2000, 97). And, in demonstrating how the social works, Colbert allows the chance to see how it can also unwork — and an opportunity for each of us to consider how we look at the world and why. Coded as the jokes may be, there is also a demystification of what is happening and what people are saying.

I Am America: Positioning Stephen Colbert

From his debut episode, Colbert audiences quickly realize that *The Col-bert Report* is more than a mere spin-off of *The Daily Show*. Colbert kicks off the show by reminding the audience that it's *his* show — and, in case the audi-ence forgets, they will be reminded of it from the myriad places his name is reflected, from the title banner above him and the background silhouette to the plasma screen below his desk and the chaser lights below that; even his desk, he reminds us, is shaped like "a 'C' for Colbert." Slowing down his pace, Colbert then confidently confirms, "But this show isn't about me. No, this program is dedicated to *you*, the heroes ... the people who watch this show." He makes a clear point to define his audience as "average hardworking Americans" rather than the country club elites (who, amusingly, wouldn't be allowed into Colbert's club — reiterating Colbert's position as outsider, a man with the people, but not necessarily of them) and promises that their voices will be heard on the program in the form of Colbert's voice. He then leaps into Tonight's Word, "truthiness," and the now famous line that he "shoots from the gut" for his answers (see, Baym 2009; Decker 2007; Griffioen 2007; Johnson 2007; Mills 2007). Here, Colbert constructs a dichotomy of truth and opinion, head from heart, which is multi-layered indeed. He is an absolutist who practices individual relativism — that is, he shows his audiences that there is no truth, or rather there *is*, only none that is universal. He shows that each person has his or her own truth — what they think — but, further complicating the matter, this is only true if Colbert says so as well. It is in this absurdity that Colbert's show forces the audience to examine (and re-examine) what Colbert is saying but also reconsider what they are thinking.

Further complicating any reading of Colbert, our host, is Colbert, the actor. Unlike Stewart, who maintains his public persona as a comic, the Stephen Colbert figure that greets audiences and guests each night is a character played by Stephen Colbert, an actor. We are living in a culture that not only celebrates the celebrity but also confuses on-screen characters with actors' screen personas, public personas, and, of course, the personal; the rise of reality television shows has only added to this trend (Dyer 1998; Turner 2004). And, at times, it can be forgotten that our egomaniacal host is just the creation of a guy who played on *The Dana Carvey Show* and *Strangers with Candy*. And this is further complicated by the similarities shared by Colbert, the actor, and Colbert, the character. For example, both were raised in South Carolina, and both are practicing Catholics, truths that often play a large role in the act. So it is easy to see how audience might be confused with whom they are watching and how these lines are to be read. But it is in this liminal space that Colbert is able to play up the ego and pull out truths — and the people behind the personality — from his guests.

The show *works* precisely because of these complicated readings and contradictory personalities of our host. How far do we believe the role of his "arch-conservative blowhard" impression of Bill O'Reilly? (Mnookin 2007). Colbert, the nemesis of intellectualism, labels learning as "elitism," and thereby becomes his own sort of everyman hero. He questions politicians, stomps on scientists and buries experts appearing on his show. In one interview, Colbert replies, "It's one thing to express your views. It's another thing for those views to be different from mine." Here, the patriotic, all-American champion of the First Amendment reminds us that the freedom of speech only goes as far as you agree with his opinion. And as the audience applauds the infectious, endearing ego of the everyman in unison, individually, each must also question the dynamic they're watching, what the host and his guests are *really* saying. This is why viewers tune in each night: they enjoy *recognizing* the double-voiced imitation of the one-dimensional, one-sided evening news stations and talk radio shows that consume the media; they enjoy, appreciate, the tension, the juxtaposition of what is said and what is meant. In the end, audiences enjoy the work of decoded messages and getting at the heart of an issue. Ultimately, this is what audiences want and why they watch.

While it can be easily argued that broadcasts on FOX, for example, don't necessarily beat around the bush in their viewpoints, daily viewers of such programs might fail to see these hosts as personalities, products, themselves. There is no mistaking Colbert as a personality. Mimicking a personality rather than a "real" person allows Colbert to skate into a criticism of both that personality and the system in which it resides. Baudrillard claims that in this postmodern world of simulations and information overload, the refusal of meaning is the only resistance possible (Baudrillard 2004, 84–86; Fiske 1989, 180). So Colbert's defiance towards science and facts and his claim that "Nothing I'm saying means anything" should be read as resistance to the established order of American politics. Again, the criticism is that politics and its coverage is filled with empty words and fallacious jargon. And Colbert's audience seeks content, meaning. For many viewers, guests brought onto the "real" news to publicize a book or film or testify and offer expert analyses on an issue never really have much to say in terms of content. Whether they agree with what's being expressed or not, audiences want to hear a clear answer to a question. Instead, they are often presented with a seemingly well-rehearsed response that is void of content or an inauthentic, disingenuous reaction from someone who is apathetic to or unaware of their audiences. The appearance is neither interesting nor engaging for those watching.

The opposite might be said for Colbert's interviews. The mode of comedy produced by the show and by the nature of the host allows him to ask the questions other broadcasts can't or won't ask. He can be celebratory, admiring, critical and just plain disruptive. Moreover, the improvisational, spontaneous temperament of comedy allows both host and guest to at times get thrown for the routine often established on such a publicity circuit and allow much more jargon-free, honest responses. In his narcissistic, anti-intellectual suit, Colbert is at the top of his game with non-fiction writers, especially the group of academics of which he claims to be most wary. Examining such interviews exposes a multitude of layers within *The Colbert Report*. First, of course we see a format familiar but somewhat detached from interviews we see on the "real" news because of the initial reversal of power. No matter who the guest may be, the star is always Colbert. In his grand entrance to be discussed later, he is able to de-center the allure and clout of their celebrity. Within this act, Colbert's guests are forced to meet and speak with their host and his audience on his terms often mixed with quick rebuttals, silly faces, heavy handed accusations and sneers, and screwball questions that are sure to take them out of their element. Some simply don't allow themselves to get in on the joke and interviews can go stale. But others are quick to play along. They hang onto their hosts' lead and are able to not only simplify their points in an everyday vernacular the audience understands and respects but also gain a larger audience worthy of the Colbert bump.

The Colbert bump refers to the boost in popularity of a personality or sales in a product that often accompanies an appearance on the show. Blackmore (2000, 8) is correct in her descriptions of memes as "selfish," "autonomous" cultural products "working only to get themselves copied. We humans, because of our powers of imitation, have become just the physical 'hosts' needed for the memes to get around." It is impossible to gauge which ideas will be remembered, passed on, and repeated, but television and the Internet are certainly the most appropriate avenues for such sharing because of its accessibility and transmutability. Humans copy programs, and programs copy humans. In reenacting "real" news broadcasts, Colbert is able to create an avenue in which the writers who visit him have the ability to quickly implant a few ideas extent in their works to a larger audience. The few minutes they are allotted on the air allows this because it is encrypted in humor rather than encoded in a sophisticated, high brow jargon the masses are much more likely to tune out or be confused by.

Memes are not a new idea. In his efforts in the nineteenth century to formulate a theory of nation-making and the evolution of culture, Walter Bagehot (1916, 100) listed words, books, monuments, symbols and laughter as artifacts of contagion that result in processes of imitation stabilized by a "the inheritance of preferred characters." He (1916, 104) argued that "the infection of imitation" is accompanied with a tendency towards "persecution" and that when patterns form and differences are distinguished, each nation practices "a kind of selective conservatism, for the most part keeping what is old, but annexing some new but like practice — an additional turret in the old style." Similarly, both Foucault (1977, 199) and Douglas (2005, 160–172) see the language of infection and contagion as a trope seen in many places, which simultaneously transmits a desire to dissent from and to accept law and social norms. The popularity and mass distribution of shows like *The Colbert Report* further reveal that this dissent, this refusal of laws and systems, is merely a part of the larger social order and serves as a means of explanation of the system called into question. These interviews and guest appearance may still just be part of a show, but that doesn't make them less valuable or influential.

Derrida might contend that contagion — once invested in socio-political meanings — becomes empty of content, but one could argue that contagion's greatest function is that it *does* inspire a line of questioning from its participants (Eagleton 2003, 111–112). On one hand, there is a loss of one's identity because of this awareness of the system in which it is a part — as seen in the audiences' collective laughter or even in their rallying around Colbert's impetus to chant, vote, or donate money to a particular cause. On the other hand, and in part because of the broad span of potential meanings and interpretations of the show's host, an individual's interpretation and action reinforces their own sense of identity and purpose within the signifying system. Fauconnier and Turner (2002, 168) refer to this process as "conceptual integration networks," which they explain as a product of several input spaces blended together, so while there are slippages in meaning, there is also the activation of new meanings. As Paul de Man (1983) suggests, interpretation is an effort at understanding a work's intention. While in this case he is referring to literature, specifically, the same may be applied to reading Colbert.

Colbert's imitation of interviewers like O'Reilly not only loosens the validity of such shows' opinions and the facts they try to critique, it can also allow a clearer insight into the heart of the ideas maintained by guests. Hence, these exposures reveal an arena for participating in popular political culture, a sphere that allows viewers to see and make sense of at least some of the ways that politics extends beyond Capitol Hill and the ruling class. This is most visible in his eccentric approach to interviews. While Stewart's format of interview can offer a space in which the public can criticize the same celebrities they idolize, Colbert and his insatiable ego subverts ideas of politicians, celebrities, and other figures of authority. Each night, he introduces his guest and then runs across the soundstage to meet them; they are already sitting on one side waiting for their host and positioned in a way that they are staring at a distinguished-looking portrait of the host which hangs above a fireplace in the background. Meanwhile, before greeting his guest, Colbert raises his arms at the cheering crowd as if it was he who had been introduced. From this not-so-subtle opening, Colbert displaces the focus away from his guest and back onto himself. Therefore, he is able to position himself in a unique place outside the discourse altogether, forcing his guests to be on their game to bring the discourse to Colbert and, to us, the audience.

On October 10, 2006, when Jane Fonda and Gloria Steinem were brought onto the show to promote their new talk radio network marketing women,

Colbert went well beyond his typical self-congratulatory approach. Sitting across the table and in a very serious tone and demeanor, Colbert poses the question, "Why a women's radio network now?" But before Steinem can respond, Colbert abruptly interrupts her, and the three are re-situated on the set of a kitchen where the interview continues as the three bake an apple pie together. Emphasizing the juxtaposition of the two sets and formats, humor and seriousness, the public and private, Baym (2009, 124–126) reads this interview as a critique of the gendered nature of television and as an example of how Colbert exemplifies a new kind of political television that defies categorization and allows the audience to recognize the fallacies of conventional cultural and political assumptions. This reading is apparent in Colbert's over-the-top misogynistic queries and demands — for example, in his questions on the difference between angry women and feminists and in his assertion that starting a women's network run by women is sexist — but it also demonstrates, again, that this *is* Colbert's show. He sets the tone and the pacing and dominates the direction of the interview, and the interview shows how each guest needs to fight for his or her points to be made clear, and, here, it is clear that Steinem and Fonda largely do not play into the Colbert system. While they do participate in the "Cooking with Feminists" sketch, their responses maintain a serious and structured tone that doesn't necessarily flow with Colbert's. Here, the audience's laughter is mostly centered around the absurdity of the Colbert and his questions. Because of this, one must wonder if these very serious responses are actually heard and processed by the viewer.

One exception arises around Jane Fonda. Perhaps because of the kitchen set-up, the interview has the feel of scripted sketch, but, at one point of the interview, attention is drawn towards Colbert's "kiss the cook" apron; Colbert looks at Fonda and urges her it, "Fight it," which prompts her to lean into him for a kiss. The act is clearly unplanned and Colbert grins largely into the camera and belts, "Oh, Boy!" He looks down into his cards, regaining composure and replies, "I like you, Fonda," as he tries to return to his persona and next line of questioning. As he refers to the network as sexist, Fonda stuffs his mouth with a spoon full of ice cream, allowing a moment for serious, extended response. Somehow, Steinem returns to the apron, and Fonda leans in for another smooch, to which Colbert returns to the camera, claiming, "I'm in huge trouble at home."

This interaction was further extended in Fonda's visit on May 9, 2007, while promoting her film *Georgia Rule*. While introducing her, Colbert remarks, "I'll remind her of my Colbert Rule: the real peach-state is South Carolina." Here, Fonda takes control of the interview, and, before the host can even begin asking questions, she seductively walks to his side of the table, sits on his lap, and begins kissing him on the mouth. Unable to respond, Colbert reverts to a clip of her new movie. When the camera returns to Colbert, Fonda is still on his lap, and Colbert nervously tries to shuffle through his cards and loosely improvises. He chuckles to himself that this isn't how he imagined the interview would happen and alludes to the trouble he'll be in upon returning home to his wife later. As Fonda returns to the title of the film, Colbert interrupts, "I have rules, too, and you're breaking several of them."

What is significant about this "rule breaking," is Colbert's willingness to play, to improv, himself. Fonda's sequences shows that the success of interviews of Colbert's comedy is based not only on mimesis in terms of his imitations of broadcasters like O'Reilly and his narcissistic and controlling persona but also in those rare yet always potential breakdowns of this model and Colbert's caricature. Moreover, it further extends the idea that a successful Colbert interview also is dependent on the guests and their willingness to come down to Colbert's level. In the case of Jane Fonda, Fonda plays the Colbert game, and the insatiable ego of Colbert, while defeated, is satisfied. This subversion of the Colbert interview construct reveals how the metaphor, the act, power is transferred. The scene shows breaks in performance for Colbert. He allows the work to un-work itself, showing that contagion — the meme — continues to operate and create new threads, even as other parts are breaking down. In other words, even as Colbert breaks character, the jokes continue without a break in continuity, thus revealing another layer of the show, another metaphor for the operative principle of systems. Again, nothing is absolute. Not even the Stephen Colbert.

Understanding the Game: Three Interviews

Stephen Colbert often boasts that he's "not a fan of books," so there is irony in the fact that he interviews so many authors. Speaking to Terry Gross on NPR's Fresh Air, he divulged that he tells his guests before the cameras roll: "You understand the game, right? I'm a total idiot." To do the interview, the author must play along. But understanding the game is one thing, and playing the role before a live audience while remaining informative and entertaining is quite another. Like it or not, an author being interviewed by Colbert must assume the parts of both actor and entertainer. While advancing the issues in their books, these writers must perform live by going with the flow of a seasoned comic actor playing a buffoon intent on misinterpreting them. As each interview progresses, Colbert misunderstands his guests on a wide range of issues — as if he has misread most of their ideas — except that in most interviews Colbert brags that has not and does not plan to read the author's book. As a construct, then, a Colbert book interview requires each author to step back and take his or her book less seriously so that Colbert can twist their ideas and leave the author a small bit of time to defend the book without seeming defensive.

Generally speaking, scripted book interviews may not sound like instant comedy. But in the hands of Colbert and his writers, laughter does ensue. Most of the guest authors seeking the "Colbert bump" are not comedians, but, on October 13, 2009, comedy writer David Javerbaum was the exception. Colbert's interview about Javerbaum's parody of popular pregnancy books, *What to Expect When You're Expected*, demonstrates a unique dynamic of collaborative writing and performing that not only promotes the book, but also gets the laugh. As lyricist for the Colbert Christmas special and as the former head writer for *The Daily Show* during Colbert's tenure there, Javerbaum had previously worked extensively with Colbert. This relationship is the butt of the first joke when Colbert infers that he doesn't remember meeting the writer, having blocked out his time on Stewart's program.

Drawing from the material in his book, Javerbaum advises any unborn babies who might be listing to the show from inside their mothers: "Hang in there. It gets better. Right now, you're spending the better part of a year between a bladder and a rectum." The anatomical punch line draws a big laugh from the audience, and both alert performers listen for the laughter to subside. Giving each other the time and space to be funny, like clockwork, Colbert replies, "That's a tough neighborhood." This time Colbert's punch line kills, and again the performers leave space and time for the other's joke to succeed. Then taking his turn at the right instant, Javerbaum rests a beat before replying: "Absolutely. But never forget, you are a miracle. A miracle that makes Mommy vomit." And so goes the theater of comedy, from setup to punch line to laughter. On the surface, these talking heads may appear to be only discussing a book; but a closer look reveals Colbert and Javerbaum to be professional comedy writers and performers doing what they do best. However, their precisely-timed setups and punch lines are noteworthy because it's divergent from the typical Colbert interview. Their tête-à-tête has the feel of a scripted comedy program rather than the spontaneous shooting match that catches guests and audiences off-guard. Perhaps it is their longstanding relationship or Javerbaum's own comedic background, but, ultimately, despite its well-received laughs, the interview is stale. While it doesn't convey some controversial political truth or subvert celebrity personas like other interviews, the segment does show how, like the shows it parodies, that the show is tied to a formula, in this case, a comedic structure audiences often forget about in other Colbert interviews.

A more successful interview aired on the June 2, 2009, when Katty Kay arrived on set to promote her book *Womenomics*. The BBC journalist sparred deftly with Colbert's predictable chauvinism by anticipating his wisecracks about women in the workplace and by taking his jabs in stride. Even before Kay's interview began, Colbert had already pretended to misread the slug line by saying, "showering" women in the workplace instead of "empowering" them. Continuing, he joked that her cover price was 25 percent less than a book he dubbed "Man-onomics." With this setup of inequity, Kay's interview began. But the journalist was so prepared for the strategy of Colbert's buffoon character that she repeatedly delivered a number of her own relaxed condescending double entendres, putting the heat back on Colbert to respond in kind. Their mutual quick reflexes and spontaneous drollery demonstrate how entertaining a "fake" (i.e. put-on) interview about a book can really be.

In keeping with Colbert's swagger about not caring enough or having enough time to actually read his guests' books, the host read Kay's entire title along with its lengthy subtitle: *Womenomics: Write Your Own Rules of Success. How to Stop Juggling and Struggling and Finally Start Living and Working the Way You Really Want.* Before conversation can focus on Kay's decision to use this title, Colbert reached across the desk to shake her hand, mocking: "Thank you so much for stopping by. All we had time for was the title of your book, I'm afraid." Not to be outdone, Kay's patronizing retort is that by the host reading the subtitle, he can now take a rest because her subtitle does the work for him, a non-subtle insinuation that the host is mentally lazy. After reminding Kay that he never reads his guests' books, again subverting the traditional model and positioning himself as subject, Colbert highlights the public's mistrust in elitist culture and similarly-marketed books by a series of attacks. He asks if the book includes dietary strategies, and bemoans it as another example of how "white middle-aged men like me are being held down." He refers to women in this case as "elites" and yet also subtlety points out that women still typically earn lower salaries than their male counterparts, despite holding more degrees and being so productive. His guests' responses were the perfect mixture of witticisms and clear, declarative highlights from the book.

Her thesis for female balance in the workforce is quickly expressed in one portion of the interview: "If you let us do that [work in the way women want to work], we'll perform for you." Colbert slowly imitates the line fading out at the word *perform* to pipe up, "I'm flattered." The double-meaning is quickly made clear and all share a laugh. Here, in maintaining his subjective position in the interview, Colbert can play the role of male victim one second and return to his patriarchal realm as aggressor, agitator, the next. This back and forth leads to his demand that Kay answer the questions: "Is this a feminist diatribe? Are you a feminist?" While she escapes answering the first time, the second series she is caught in her own trap. Explaining that women no longer have to choose between work and children only sets up Colbert who interrupts, shouting, "Work or children? ... Baby-buggy on a cliff? / Big promotion?" In doing so, Colbert emphasizes a power struggle this is still extent between the genders, the modern feminine predicament that not all women have the luxury to surpass. By the end of the interview, Kay is completely infected by Colbert's rhetoric. She breaks down: Yes, she is a feminist. Even better, engulfed by the interviewer's line of fire, she admits that she didn't have to choose in real life, but, if she had to, she has one job and four children, "maybe I could lose just one of the children."

While visiting the program to promote his book *In Defense of Food*, UC, Berkeley professor, Michael Pollan found himself caught in a Colbert trap similar to that of Kay. The interview took a strange but humorous turn where the host, audience, guest, and guest's mother all enjoyed a moment of hilarious spontaneity. After the preliminary discussion of the dangers of processed, synthetic food, and Sierra Mist's "lime-like" quality (which Colbert pulls out and both men drink during the interview), an unscripted detail spun the interview in a new direction. When Pollan began to tell Colbert about the superiority of breast milk over formula, Colbert probed, "Were you breast-fed?" Pollan shrugged, "I don't know. My mom is here. Let's ask her." Her reply was "formula," and Mrs. Pollan's surprising answer struck a chord of irony throughout the studio. Taking offense on behalf of Mrs. Pollan, Colbert commanded Pollan: "I demand you apologize to your mother" for contending that babies on formula "don't do as well."

Laughing heartily about the improvisational element that he himself started, Pollan goes with Colbert's flow, guiltily admitting that once he was caught buying Fruity Pebbles cereal for his son (and never returned to that grocery store again). The two even return to the formula jokes at the interview's close when Pollan jeers processed food for "pasty complexions," to which Colbert reminds his bald guest that he has wavy hair, implying that synthetic food might not be so bad after all: "You notice I have wavy hair, Mr. Pollan. This is what high fructose corn syrup gets you. Physician, heal thyself." To which the laughing Pollan replies, "Formula, formula" as he smiles and enjoys the good natured judgment he has brought on himself. Only a few authors enjoy getting the "Colbert bump" enough to go this far and long with a joke, and for that, Pollan's interview is memorable; Pollan "gets" Colbert. In citing the powers of comedy, imitation, and contagion, Bagehot claimed that in any age, "most men catch the words that are in the air ... an unconscious imitation determines their words, and makes them say what of themselves they would never have thought of saying" (36). The Pollan interview demonstrates how a Berkeley professor and professor not only shifts gears from lecture-mode to a vernacular the masses is willing and happy to follow.

He is able to maintain the root of his book's argument, but also plays along with Colbert, seemingly contradicting his thesis by sipping on the high-fructose soda and revealing that he was raised (and has raised his son) in a way that does the same. Like Kay's insistence on balance, Pollan calls for moderation. Within the binary principles upon which the Colbert character insists, the Pollan interview reveals the dangers of ideologies drawing sharp distinctions between conceptual opposites.

In doing so, Colbert's interviews poke holes through the egos of the commentators and columnists he parodies. By imitating such personalities, he exposes the logical fallacies and empty jargon often used to rile the masses. For Colbert, it is all about meme, exploring how such ideas are passed along, inciting fear or anxiety or patriotism. His contagion of comedy can also expose flaws and gaps in systems like politics and show how these problems may be corrected using the same system deemed broken. While not all of his guests are willing to get the format, to be in on the joke, Colbert sets up a format that allows an array of layers and interpretations. In breaking down his guests, himself, and the complex issues of our time, he creates a forum through which his viewers cannot only recognize the paradox of language and politics but also envision alternative possibilities and configure their own beliefs and their positions within a larger context. Like Stewart, he demonstrates that television, technology, and our political system are not necessarily devils preying upon the average citizen but rather places to be engaged, places that are able to promote an awareness of ourselves and the world around us. He shows systems that maintain social order as much as encourage freedom. In a time labeled by terms like "the Me Generation" and "cyberselfish," the destabilizing character of Colbert and his insatiable ego shows that it's not all about *me*.

References

Bagehot, W. 1916. *Physics and Politics*. New York: D. Appleton.

Bakhtin, M. 1981. *The Dialogic Imagination*, trans. C. Emerson and M. Holquist. Austin: University of Texas Press.

Baudrillard, J. 2004. *Simulacra and simulation*, trans. S. F. Glaser. Ann Arbor: University of Michigan Press.

Baym G. 2009. "Stephen Colbert's Parody of the Postmodern." In *Satire TV: Politics and Comedy in the Post-Network Era*, eds. J. Gray, J. P. Jones, and E. Thompson. 124–144. New York: New York University Press.

Day A. 2009. "And Now ... the News?" In *Satire TV: Politics and Comedy in the Post-Network Era*, eds. J. Gray, J. P. Jones, and E. Thompson. 85–103. New York: New York University Press.

Decker, K. S. 2007. "Stephen Colbert, Irony, and Speaking Truthiness to Power." In *The Daily Show and Philosophy: Moments of Zen in the Art of Fake News*, ed. J. Holt. 240–251. Malden, MA: Blackwell.

Douglas, M. 2005. *Purity and Danger: An Analysis of Concept of Pollution and Taboo*. London: Routledge.

Douthit, R., Davis, R. and Feist, S. (Executive Producers). 2004. Interview with Jon Stewart. *Crossfire*. With Paul Begala and Tucker Carlson [Television broadcast]. October 15. New York: CNN.

Dyer, R. 1998. *Stars*. London: BFI.

Eagleton, T. 2003. *Literary Theory: An Introduction*. Second edition. Minneapolis: University of Minnesota Press.

Erion, G. J. 2007. "Amusing Ourselves to Death with Television News: Jon Stewart, Neil Postman, and the Huxleyan Warning." In *The Daily Show and Philosophy: Moments of Zen in the Art of Fake News*, ed. J. Holt. 5–15. Malden, MA: Blackwell.

Fauccioner, G. and Turner, M. 2002. *The Way We Think: Conceptual Blending and the Mind's Hidden Complexities*. New York, Basic Books.

Fiske, J. 1989. *Reading the Popular*. Boston: Unwin Hyman.

Foucault, M. 1977. *Discipline and Punish: The Birth of the Prison* (A. Sheridan, Trans.). New York: Random House.

Freud, S. 1960. *Jokes and Their Relation to the Unconscious*, trans. J. Strachey. London: Hogarth.

Gray, J. 2009. "Throwing Out the Welcome Mat: Public FIgures as Guests and Victims." In *Satire TV: Politics and Comedy in the Post-Network Era*, eds. J. Gray, J. P. Jones, and E. Thompson. 147–166. New York: New York University Press.

Griffioen, A. L. 2007. "Truthiness, Self-Deception, and Intuitive Knowledge." In *The Daily Show and Philosophy: Moments of Zen in the Art of Fake News*, ed. J. Holt. 227–239. Malden, MA: Blackwell.

Hegarty, P. 2000. *Georges Bataille: Core Cultural Theorist*. London: Sage.

Johnson, D. K. 2007. "Colbert, Truthiness, and Thinking from the Gut." In *Stephen Colbert and Philosophy: I Am Philosophy (And So Can You!)*, ed A. A. Schiller. 3–18. Chicago: Open Court.

de Man, P. 1983. *Blindness and Insight: Essays in the Rhetoric of Contemporary Criticism*. Minneapolis: University of Minnesota Press.

Mills, E. 2007. "Truthiness of the Appearances." In *Stephen Colbert and Philosophy: I Am Philosophy (And So Can You!)*, ed A. A. Schiller. 95–113. Chicago: Open Court.

Mnookin, S. 2007. "Captain America: The Man in the Irony Mask" [Electronic version]. Available at: http://www.vanityfair.com/culture/features/2007/10/colbert200710 (accessed February 4, 2010).

Morreale, J. 2009." Jon Stewart and The Daily Show: I Thought You Were Going to Be Funny!" In *Satire TV: Politics and Comedy in the Post-Network Era*, eds. J. Gray, J. P. Jones, and E. Thompson. 104–123. New York: New York University Press.

Noys, B. 2000. *Georges Bataille: A Critical Introduction*. London: Pluto Press.

Postman, N. 1985. *Amusing Ourselves to Death: Public Discourse in the Age of Show Business*. New York, Penguin.

Turner, G. 2004. *Understanding Celebrity*. Thousand Oaks, CA: Sage.

Watts, H. 1981. "The Sense of Regain: A Theory of Comedy." In *Comedy: Meaning and Form*, 2nd edition. Ed. R. W. Corrigan. 115–119. New York: Harper & Row.

Real Ethical Concerns and Fake News

The Daily Show *and the Challenge of the New Media Environment*

Bruce A. Williams *and* Michael X. Delli Carpini

On August 29, 2008, *The Daily Show* aired a story lampooning Republicans for ostentatious displays of wealth during a time of financial struggle for most Americans. Jon Stewart began by saying that politicians had been trying to show support for their contituents struggling with high gasoline prices, "...which is why it was so surprising that Virginia Congressman Virgil Goode, whose opponents have accused him of being in the pocket of big oil, showed up for a 4th of July parade in a Hummer." As Stewart spoke, a brief clip of a slow moving gray Hummer adorned with Goode election stickers was shown. Stewart then introduced "Senior Political Image Consultant" Wyatt Cenac. Cenac, who is African-American says, "I love this. Virgil Goode is pimp. The dude is like, gas is four dollars a gallon, I'm Virgil Mother-(bleep)ing Goode, I make it rain." Cenac accompanies this by throwing fake money into the air. The segment continues with Cenac arguing that there is no difference between Rappers and Republicans, "...they both love money, they love guns, gay people scare the shit out of them, and every other word out of their mouth is nigger." Stewart is then asked a series of quiz show-like questions describing people and asking him to say whether the answer is "rapper" or "Republican." He gets none of the questions right (e.g., "This business man owned 10 percent of Vitamin Water and is now worth about 400 million after its sale to Coca Cola": Stewart answers Mitt Romney, but the correct answer is 50 Cent.).

In most respects this was a standard *Daily Show* story. The video clip of the parade established the basic "facts" of the issue and invited viewers to conclude that Congressman Goode had ridden in a Hummer. The reliance on video, usually taken from television news (although not in this case), is a key component of the show, assuring the viewer that reliable sources have been used and the ensuing comedy is based on actual events. Even when the point of a story is to lampoon the ways in which journalists (and those who claim the mantle of journalism) cover issues, the show uses actual clips to establish that their targets are actually guilty of the behavior satirized. Similarly, the cutback to the studio and the repartee between Stewart and Cenac clearly signaled the move into the realm of political satire. In short, the *Daily Show* uses a set of well-established signals, understood by the regular viewer, to indicate the status of the different components of any segments. This tacit commitment to getting the facts right is an important part of the show's appeal and central to the significant role it plays in American political discourse.

But what happens when the tacit agreement between the producers and viewers of the show are violated? According to the local newspaper and sources within the campaigns of both Goode and his Democratic challenger Tom Periello, the congressman didn't ride in the Hummer during the parade, instead he walked and handed out campaign literature to the crowd. The story that he rode in the gas guzzler was apparently planted by the Periello campaign, posted on *YouTube* and then picked up by *The Daily Show* (Baker 2008). It should also be added that the election was decided by less than 1,000 votes and required a recount before Periello was declared the winner.

We are not claiming that this is a particularly egregious distortion of the facts, nor are we arguing that such errors are frequent (see, Williams and Carpini forthcoming). Rather, it indicates the unsurprising, but rarely discussed reality that like any attempt to address issues of the day, the show makes mistakes. Additionally, like any other show, decisions are made about what issues to cover, what issues to ignore and what perspective to take. The Project for Excellence in Journalism, for example, found that *The Daily Show* news agenda mirrored cable news talk shows and shared the same limitations (e.g., slighting local stories, a focus on Washington elites), but almost completely ignored tragic events (unsurprising given the comedic slant of the show). While comedy is always central, it seems obvious that the show aims for more than a quick laugh. As the same report put it: "In its choice of topics, its use of news footage to deconstruct the manipulations by public figures and its tendency toward pointed satire over playing just for laughs, *The Daily Show* performs a function that is close to journalistic in nature — getting people to think critically about the public square" (Project for Excellence in Journalism 2008).

One of the great strengths of American journalism as it developed in the

20th century, was its explicit rules for the construction of stories (e.g., reliance on reliable sources, non-partisanship, distinguishing between news and opinions). This allows both criticism of whether reporters actually followed the rules and debate over the adequacy of the rules themselves. But how do we hold *The Daily Show* accountable for mistakes or evaluate its role in shaping public discourse? More generally, what criteria are appropriate to critique satirical shows, or other genre busting sources of political information, on questions of accuracy, content, and style?

Saying "My Show Follows Puppets" Doesn't Solve the Problem

While clearly relishing his role as a critic, Jon Stewart himself has resisted attempts to define his show's role in the new information environment, calling it "fake news" and claiming that, as a comedy show, it is beneath serious criticism. In his well publicized 2006 argument with Tucker Carlson on CNN's *Crossfire*, when criticized for being too easy on guests he agreed with, Stewart's response was not to defend his approach to interviewing, but rather to ridicule the very idea of such criticism, arguing that his show followed puppets on Comedy Central. It was this confrontation that firmly established Stewart's role as media watchdog. His criticism of Tucker Carlson, in particular, and the vacuous arguing talking heads of cable news, more generally, contributed to the decision to cancel *Crossfire*. In a similar vein, during his 27 April 2007 appearance on *Bill Moyers' Journal*, Stewart said, "we feel no obligation to follow the news cycle ... because ... we're not journalists."

Another example of the strategy of defining satirical shows as outside the realm of "serious" political communications occurred in October 2009 when CNN aired a segment fact-checking the political sketches on *Saturday Night Live* (in particular the claim on one that President Obama had accomplished nothing in his time in office). The next day, *The Daily Show* ran a story ridiculing CNN for paying attention to the comedy on *SNL* when they often let their own guests make false claims and there were so many more important stories to cover. Referring to an old *SNL* sketch, Stewart asked, for example, whether CNN had also discovered that sharks only lived in water and did not really deliver candy grams.

Insisting that satirical shows are beneath serious criticism precisely because they are satire/comedy is useful for some purposes. As Geoff Baym argues, it allows the shows to position themselves as outsiders, speaking for the ordinary citizen, unconstrained by the significant limitations in the way much of professional journalism and other more "serious" outlets operate (see

Baym 2008). Satirical shows are thus able to keep the spotlight firmly focused upon their targets and not themselves.

Yet this strategy has significant disadvantages, especially if we consider the broader information environment. In demonstrating the failure of journalists or other "serious" commentators (and those who claim either title), while at the same time deflecting criticism by claiming to be neither, *The Daily Show* assumes a clear distinction between serious and non-serious sources of information. Even if we accept this distinction, which we do not, it leads to a basic contradiction. The undeniable fact that the show is taken seriously enough for its stories to be routinely used on a wide range of "serious" media and for Stewart to become a widely respected critic would seem to make it serious by definition. However, recent changes in the media environment have rendered such distinctions outmoded and virtually useless (see, for example, Carpini and Williams 2000; Williams and Carpini 2009). Political information no longer comes to us primarily from news broadcasts or newspapers, nor are the myriad sources through which it does flow clearly and consistently labeled. Indeed, even traditional sources, like the television news shows and most newspapers, have been transformed almost beyond recognition in an attempt to preserve audiences in this changing environment.

It is no longer possible, if it ever was, to make a priori distinctions between the serious and the non-serious or between the political and the non-political. Rather, the belief in the naturalness of such dichotomies is itself rooted in the media system of the mid to late 20th century, what we call "The Age of Broadcast News" (see Williams and Carpini forthcoming [b]). During this period, professional journalists assumed their unquestioned and authoritative role as gatekeepers of the public agenda, the source of information about pressing issues of the day, and the public space in which (mainly elites) debated these issues. While there is much to be valued in The Age of Broadcast News, especially when journalists actually lived up to their professional values, it also left much to be desired. But whether one agrees with this assessment or not, there is no returning to the past system. In the current media environment, we need to be clear about the role played by all sources of political information.

There simply is no denying that programs like *The Daily Show,* along with Fox News, MSNBC, talk radio, myriad blogs and social networking sites, have become significant sources of political information. For a large and relatively young audience, shows like *The Daily Show, Colbert Report,* and on occasion *Saturday Night Live,* hold the media and political elites accountable, and help to set the public agenda and provide a basic summary of the most important events of the day. Similarly, Fox News is now a significant source of political information for a large and older audience. The average age of a

Fox News viewer is 65, while *The Daily Show* audience average is 41 years old. In such a changed and greatly expanded universe of political information questions of public responsibility fall on a wider range of media than in the past. This responsibility is clearest perhaps in the case of journalists, but applies as well to any source upon which large numbers of citizens come to rely as they negotiate a mediated political world. The declining audience for traditional information sources like newspapers and broadcast news, coupled with the increasing use of a wide range of changing sources of all kinds (many with unclear claims about the rules used to produce the information they disseminate), makes it vital to develop ways of evaluating the full range of sources of political information confronting citizens in the 21st century.

At their best, shows like *The Daily Show* and *The Colbert Report* help viewers better negotiate the new media environment by providing a critical perspective on the media and holding journalism (whatever form it takes) accountable. However, there is no guarantee that these shows, or newer imitators, will continue to live up to this potential. Currently, the positive role of satirical shows depends upon little more than the good intentions of their creators, networks, and advertisers. This is a particularly thin reed, given the likelihood of imitators, the explosive growth of cable programming and internet sites on the left and right, and the increasingly blurred line between news and other forms of politically-relevant programming. How slim this reed can be was illustrated by ABC's 2002 decision to cancel Bill Maher's *Politically Incorrect* in the wake of the host's unpopular comments on the 9/11 terrorists. What's needed are ways of thinking about the new media environment which do not unreflectively adopt (or reject) the values of the collapsed Age of Broadcast News. How do we articulate the criteria of evaluation which would include satirical shows, in particular, but also other traditional and non-traditional sources of political information?

Articulating the nature of such responsibilities is especially important in the case of media figures like Stewart and Colbert who have attained a significant level of trust and respect. Giving a pass to those who call themselves comedians, entertainers or any other label (e.g., "ordinary folks" "soccer mom") designed to deflect accountability and criticism is dangerous. If we fail to develop critical perspectives for media we like (for reasons we do not articulate), what do we do when other sources, either new or already established, to which we object, also claim to lie outside the boundaries of serious criticism? In a media environment which threatens to devolve into ideologically isolated echo chambers, the need to develop critical perspectives applicable across a wide variety of sources of political information is especially acute.

What Are the Ethical Responsibilities of Fake News?

What criteria can we use to evaluate whether these varied sources further or discourage the development of an informed citizenry, civil debate, and political engagement? Moreover, any criteria must be flexible enough to apply to a wide range of sources while appreciating their unique characteristics. For example, in the case of *The Daily Show*, any evaluation must always keep in mind the centrality of humor. Expecting the show to carefully cite sources, present opposing perspectives and the like, as we expect of journalists, would clearly destroy the very essence of what accounts for the show's appeal in the first place. Answers to these questions need to be developed in the context of open public debate. As in the past, journalists, political elites and scholars have a role to play in this public debate, but so too do movie and television producers, bloggers, and musicians — as well as, most importantly, ordinary citizens themselves.

To begin exploring how these questions may be explored, we suggest four qualities of politically-relevant media that are likely to influence the practice of democratic politics (see, for example, Williams and Carpini forthcoming [b]). We have argued elsewhere that these qualities — what we label transparency, pluralism, verisimilitude, and practice–salvage the spirit and intent of past efforts to create a democratic media environment, especially the stated of professional journalism in the mid to late 20th century (if often honored only in the breach), while taking into consideration both the limitations of these earlier efforts and the unique promise and pitfalls of the new media environment. We offer these criteria not because they are the only ones possible, but rather as a starting point for developing a way of evaluating and holding accountable the increasing number of sources of political information, including satirical shows, upon which Americans now rely for political information.

Transparency

By this term we mean that the audience of any mediated message must know who is speaking to them. It is related to the traditional journalistic norms of revealing one's sources, including a byline, and acknowledging when a story involves the economic interests of the media organization. But transparency is more encompassing. First, it now extends across a much broader range of media, not simply the news. It is just as important to know the sources, biases, and intentions of Jon Stewart as Brian Williams; to know the economic interests of a movie studio as a newspaper chain; and to know the "sources" of a screen writer as a reporter. Second, the ways in which information is produced by many new sources of political information are often unclear. The value of transparency recognizes that to critically evaluate the quality of any source of political information the specific rules used to produce it must be available.

When it comes to transparency, *The Daily Show* does an admirable job of exposing the ways in which mainstream media, especially those claiming to adhere to the rules of journalism, actually cover issues of the day. The show regularly satirizes the failures of professional journalism which have been identified by many (especially academic) critics: pack journalism, over-reliance on unchallenged elite sources, failures to investigate the factual basis of claims made by politicians and other sources, and a focus on superficial and sensational issues at the expense of coverage of serious and complex issues. By taking seriously the rules of journalism and using them as the bases of critique (as opposed to the ideologically driven criticism found on Fox, MSNBC, and numerous blogs), *The Daily Show* plays an important role in exposing the systematic failures of the media. In this focus on the media itself, the show plays a unique role: *The Daily Show* devotes 8 percent of its time to the press and news media, twice the percentage of coverage in the mainstream news media (Project for Excellence in Journalism, 2008).

On the other hand, when it comes to the rules it uses, *The Daily Show* is far from transparent. As we have noted, Stewart himself has been reluctant to consider serious analysis of his show. Consequently, we have little idea of how guests, stories, and issues are chosen; the sort of fact-checking that goes on; and the degree to which values other than humor enter into the equation (e.g., getting viewers to think critically about the public square, as The Project for Excellence in Journalism put it). An explicit willingness to discuss these issues in ways that do not cramp the show's style, would go a long way. It would certainly help to distinguish the show from ideologically driven sources claiming the mantle of professional journalism (e.g., Fox News's claim to be "fair and balanced") which have become, like *The Daily Show*, alternatives and/or supplements to more traditional sources of information.

Pluralism

This quality refers to the openness of the media environment to diverse points of view and the ease of access to these views. It is related to the traditional notions of balance and equal time, but we see pluralism as a much broader concept. New technology and the blurring of out-dated distinctions between genres increases the possibility for either a much richer conversation that includes a more diverse set of viewpoints or a more ideologically polarized environment of homogeneous echo chambers.

The Daily Show has been accused, as in Stewart's 2006 appearance on *Crossfire*, of letting its liberal politics shape the way it treats guests, specifically, and its approach to satire, more generally (Dickens 2006). While the show's liberalism is undeniable, that does not mean that it fails to present a wide range of views. The interview segment, for example, is a model of civil discourse and often hosts guests with decidedly conservative values (e.g., John McCain, Ron Paul, Mike Huckabee and John Yoo to name a few). Guests are provided the time to discuss their ideas, even when Stewart disagrees. Further, it is undeniable that the show was a consistent critic of the Bush Administration, but this may be at least as much a result of the show establishing itself during a period of Republican dominance as any liberal slant. Recently, the show has taken more than its fair share of shots at the Democratic controlled Congress and the ineptness of the Obama Administration. At its best, the show's role as satirical gadfly trumps ideology. When it comes to targeting the media, *The Daily Show*'s criticism is based on journalistic standards rather than ideological favoritism, and routinely uses these standards to lampoon CNN, MSNBC, and a host of other print and electronic news outlets. One could not say the same thing about Fox News, whether in its shows labeled as opinion (e.g., *The O'Reilly Factor* or *Glenn Beck*) or news (e.g., *Special Report with Bret Baier*). Again and again, the network, in Stewart's own words, "...alters[s] reality. You are sold a preconceived narrative."

Verisimilitude

We use the word verisimilitude not in its meaning as "the appearance or illusion of truth" (though this definition should always be kept in mind), but rather "the likelihood or probability of truth." It acknowledges the uncertainty of things, while also recognizing the importance of seeking common understanding through efforts to approach the truth.

When we talk about verisimilitude in the media, we mean the assumption that sources of political communications take responsibility for the truth claims they explicitly and implicitly make, even if these claims are not strictly verifiable in any formal sense. This is as applicable to a newspaper or network news broadcast as it is to documentaries like *Fahrenheit 9/11* and *An Inconvenient Truth*, more traditional Hollywood movies like *Good Night, and Good Luck* and *Breach*, and to satirical news shows.

As with transparency, *The Daily Show* does a much better job shining a light on the foibles of others than it does taking responsibility for its own choices. The show performs the vital task of pointing out the mistaken truth claims made in other media. While much of journalism is rightly criticized for a "he said, she said" approach which uses ideological balance to avoid the job of independently checking the factual claims of sources, *The Daily Show* demonstrates the absurdities that can result. CNN's failure to fact-check its own guests was a point made by Stewart in his criticism of the network for turning its attention on *SNL*. While we disagree with the idea that political satire should be immune from fact-checking, reminding viewers that CNN needs to put its own house in order is a point well taken. The show repeatedly skewers political elites (and by implication the journalists who pass on their statements) by simply juxtaposing what they have said recently with video of what they said about the same issue in the past. The show is even tougher on the often absurd claims that are taken for granted in more ideological venues which then too often set the agenda for the more mainstream media. The recent case of Shirley Sherrod, who was forced to resign from her position as Georgia State Director of Rural Development for the United States Department of Agriculture on 19 July 2010, provides yet another example of this process. A misleadingly edited video of her speech to the NAACP, designed to cast her as a black racist by the unscrupulous right wing blogger Andrew Breitbart, aired on Fox News. It was then repeated in a wide variety of other mainstream outlets and led to her firing by the panicked Obama Administration. Shamefully, neither the mainstream media nor the administration did even the most cursory fact-checking before a rush to judgment. Once Sherrod's background and the actual context of her speech emerged, everyone involved (except Breitbart and Fox) was forced to apologize. Returning from vacation, *The Daily Show* wickedly parodied both the failures of the press and the Obama Administration, comparing the president to Donald Trump in his willingness to fire people.

On the other hand, *The Daily Show* is, much like many other parts of the new media environment, parasitic upon the work of journalists, depending upon them for both a basic understanding of the day's significant events and the specific stories upon which their satire is based. Yet, the show fails to acknowledge this dependence, rarely praises high quality reporting, or recognizes the current crisis of journalism to say nothing of suggesting solutions.

Finally, the degree to which the show takes responsibility for its own truth claims, or makes it easy for viewers to check for themselves is uneven. Video clips are usually shown with the source clear (e.g., leaving in the logo of Fox News, CBS, or Yahoo News), but this is not a hard and fast rule, as was the case with the story on Virgil Goode. Even more problematic is the show's resistance to outside scrutiny, as we saw with its criticism of CNN for fact-checking skits on *SNL*. Rather than deserving scorn, CNN at least recognized that the truth claims of satirical shows can play an important role in political discourse and deserve to be scrutinized. Consider, for example, the significant role played in the 2008 campaign by *SNL's* parodies. They both helped unravel Sarah Palin's candidacy and were used by Hillary Clinton to make the claim that the press was uncritical of candidate Barack Obama. In our view, efforts to verify the factual claims of non-traditional sources of information, from satirical shows to web pages to movies claiming to be "based on real events," is to be lauded. Indeed, in a changing media environment, expanding the targets of fact-checking to the increasing array of sources of political information may be a new and significant role for traditional news sites. It would be one way to both provide critical information for evaluating such sources and a way of encouraging them to take responsibility for the truth claims made.

Practice

Finally, we suggest the concept of *practice*. We mean this in two senses. First, as in modeling, rehearsing, preparing, and learning for civic engagement. And second as actual engagement and participation, be it in further deliberation or more direct forms of political activity.

Here again, *The Daily Show* record is mixed. In the sense of providing a model of civil debate, the interviews between Stewart and his guests in the last segment of each show are exemplary. While there are certainly many celebrities flogging their latest films of television shows, the interview segment is one of the few places on television where books, authors (even relatively unknown academics) and ideas matter. Stewart seems to have read the books his guests have written and provides a space for back-and-forth discussion, even when he seems to disagree. Indeed, it is disappointing that when Tucker Carlson criticized the softball questions asked of liberal guests, Stewart didn't defend his interview style, but ducked the whole issue by claiming he was only a comedian. From the vantage point of practice, what Carlson and the angry talking heads of cable television see as "softball" questions, is actually an alternative to pointless partisan bickering. Stewart's respectful (and often humorous) approach elicits some of the most thoughtful discussion available in the media. For example, in his 2009 interview with Tony Blair he gave the former prime minister the opportunity to make a reasoned argument in defense of his decision to support the invasion of Iraq. The defense might not have convinced skeptical viewers (it clearly did not convince Stewart) but it did make clear that the decision was not taken lightly and shed light on the dilemma that policymakers faced at the time. Such an interview style stands in stark contrast to the shouting matches which regularly occur in echo chambers like Fox News, or distressingly more often on supposedly non-ideological sites like CNN (see, Jamieson and Cappella 2008).

On the other hand, the show seems much less oriented toward fostering actual political participation. Right-wing hosts like Glenn Beck, Sean Hannity, and Rush Limbaugh regularly encourage their audience to participate in politics through traditional channels like voting, but also by serving as facilitators of new movements like the Tea Party. *The Daily Show*, in contrast, has little to say in support of political participation of its viewers. In the face of this silence, it is possible that the political satire of the show encourages a "hip aloofness" which supports cynicism about and disengagement from politics (see, Baumgartner and Morris 2006). So not unlike left-leaning critiques of *Fox News*, satirical news shows might legitimately be accused of cultivating knee-jerk cynicism about both politics and the press.

Conclusion

Our application of explicit evaluative criteria to *The Daily Show* is both tentative and preliminary. We offer it as a way to encourage a broader discussion of how to analyze and hold accountable the expanding range of media which now provide political information to Americans. While our specific criteria and the ways they are applied are, obviously, open to criticism, we hope that our broader points are accepted: dubious distinctions between entertainment and news, serious and non-serious media and so forth are increasingly inapplicable in the new media environment; relying upon these distinctions to *a priori* exempt some politically-relevant media from serious scrutiny is a serious mistake.

With this in mind, our four criteria would ideally be applied to all politically-relevant media. This raises the interesting question of how programs like *The Daily Show* and other satirical shows compare to many other sources of political information, both traditional (e.g., television news and newspapers) and new (e.g., ideological cable stations and blogs)? There is reason to believe that *The Daily Show* in some ways does better than many traditional sources of political information. As Tom Brokaw observed, "There are more facts and more truths told in the first eight minutes of *The Daily Show* than most political news conferences in Washington" (Dickens 2006). Yet, the absence of clear criteria for evaluation makes it difficult to get past the idea that liberals like the show because it reflects their values. Indeed, the words of praise from Brokaw were used on the conservative blog *Newsbusters* as evidence of the liberal bias of both *The Daily Show* and the mainstream media, personified by the former anchor of the *NBC Nightly News*. Whether this praise or criticism is deserved is and should be an open, debatable question. But to have such a debate, we must acknowledge the fundamentally changed nature of the new information environment, the public interest obligations of both professional journalists and other political information providers in this new environment, and the need for establishing appropriate standards for holding these various players accountable.

References

Baker, Bernard. 2008. "Virgil Goode Unhappy with 'The Daily Show' clip." *Lynchburg News and Advance*. Available at: http://www2.newsadvance.com/lna/news/local/article/virgil_goode_unhappy_with_the_daily_show_clip/7112/ (accessed July 25, 2010).

Baumgartner, Jody and Jonathan S. Morris. 2006. "*The Daily Show* Effect Candidate Evaluations, Efficacy, and American Youth." *American Politics Research*. 34.3: 341–367.

Baym, Geoffrey. 2008. "Serious Comedy: Expanding the Boundaries of Political Discourse." In *Laughing Matters: Humor and American Politics in the Media Age*, ed. Jody C. Baumgartner and Jonathan S. Morris. New York: Routledge.

Carpini, Michael X. Delli and Bruce Williams. 2000. "Let Us Entertain You: Politics in the New Media Environment." In *Mediated Politics: The Future of Political Communication*. Ed. Lance Bennett and Robert Entman. Cambridge: Cambridge University Press.

Dickens, Geoffrey. 2006. "Brokaw Praises Obama, Stewart and Colbert, Attacks Reagan for Neglecting 'Mother Earth.'" *Newsbusters.org*. Available at: http://newsbusters.org/node/9457 (accessed July 30, 2010).

Jamieson, Kathleen Hall and Joseph N. Cappella. 2008. "*Echo Chamber: Rush Limbaugh and the Conservative Media Establishment*." New York: Oxford University Press.

Project for Excellence in Journalism. 2008. "The Daily Show: Journalism, Satire or Just Laughs?" May 8. Available at: http://pewresearch.org/pubs/829/the-daily-show-journalism-satire-or-just-laughs (accessed July 29, 2010).

Williams, Bruce A. and Michael Delli Carpini. "The Eroding Boundaries between News and Entertainment and What they Mean for Democratic Politics." In *Handbook of Mass Media Ethics*, ed. Clifford Christians and Lee Wilkens. New York: Routledge.

_____. Forthcoming [a]. *The Daily Show* And *Colbert Report*. In A Changing Information Environment: Should "Fake News" Be Held To Real Standards? *The Crisis in Journalism*. ed. Robert McChesney and Victor Pickard. New York: Nation Books.

_____. Forthcoming [b]. *After the News: The Legacy of Professional Journalism and the Future of Political Information*. Cambridge: Cambridge University Press.

About the Contributors

Jody C. Baumgartner is an associate professor of political science at East Carolina University. He has authored or edited five books on American and comparative politics, and has written or co-written more than two dozen articles and book chapters.

Amy B. Becker is an assistant professor in the Department of Mass Communication and Communication Studies at Towson University in Towson, Maryland. Her research focuses on public opinion and citizen participation on controversial political issues, and the effects of exposure to political comedy programming and celebrity political involvement.

Randy S. Clemons is a professor of political science and dean of the School of Social Sciences at Mercyhurst College. He is the coauthor of *Public Policy Praxis* (Longman, 2nd ed., 2009). Other recent publications include an article in *Journal of Public Affairs Education*. He has also presented extensively at major conferences and in 2007 won the "Distinguished Teaching Award" at Mercyhurst.

Josh Compton is a senior lecturer in speech for the Institute for Writing and Rhetoric at Dartmouth College. His scholarship in persuasion, political communication, and speech pedagogy has been published in *Human Communication Research*, *Communication Theory*, *Journal of Applied Communication*, and *Communication Yearbook*, among other journals.

Michael X. Delli Carpini is dean of the Annenberg School for Communication at the University of Pennsylvania. His research explores the role of the citizen in American politics, with particular emphasis on the impact of the mass media on public opinion, political knowledge and political participation.

Sarah E. Esralew is a doctoral student in the School of Communication at Ohio State University. She is interested in studying political entertainment. Her undergraduate thesis explored whether Tina Fey's caricatures of Sarah Palin on *Saturday Night Live* affected perceptions of Palin.

Lauren Feldman is an assistant professor of communication at American University. Her research examines the effects of the media on political knowledge, attitudes, and behavior. She is particularly interested in the nexus between entertainment and politics, and how less traditional sources of political information contribute to political learning and engagement. Her work has appeared in a number of edited volumes and peer-reviewed journals, including *Communication Research*, *Political Communication*, and *Journal of Communication*.

Julia R. Fox is associate professor in the Department of Telecommunications at Indiana University. She is the lead author of a study comparing broadcast networks' newscasts and *The Daily Show* that received international attention in the Associated Press, United Press International, CBS, NPR, *The Washington Post*, MSNBC, and *Rolling Stone*.

Anthony Leiserowitz is director of the Yale Project on Climate Change Communication at the School of Forestry and Environmental Studies at Yale University. He is an expert on American and international public perceptions of climate change risks, support and opposition for climate policies, and willingness to make individual behavioral change.

Edward Maibach is a university professor and director of the Center for Climate Change Communication at George Mason University. His research focuses on how to mobilize populations to adopt behaviors and support public policies that reduce greenhouse gas emissions and help communities adapt to the unavoidable consequences of climate change.

Mark K. McBeth is a professor of political science at Idaho State University. He is the coauthor of the widely adopted public policy analysis text *Public Policy Praxis* (Longman, 2nd ed., 2009) and publishes in public policy.

Jonathan S. Morris is an associate professor of political science at East Carolina University. He has published dozens of articles and book chapters on the influence of cable television in American politics.

Patricia Moy is the Christy Cressey Professor of Communication and an adjunct professor of political science at the University of Washington. Her research examines how communication shapes our conceptions of citizenship; specifically, she studies media effects on public opinion, political knowledge, and various forms of political behaviors.

Robert T. Tally, Jr., teaches American and world literature at Texas State University. He is the author of *Melville, Mapping and Globalization: Literary Cartography in the American Baroque Writer, Kurt Vonnegut and the American Novel: A Postmodern Iconography*, and *Spatiality (The New Critical Idiom)*; he is also the translator of Bertrand Westphal's *Geocriticism: Real and Fictional Spaces*.

Richard Van Heertum is a visiting assistant professor of education at UCLA, where he received his Ph.D. in education and cultural studies in 2009. He has published 20 academic essays, and more than 130 articles in the popular press. He is also co-editor of *Hollywood's Exploited* (Palgrave, 2010) and *Educating the Global Citizen* (Bentham, 2011).

Bruce A. Williams teaches in the Department of Media Studies at the University of Virginia. His most recent books are (with Andrea Press) *The New Media Environment: An Introduction* (Blackwell, 2010) and (with Michael X. Delli Carpini) *After Broadcast News: Media Regimes, Democracy and the New Information Environment* (Cambridge University Press, 2011).

Kevin A. Wisniewski lectures in English and political science at Cecil College in North East, Maryland. A recent Lord Baltimore Fellow at the Maryland Historical Society, he is editor of *The Comedy of Dave Chappelle: Critical Essays* (McFarland, 2009).

Michael A. Xenos is an associate professor in the Department of Communication Arts at the University of Wisconsin Madison, where he also serves as director of the Center for Communication Research. He has research interests in political communication, civic engagement, public opinion, and new media.

Dannagal Goldthwaite Young is an assistant professor of communication at the University of Delaware. She studies the content, audience, and effects of political humor. Her research on the psychology and influence of humor has appeared in numerous journals including *Media Psychology, Political Communication, International Journal of Press/Politics, Journal of Broadcasting and Electronic Media, and Mass Media and Society.*

Index

197